450 AC
nd

INDUSTRIALIZATION, IMMIGRANTS
AND AMERICANIZERS

Gerd Korman

INDUSTRIALIZATION

❋ ❋ ❋ ❋ ❋ ❋ ❋ ❋ ❋ ❋ ❋

IMMIGRANTS

✠ ✠ ✠ ✠ ✠ AND ✠ ✠ ✠ ✠ ✠

AMERICANIZERS

▬ ▬ ▬ ▬ ▬ ▬ ▬ ▬ ▬ ▬ ▬

THE VIEW FROM MILWAUKEE, 1866–1921

1967
THE STATE HISTORICAL SOCIETY OF WISCONSIN
MADISON

In Memory of My Father

MAX O. KORMAN

*He outlived the beasts
by remaining a man.*

Preface

TOWARDS THE END of the nineteenth century there emerged in this country the intricate social relations that slowly accustomed us to professions, bureaucracies, and standardized forms of behavior. To Jacques Ellul, a French sociologist and social philosopher, the product of this kind of development represents something new. It represents a society responding to ever-accelerating demands for techniques— unplanned, unwilled methods, forms, and devices—to convert "spontaneous and unreflective behavior into behavior that is deliberate and rationalized." So new is our epoch to Ellul, in fact, that he is no longer concerned with the determinisms of the past: "They are finished and done with."*

The historian had best leave the problem of ultimate determinisms to the social philosophers, but he must examine the processes they identify. If he does not, he neglects opportunities for enriching historical scholarship. He also shirks his responsibility to analyze in detail their generalizations about the past.

Actually the charge of responsibility need not be so vigorous. Imperceptibly the insights of social philosophers, past and present, so blend with the environment in which the

---

* Jacques Ellul, *The Technological Society*. Translated by John Wilkinson. Foreword by Robert K. Merton. (New York, 1964.) The quotations are from pages vi and xxix.

historian works that unknowingly he often studies problems already identified outside of his discipline. Thus, this study was conceived and executed in blissful ignorance of Ellul's work. But surely my book, which examines the process by which a polyglot population evolved the techniques for coping with the problems of an emerging industrial society, reveals implicitly its indebtedness to men like Ellul.

Scrutinizing industrialization and related processes such as the absorption of immigrants, patterns of occupational change, or the rationalization of social relations demands from the historian a microscopic approach. In our time he is akin to the biologist who, utilizing knowledge and tools acquired in the fields of physics, chemistry, and genetics, now knows so much that he tackles the mysteries of life itself by studying bacteria and viruses. The contemporary historian is also turning to the microscope for the study of macroscopic problems to acquire the details demanded by his calling.

The comparison with the biologist can be extended one step further in order to amplify one aspect of the microscopic approach to macroscopic problems. A very few bacteria and viruses are being used to penetrate the mystery of inheritance. Biologists chose these because they had particular properties which especially lent themselves for solving specific problems; the typical representative, after all, is not always the most revealing one. Thus, historians also turn to atypical subject matter in order to examine specific problems: some turn to the lives of particular men because they especially reveal so much about the generation in which they lived; some choose a particular city because it reveals so much about the society in which it developed.

Milwaukee is especially suitable for a fine-structure analysis of complex processes attending industrial growth, for it held a special place in the modernization of America's industrial relations. This status came to Wisconsin's largest city because the state was one of the first in the nation to cope systematically with the social consequences of burgeon-

ing growth of population and industry so characteristic of
the last third of the nineteenth century.

The place of immigrants in this study deserves special comment. From the beginning my organizing principle was the
social relationship between industrial growth and immigrants.
Yet I soon found myself studying the men and women who
mediated that changing relationship. In fact, though the organizing principle remained rooted to the initial design, I
ended by examining a significant chapter in the history of
industrial relations.

I have benefited from many kind acts. John Dierbeck, Jr.,
led me to the records of International Harvester, the late T.
C. Turner to those of Phoenix Hosiery, and the late Mrs.
Alberta Price to the books and papers of Allis-Chalmers. The
staff of the Wisconsin Secretary of State helped me work
among volumes of the state manuscript census of 1905. The
staff of the State Historical Society of Wisconsin was patient
and co-operative, and I had in addition the special assistance
of two of its now retired ladies: Mrs. Lucile O. Kellar, the
custodian of the McCormick Collection, and the incompar-
able Alice E. Smith. The Social Science Research Council
provided two and a half years of support in the form of pre-
doctoral training fellowships. My home institution, the New
York State School of Industrial and Labor Relations at Cornell University, made available secretarial service which Mrs.
Marilyn Hickok and Mrs. Elsie Cole always supplied in the
best of spirits. The *Industrial and Labor Relations Review*
granted permission to publish as Chapter Six an article of
mine which appeared in its issue of April, 1965.

I acknowledge gratefully the help of teachers, colleagues,
and friends. Some cannot remain nameless: Burton Fisher
of the University of Wisconsin and Arthur Waskow of the
Institute for Policy Studies helped with earlier versions of this
study. John Burnham of Ohio State University and Maurice
Neufeld, fellow historian and colleague, made invaluable

comments on later drafts. Forrest McDonald of Brown University, who reviewed the final manuscript, made important suggestions about its organization. And I recall with affection and esteem the late Howard K. Beale, my mentor.

My wife, Ruth, helped far more than she is willing to acknowledge. Each of our children, Arona, Joshua, and Ezra, endured patiently.

Gerd Korman

Ithaca, New York
May, 1966

Contents

Introduction

DURING THE FIFTY YEARS from 1870 to 1920, when Americans began to rationalize their means of production and distribution, they also groped for the ways and means to rationalize their social relations. These efforts to organize, centralize, and systematize were especially evident in the complex realm of industrial relations. There, in the context of an expanding and competitive economy and in the name of progress, factory masters, engineers, reformers, educators, academicians, nurses, secretaries, bookkeepers, and Americanizers of immigrants struggled with the new technology of factory production, the heterogeneous labor force, and the values and ideals of a republican society. By the time the nation emerged triumphant from World War I, these amateurs were on the way to becoming professionals, and, because of their involvement with immigrants, they had laid the foundations of the industrial relations of welfare capitalism.

Late nineteenth-century attempts to improve relations between industrial employers and their workers were a manifestation of a national effort to make American society function harmoniously. In the 1890's, when Frederick W. Taylor began to publish his time-and-motion studies of American factory workers, the use of statistical data, especially by government agencies, was becoming more widespread, and a science of statistics was emerging for explaining data systematically. By this time, rationalization of the means of production and distribution had already become commonplace, labor was demonstrating the viability of the national union for organizing workers into effective bargaining units, farmers were seeking to protect and advance their interests through their alliances and the Populist party, and the United States Army was looking to the "scientific" Prussian model when it reorganized itself in the name of efficiency.[1]

After the turn of the century, manifestations of the trend became more pronounced. Frank B. Gilbreth and Harrington Emerson joined Taylor in publicizing principles of efficiency and scientific management. Harvard University founded its Graduate School of Business Administration. The output of books and articles about business management increased significantly. Wisconsin and some other states inaugurated techniques for making political democracy more efficient and instituted commissions to regulate the economy. Conservationists accepted the gospel of efficiency, especially in forest management. Urban health crusaders, responding to scientific findings made by bacteriologists, organized anti-tuberculosis, anti-syphillis, and anti-spitting campaigns. Some groups concentrated on urban housing reform, seeking in particular to alleviate overcrowding and the "tenement house evil"; others focused on municipal government, hoping to make it efficient and representative. In education, there were efforts to integrate curricula with the economic and social needs of a community, and some educators strove to train youngsters to become efficient workmen. "Schools," said the director of the United States Board of Vocational Education in 1917, should be "human efficiency producing plants."

[1] Henry S. Commager, *The American Mind: An Interpretation of American Thought and Character Since the 1880's* (New Haven, 1950), 327; Paul F. Lazarsfeld, "Notes on the History of Quantification in Sociology—Trends, Sources, and Problems," in Harry Woolf, editor, *Quantification* (New York, 1961), 202–203; Samuel P. Hays, *The Response to Industrialism, 1885–1914* (Chicago, 1957), 24–70; Lloyd Ulman, *The Rise of the National Trade Union: The Development and Significance of its Structure, Governing Institutions, and Economic Policies* (Cambridge, 1955), *passim*; Walter Millis, *Arms and Men: A Study in American Military History* (New York, 1956), 154–162.

Sociologists, psychologists, and psychiatrists often thought and spoke of social control as necessary for coping with problems of community life.[2]

With the outbreak of war in Europe, efforts to organize and make the work force produce more efficiently were accelerated. Faced with the task of harnessing America's manpower at a time when the influx of European workers decreased and the demand for labor increased, advocates of industrial welfare and safety, agencies of government, and employers responded according to their own particular assessments of the situation.

Influenced by applied psychology, the professionalization of social work, and scientific management, industry's pioneer welfare and safety experts sought professional status for themselves and for their craft. Advocates of Taylor's gospel particularly urged making welfare work more scientific. The year that the scientific managers of production founded the Taylor Society, 1914, also brought the appearance of the periodical *Industrial Management*. Next year, Richard A. Feiss of the Joseph Feiss Company in Cleveland told the

---

[2] Frank B. Gilbreth, *Primer of Scientific Management* (New York, 1912), *passim*; Harrington Emerson, *The Twelve Principles of Efficiency* (New York, 1912), *passim*; Raymond E. Callahan, *Education and the Cult of Efficiency: A Study of the Social Forces That Have Shaped the Administration of the Public Schools* (Chicago, 1962), 1–240; Harold U. Faulkner, *The Quest for Social Justice, 1898–1914* (New York, 1931), *passim*; Lincoln J. Steffens, *The Autobiography of Lincoln Steffens* (New York, 1931), 344–627; Samuel P. Hays, *Conservation and the Gospel of Efficiency: The Progressive Conservation Movement, 1890–1920* (Cambridge, 1959), *passim*; Merle E. Curti, *The Social Ideas of American Educators* (New York, 1935), 230–231, 518–533; John Dewey, "Address to Parent's Association of the University of Chicago Elementary School, January, 1899," typescript of notes taken of Dewey's address by Laura L. Runyan, recorder and librarian of the school, enclosed in a letter of Runyan to Mrs. Emmons Blaine, May 17, 1899, in the Emmons Blaine Papers, in the McCormick Collection in the State Historical Society of Wisconsin; Charles A. Prosser in the *Proceedings of the National Safety Council, 1917*, p. 296; John C. Burnham, "Psychiatry, Psychology, and the Progressive Movement," in the *American Quarterly*, 12: 457–465 (Winter, 1960). For a recent interpretation of the efficiency nexus, see Samuel Haber, *Efficiency and Uplift: Scientific Management in the Progressive Era, 1890–1920* (Chicago, 1964), *passim*.

Taylor Society that the handling of men should be as scientific as the manufacture of goods. During the same year and again in 1916 the Academy of Political and Social Science devoted special issues of its *Annals* to discussions by industrial and academic experts of various aspects of the systematic handling of factory workers. In 1916 a national association of "employment managers" was founded; in 1919 it became an association of "industrial managers." These terms, and such other new phrases as "personnel management," "industrial relations," and "industrial service work," began to replace the older terms of "welfare" and "industrial betterment" as descriptions of departments and practitioners concerned with aspects of welfare and safety and with innovations in hiring and classifying employees.[3]

During the war decade the number of workers who came under industrial service programs of one type or another more than doubled. Many companies instituted departments of industrial management, personnel, or industrial relations. In companies that had for some time conducted welfare programs, the new departments were usually the outgrowth of welfare and safety organizations. These new departments expanded their earlier efforts to stabilize a company's work force, achieve harmonious relations between management and labor, and to increase production. They worked to broaden and refine their methods of controlling behavior within the plant, and to influence the ways that workers spent their leisure time.[4]

[3] "Proceedings of the Employment Managers' Conference, 1916," in the *Bulletin of the Bureau of Labor Statistics*, no. 196 (Washington, 1916); Richard A. Feiss, "Personal Relationship as a Basis of Scientific Management," in the *Bulletin of the Taylor Society*, 1: 1–15 (November, 1915); *Annals of the American Academy of Political and Social Science*, 61: *passim* (September, 1915), and 65: *passim* (May, 1916); Loren Baritz, *The Servants of Power: A History of the Use of Social Science in American Industry* (Middletown, 1960), 35–37; John R. Commons and others, *History of Labor in the United States* (4 vols. New York, 1918–1935), 3: 330; Thomas Cochran and William Miller, *The Age of Enterprise: A Social History of Industrial America* (New York, 1956), 244–245.

[4] "Welfare Work for Employees in Industrial Establishments in the United States," in the *Bulletin of the Bureau of Labor Statistics*, no. 250 (Washing-

Government agencies also intensified their efforts to regulate and systematize industrial life after the United States entered the war. Besides dealing with workmen's compensation, industrial safety, and sanitation, federal and state bureaus grappled with problems about the distribution of labor. Since the turn of the century Wisconsin had sought to make order out of the chaos that characterized the labor market. Initially the state had required private employment offices to be licensed, and it soon tightened its control over their activities. This was followed by the establishment of a state employment agency. In 1911 when the Wisconsin Industrial Commission came into being, the state employment agency was placed on a firm basis, but it did not significantly cut into the business done by private offices. Only after 1914, when the state agency enlarged its staff to include interpreters for immigrant workers, did it begin to make inroads into the business of private bureaus. Unscrupulous private agencies which had abetted the high rate of turnover among workers suffered particularly from state competition.[5]

America's entry into the war strained the capacity of state employment agencies in Wisconsin and other states to meet the demands that were made on them, and the war served as a powerful stimulus to the development of a federal employment service. In their efforts to secure workers, foremen and superintendents resorted even more frequently than in peacetime to intra- and inter-company raiding.[6] To prevent

---

ton, 1919), *passim*; Cyrus McCormick, Jr., "The Advantage of a Superintendent of Labor," in the *Harvester World*, 9: 4 (April, 1918); H. F. Perkins in *ibid.*, inside front cover; *ibid.*, 9: 11 (June, 1918); Cyrus McCormick, Jr., "Co-operation and Industrial Progress," in *ibid.*, 10: 23–25 (December, 1919); interview with William M. Leiserson, 1956.

[5] Wisconsin Bureau of Labor and Industrial Statistics, *Biennial Report, 1899–1900*, pp. xxii–xxiv, 34–35; *1901–1902*, p. 773; Wisconsin Industrial Commission, *Bulletin*, 2: 195–196, 199–200, 202, 212–213, 216–217, 218, 220 (1913); Wisconsin Industrial Commission, *Report on Allied Functions, 1914*, pp. 29, 41; Citizens Committee on Unemployment and the Milwaukee Free Employment Office, *Annual Report, 1913*, pp. 6–7, 231; William M. Leiserson, *Adjusting Immigrant and Industry* (New York, 1924), 60–62; *Milwaukee Leader*, March 31, April 20, 1914.

[6] Don D. Lescohier, *The Labor Market* (New York, 1919), 177–185. For

such practices as well as to harness the nation's labor power, the federal government turned for help to the Bureau of Naturalization, then part of the Department of Labor. The bureau was one of the few federal agencies that before 1917 had given some thought to the problem of distributing immigrants throughout the economy. During the early days of the war a number of its officials tried to place immigrants in communities where the labor shortage was particularly acute.[7] At the same time the federal government encouraged the expansion of industrial service work in factories.[8]

In their efforts to reduce the waste of manpower, industrial organizations and governmental agencies relied increasingly on the counsel of academic specialists. A number of universities instituted courses dealing with the management of labor. The Harvard Graduate School of Business Administration continued to publish books and articles on this subject; it also began to advise some companies on techniques of industrial management. Other schools approached these problems from a different perspective. At the University of Wisconsin, John R. Commons and his students examined protective labor legislation, administration of labor laws, trade union history, and collective bargaining, generally from a

---

Milwaukee, see Willits Pollock, Milwaukee County Council of Defense, typescript "Weekly Reports," July 5, 14, 21, September 22, October 13, 20, December 4, 1917; February 26, August 18, 1918, Series 76/1/2, in the Wisconsin State Archives, in the State Historical Society of Wisconsin; Milwaukee County Council of Defense, *Official Bulletin,* September 22, 1917, p. 3; Citizen's Committee on Unemployment and the Milwaukee Free Employment Office, *Annual Report, 1919,* pp. 5–6; *1920,* pp. 8–9. For raiding practices, see W. J. Whiteside, Circular letter no. 46, April 15, 1910, in the Allis-Chalmers Archives, West Allis, Wisconsin.

[7] These officials administered an organization that was the forerunner of the United States Employment Service. On June 3, 1918, the Secretary of Labor separated the employment service from the Bureau of Naturalization. Lescohier, *Labor Market,* 186–187; interview with Leiserson.

[8] May W. Simons to William H. Lighty, July 6, 1918, in the William H. Lighty Papers, in the State Historical Society of Wisconsin. Applied psychology for factory personnel was popularized by the work of army psychologists during the First World War; see Baritz, *Servants of Power,* 110–117.

viewpoint that was sympathetic to the workers and to the principle of collective bargaining.[9] Commons' studies of *Races and Immigrants* (1907) and *Industrial Goodwill* (1919) were especially broad in scope and discussed methods for making the economy and nation operate more harmoniously.

Other studies concerned themselves directly with managerial problems. Foremost among them was Sumner H. Slichter's classic analysis of *The Turnover of Factory Labor.* Begun in 1913 and published in 1919, the book dramatized the problem of labor turnover and demonstrated to management the "neglected truism that a definite plan and specific responsibility for creating and executing the plan are as necessary in dealing with labor as in controlling manufacturing operations." In his introduction, Commons declared that Slichter's work had "the highly important practical purpose of guiding the employer in his efforts to reduce labor turnover." Those in management who fully grasp "all that is implied in this profound subject," said Commons, "will be in a position to meet the critical problems of the future." Slichter had performed a great service for American industry.[10]

To Commons and other rationalizers of social relations a variety of approaches occurred as ways to change existing conditions. Many reformers relied on the political process. They were convinced that the intimate relationship between private capital and government could be broken by increasing the power of the electorate and giving the voters more direct control over government, at the same time establishing regulatory commissions staffed by experts. Such changes would

[9] *Ibid.*, 100–106, 110–117; *Immigrants in America Review,* 1: 98 (September, 1915); *Bulletin of the Bureau of Labor Statistics,* no. 518 (Washington, 1930), 151–158; Commons, *History of Labor,* 3: 330; Allan Nevins and Ernest Hill, *Ford: The Times, the Man, the Company* (New York, 1954), 527; Merle Curti and Vernon Carstensen, *The University of Wisconsin: A History, 1848– 1925* (2 vols. Madison, 1949), 2: 339–341.
[10] Sumner H. Slichter, *The Turnover of Factory Labor* (New York, 1919), vii, viii, xiii–xiv.

lead to enactment of remedial legislation, particularly statutes dealing with protection of industrial workers.[11]

Political action, however, was only the most publicized method used by reformers. A number of groups and individuals sought to bring their techniques directly into industrial organizations. John Dewey wanted to use factory classes for industrial education. Commons considered company-sponsored welfare programs part of the general effort to ameliorate the conditions of employment. Indeed, he looked to factories as one of the most effective instruments for bringing about social change.[12] A host of social and governmental workers joined in the industrial safety campaign because, like Frances Perkins, they hoped to improve working conditions. Temperance groups carried on proselytizing activities in factories, as did the Young Men's Christian Association, which had its agents talk to workers during their lunch hours, a technique that politicians had used for many years. One crusader against venereal disease hoped to distribute bulletins about the delicate subject among male factory workers.[13]

There was a more fundamental reason why factories became a focal point for advocates of social change. Temperance, health, housing, sanitation, and safety crusaders alike found their efforts impeded rather than facilitated by the machinery of democratic government. Opposition groups often blocked or delayed enactment and enforcement of municipal, state, and federal legislation.

Factory managers, on the other hand, had the power of coercion over their employees. If management could be convinced of the virtues of this or that program, then it could impose upon its workers all sorts of requirements not

---

[11] Steffens, *Autobiography*, 344–627; Robert M. La Follette, *La Follette's Autobiography: A Personal Narrative of Political Experiences* (Madison, 1913), *passim*; Cochran and Miller, *The Age of Enterprise*, 276–280.

[12] Commons, *Industrial Goodwill*, 129–142.

[13] The executive secretary of the Wisconsin Anti-Tuberculosis Association wanted a campaign in factories against venereal disease. See H. E. Dearhoet to William H. Lighty, October 2, 1918, in the Lighty Papers.

prohibited by protective labor legislation. Only unions in well-organized shops or informally but effectively organized groups of workers could successfully oppose such management-sponsored programs. Until the military draft of World War I, there was no American organization in which so few ruled so many adults, for the factory master wielded extraordinary power over his employees.[14]

In Milwaukee these groups and forces interacted with singular importance on the modernization of America's workshops and factories. The city's industrial workers, especially the immigrants among them, first felt the thrust of this interaction. But what transpired in Milwaukee ultimately had profound implications for the nation's emerging system of industrial relations.

---

[14] Cochran and Miller discuss one aspect of this problem by suggesting that autocracy in factories functioning within a democratic society was at the heart of the difficulty between labor and capital before 1920; see *The Age of Enterprise,* 247–248.

PART ONE

MILWAUKEE

1

The Industrial Matrix

TO THE IMMIGRANT who arrived in the last third of
the nineteenth century, the densely settled parts of the United
States of America might, at first glance, have seemed the same.
Everywhere one looked, rapid urbanization and industrialization were absorbing, albeit with acute indigestion, millions
of newcomers from the farms of America as well as the cities
and villages of Europe.

The production of nearly everything doubled, trebled,
quintupled; and the population of cities grew apace. The
number of cities of more than 8,000 population doubled.
Older communities, Boston and Baltimore and New Orleans,
grew three times and yet slipped in the population rankings
of major cities. They lost to the burgeoning cities farther
west and north—Buffalo, Pittsburgh, Cleveland, Chicago, Milwaukee, Minneapolis, St. Louis—where the basic components
of the revolution in heavy industry were centered, and where
most of the hundreds of thousands of new immigrants gravi-
tated. These places, particularly, seemed all of a piece.

But similar as these cities appeared in the broad view,
they differed in detail, and it was in detail that immigrants
would live. The details that distinguished one city from
another were countless, but to the newcomer the most important were two: the composition of local leadership and
the pattern of local industry. That is, who ran the community, and what jobs were available in it.

In Milwaukee, when large-scale industrialization began

in 1866, those who stood ready to greet and exploit new arrivals were themselves scarcely old-timers. The city was populated and dominated largely by first- and second-generation immigrants from northwestern Europe, particularly Germans, Scots, and Irish. These immigrants had, in their turns, encountered some nativist discrimination, but in the main they had shared in the opportunities provided by an expanding commercial economy before the Civil War. Together with native Americans they had laid the foundations for Milwaukee's industrial growth. They helped develop the city's harbor and rivers and its rail connections to the Mississippi River and to Chicago. They expanded its labor force and brought special skills for pioneering ventures in brewing and manufacturing. They provided a growing consumer market for the small processing and manufacturing establishments that sprang up before the war. They turned the profits of the city's trade with the hinterland to permanent advantage by accumulating capital and investing it in manufacturing.

So, when the first great wave of post-Civil War immigrants arrived in the late 1870's—Poles, other eastern Europeans, and southern Europeans as well—leadership in Milwaukee was firmly in the hands of the ethnic groups which had built the city. High in the ranks of the dominant group were native Americans, Eber Brock Ward, Edward P. Allis, and John Plankinton; Scots, Alexander Mitchell and John Johnston; and Germans, Frederick Pabst, August Uihlein, Phillip Best, Guido Pfister, and Frederick Vogel. Skilled occupations, especially in brewing, tanning, and the metal trades, were usually in the hands of Germans, Englishmen, or native Americans. Labor unions, as well as political parties, municipal government, and the churches, were likewise in the hands of native Americans or immigrants who had come before the war or during the first years of industrialization.[1]

---

[1] The foregoing is based on A. Gerd Korman, "A Social History of Industrial Growth and Immigrants: A Study with Particular Reference to Milwaukee, 1880–1920" (Ph.D. dissertation, University of Wisconsin, 1959), 1–47, 365–380. The author is now engaged in a study of the entire subject of industrialization and the occupations of immigrants in the United States from 1850 to 1910.

The patterns of industrial development were established early. Handicraft industries, requiring workers, buildings, and access to markets, logically clustered in the old commercial part of the city, the narrow peninsula between the Milwaukee River and Lake Michigan. Cigar works, clothing factories, knitting mills, and other small factories had begun to develop there before the war, and in succeeding decades they mushroomed. Heavy industry, dependent upon steam power and therefore upon access to an abundant water supply, developed first on the lake shore south of the city. Before 1870 the Milwaukee Iron Company set the pattern by erecting its rolling mills and blast furnaces on the lake shore in Bay View, just beyond the city limits. In the 1870's and 1880's Bay View spawned railroad shops, brickyards, machine shops, and foundries, and attracted the Filer and Stowell Cream City Iron Works and branch plants of the Schlitz Brewing Company, the Best Brewing Company, and E. P. Allis' Reliance Iron Works. Medium-heavy industries developed inside the city along the banks of the Menomonee River, which flows from the west, and the Milwaukee River, which flows from the north. In this area tanneries, warehouses, icehouses, lumber and coal yards, meat-packing plants, and railroad yards burgeoned; by 1880 these and other such establishments already had pre-empted the bed of the Menomonee River Valley beyond Milwaukee's western limits. Factories had become especially prominent in the area surrounding the confluence of the Menomonee and Milwaukee Rivers. Just south of the juncture, Allis' Reliance Iron Works occupied one entire city block; north of it were the breweries of Pabst and Schlitz.[2] These patterns prevailed until after the turn of the century. Then when electric power made it possible to establish heavy industry away from water, they

---

[2] In general, for the years after 1883, data about the location of factories presented in this chapter were obtained from the factory inspection reports in the *Biennial Report* of the Wisconsin Bureau of Labor and Industrial Statistics. See also Bayrd Still, *Milwaukee: The History of a City* (Madison, 1948, 1966), 187–194, for data for the ante bellum period; and Bernard C. Korn, "The Story of Bay View" (unpublished master's thesis, Marquette University, 1936), 182–185.

were supplemented by the development of the industrial suburbs of Cudahy, South Milwaukee, West Allis, and North Milwaukee.[3]

Expansion of factory production and a concomitant concentration of employment developed rapidly. As early as 1870 the Milwaukee Iron Company employed around 1,000 men, produced more than 35,000 tons of pig iron—about half the Wisconsin production—and manufactured products valued at some $3,000,000.[4] The Reliance Works had become a "confusion of pulleys, shaftings, wheels, chains, engines, patterns, and mouldings," employed about 350 men, and produced about $1,000,000 worth of goods a year.[5] The city's meat-packing plants, especially those of John Plankinton and Phillip Armour, rivaled the largest in the nation; in 1871 they made Milwaukee the fourth largest pork-packing center in the United States.[6] Among the city's tanners, the Wisconsin Leather Company and Pfister and Vogel had become firms of national eminence.[7] The Phillip Best Company was one of the largest breweries in the nation.[8]

To be sure, most jobs still were found in commerce and most manufacturing jobs still were in small shops. But the change already had begun, and already Milwaukee's total manufacturing output was sizable. Altogether in 1870, the

[3] Patrick Cudahy, *Patrick Cudahy: His Life* (Milwaukee, 1912), 115; Wisconsin Bureau of Labor and Industrial Statistics, *Biennial Report, 1901–1902*, p. 133; *1905–1906*, pp. 673–674; *Milwaukee Journal*, October 26, 1907; Harold F. Williamson and Kenneth H. Myers II, *Designed for Digging: The First 75 Years of Bucyrus-Erie Company* (Evanston, 1955), 44–45.

[4] Milwaukee Chamber of Commerce, *Report, 1866*, p. 5; *1870*, pp. 13–14; Victor S. Clark, *History of Manufactures in the United States* (3 vols., Washington, 1929), 2: 65, 67.

[5] *Milwaukee Sentinel,* May 16, 1872; Frederick Merk, *Economic History of Wisconsin During the Civil War Decade* (Madison, 1916), 144.

[6] Milwaukee Chamber of Commerce, *Report, 1869*, p. 25; *1871*, pp. 71–72; *1872*, p. 21.

[7] Merk, *Economic History of Wisconsin*, 149; Milwaukee Chamber of Commerce, *Report, 1869*, pp. 63–64; *1870*, pp. 14–15; Clark, *History of Manufactures*, 2: 121, 506–507.

[8] Thomas C. Cochran, *The Pabst Brewing Company: The History of an American Business* (New York, 1948), 54–99; Milwaukee Chamber of Commerce, *Report, 1867*, p. 49; *1871*, p. 23.

city's manufacturers used 120 steam engines producing some 5,000 horsepower, employed some 8,000 workers (more than a third of the city's work force) in 800 establishments, and made products valued at nearly $20,000,000.[9]

In the 1870's, despite a long depression that beset most of the nation, Milwaukee's industries continued their rapid expansion. By 1880 the value of their manufactured products was more than $80,000,000 a year, fourteenth among American cities. In milling of flour, tanning of leather, brewing of malt, distilling of liquor, and production of iron and steel Milwaukee ranked among the nation's first seven cities. So greatly had heavy, steam-powered industry expanded that the city now imported a million tons of coal annually, a five-fold increase in a decade. With that expansion and with increased mechanization in virtually all industries came increased concentration of jobs in fewer and bigger plants. So marked was this tendency that, while the number of manufacturing establishments had remained about the same, the number of workers they employed had nearly trebled to more than 20,000 persons and to half the city's work force.[10]

In subsequent decades, as Milwaukee's entrepreneurs responded to the spurs of demand and opportunity, factory production and concentration of economic power continued unabated. Rapid urban growth especially affected the market for Milwaukee's industries. The city itself grew from about 71,000 population in 1870 to more than 200,000 in 1890; other cities grew comparably, but the nearby market of Chicago increased at an almost incredible rate. This urban growth brought large numbers of customers to such Milwaukee industries as brewing, tanning, meat packing, flour milling, and the metal trades. By 1890 brewers sold their beer in every major population center in the United States; the three

[9] *Milwaukee Journal of Commerce,* quoted in the Milwaukee Chamber of Commerce, *Report, 1871,* pp. 14, 81; *United States Census, 1870,* 3: 582.

[10] Milwaukee Chamber of Commerce, *Report, 1882,* p. 24; *1885,* pp. 26–27; *1909,* p. 156; *United States Census, 1880,* 2: xviii, xxiv, xxvi; Wisconsin Bureau of Labor and Industrial Statistics, *Biennial Report, 1883–1884,* p. 49; E. E. Barton, *Industrial History of Milwaukee* (Milwaukee, 1886), 56.

leading tanners had important customers all over America; the meat packers, flour millers, and machine shops all shipped much of their output to buyers in the nation at large. Indeed, a number of Milwaukee companies bought raw materials and sold manufactured goods in an international market; E. P. Allis had an agency in Scotland selling patent flour roller crushers.[11]

Accordingly, more and more of the jobs available in the city were in fewer and fewer plants. True, as late as 1891 nearly 60 per cent of the city's manufacturing establishments were small shops, used for making women's clothing and millinery goods, men's and boys' clothing, cigars, boots and shoes, bread and bakery goods, and wood products. But the figure is deceptive. For one thing, 41 per cent of the work force was employed in six industries, four of them large-scale industries operating in relatively few shops: iron, steel, and heavy machinery (considered as one), leather, beer, and railroad equipment and supplies. For another, the 'nineties brought still further concentration, and by 1900 light manufacturing represented only 32 per cent of all industrial establishments.[12]

The concentration of labor was especially evident in particular factories. By the middle of the 1880's some small shop manufacturing plants housed as many as 300 workers. Some employed even more. William Graff and Company had about 350 men and women making cigars under a single roof. The Herman Segnitz Cigar Manufacturing Company employed 700 men and women in a four-story building, 500 of them on the second and third floors, 150 on the fourth

[11] Cochran, *Pabst,* 71, 129–179; *Milwaukee Sentinel,* May 16, 1872; September 23, 1886; April 2, 1889; *Fortschritt der Zeit* (Milwaukee), 19: 131 (May 10, 1890); Henry Eskuche, "Leather and the Tanning Industry," in William J. Anderson and Julius Bleyer, *Milwaukee's Great Industries* (Milwaukee, 1892), 157; Ray H. Whitbeck, *The Geography and Economic Development of Southeastern Wisconsin* (Madison, 1921), 90–109; Frank A. Flower, *History of Milwaukee, from Prehistoric Times to the Present Day* (Chicago, 1881), 1289.
[12] Compiled from the manufacturing census taken annually by the *Milwaukee Sentinel* from 1890 to 1910. The returns were reprinted in the reports of the Milwaukee Chamber of Commerce.

floor. The boot and shoe firm of Bradley and Metcalf employed more than 400 men and women in a single building.[13]

In large-scale manufacturing enterprises the concentration of employees was even more pronounced. Here the enterprises used hundreds of workers distributed among their various installations. E. P. Allis employed about 1,400 persons; the Chicago, Milwaukee, and St. Paul Railway Company employed about 1,800 in its buildings in the Menomonee River Valley; the Bay View Works, in the mid-1880's owned by the North Chicago Rolling Mill Company, employed between 1,000 and 1,400. The meat-packing plants of the Cudahy Brothers and John Plankinton and Company, located in the Menomonee River Valley, used a work force ranging between 400 and 1,200 persons depending upon the season of the year. The Pfister and Vogel Leather Company employed about 360 men in the Menomonee Valley. The big brewers also used large labor forces. Pabst employed more than 700 persons; Schlitz, 500.[14]

Milwaukee's industrial expansion required more manpower than was available among the native born in the Middle West; so its manufacturers, like those in most of the booming industrial centers, obtained their workers from the fluid international labor market. From the second half of the nineteenth century until World War I, the population of Europe and America was on the move. Europeans left their rural homes for the industrializing urban centers of the Atlantic community or for agricultural lands in the New World.[15] Millions came to the United States and joined thousands of

[13] Factory inspection report in Wisconsin Bureau of Labor and Industrial Statistics, *Biennial Report, 1887–1888*, pp. 282, 514.

[14] Factory inspection report in *ibid., 1885–1886*, pp. 515, 508, 509; *1887–1888*, p. 280; *1889–1890*, p. 55a.

[15] Brinley Thomas, *Migration and Economic Growth: A Study of Great Britain and the Atlantic Economy* (Cambridge, 1954), 25, 30–31, 152–153; Charlotte Erickson, *American Industry and the European Immigrant, 1860–1885* (Cambridge, 1957), 67–87; Fritz Josephy, *Die deutsche ueberseeische Auswanderung seit 1871* (Berlin, 1912), 34, 48–52, 71, 79–80; Leopold Caro, *Auswanderung und Auswanderungspolitik in Oestereich*, in *Schriften des Vereins fuer Sozialpolitik* (Leipzig, 1909), 131: 52–56; Arnold Schrier, *Ireland and the American Emigration, 1850–1900* (Minneapolis, 1958), 3–42.

native Americans moving from East to West, or from rural to industrial areas.

Thousands upon thousands of immigrants came to Milwaukee in the years when the city industrialized.[16] For many it was their first American home after leaving rural communities on the continent. For some it was the end of a particularly long journey that had taken them first to Brazil, then to Canada, and then to Eastern and other Midwestern states in this country. Others arrived in the city after first attempting to settle elsewhere in the United States, particularly in New York, Pennsylvania, Illinois, and Michigan. Many came to Milwaukee after having left agricultural villages in central Europe for industrializing parts of Germany; only when they could not find work there did they leave for the New World. Some came directly from the workshops of Great Britain. Still others went first to rural Wisconsin before coming to the state's leading manufacturing center.[17]

The state government played a part in bringing the foreign born to the city. In the 1870's and 1880's a state agency, though largely interested in agricultural settlement, advertised in northwestern Europe for factory workers as well. Thousands of pamphlets were sent abroad in the hope of attracting immigrants from England, Belgium, Holland, France, the Scandinavian countries, and Germany.[18] "As there are no public

---

[16] For estimates of immigrants arriving in or passing through Milwaukee by rail, see Wisconsin Commissioner of Immigration, *Report, 1871*, p. 11; *1872*, pp. 12–13; *1873*, p. 7; *1874*, p. 2; Wisconsin Board of Immigration, *Report, 1880*, p. 4; *1881*, pp. 8–9; *1882*, p. 8; *1884*, p. 9.

[17] The best evidence for migration by native Americans and foreign immigrants to Milwaukee is found in the pages of the state manuscript census. Families were usually large in the nineteenth century and the children were often born in various places en route to Milwaukee. The birthplaces of the children thus give an excellent picture of migration routes of settlers coming to the city. The manuscript copy of the Wisconsin census of 1905, Ward 12, precincts 2–4, in the office of the Wisconsin Secretary of State, Madison, provided examples cited in the text. For Germany, see Josephy, *Deutsche ueberseeische Auswanderung*, 57, 64, 79.

[18] Wisconsin Commissioner of Immigration, *Report, 1871*, pp. 10, 14; *1872*, p. 16; *1873*, p. 9; Wisconsin Board of Immigration, *Report, 1880*, p. 13; *1881*, p. 11; *1882*, pp. 9–10; *1883*, pp. 10–11; *1886*, p. 11.

lands in Milwaukee County," the agency said, "its statistics will be chiefly of interest to immigrants as they set forth the opportunities for procuring a livelihood in the different mechanical arts and occupations attendant thereon."[19] The pamphlets told of rolling mills, breweries, tanning factories, machine shops, and the factories of the woodworking, clothing, cigar, and shoe industries, all of which needed skilled workers. They described, too, the docks and lumber and freight yards, where there was a need for common labor.[20]

Private agencies and promoters also fostered the immigration of Europeans, particularly Germans and Poles. Before the Civil War the Lutheran and Catholic churches helped to establish communities in Milwaukee, and brought spiritual leaders directly from Europe. The propaganda literature of Wisconsin assured potential immigrants that in Milwaukee and the rest of the state they would have their religious institutions.[21] Before the Civil War townsite promoters had been eager to attract settlers, and on occasion had recruited them.[22] Real estate brokers participated in the work of the state's immigration agency. In the 1870's James A. Becher, a Milwaukee real estate broker, was a member of the agency and went to Europe to propagandize in behalf of the state.[23] Railroad companies with lands to sell also recruited settlers. In the early 1880's the president of the Wisconsin Central

[19] Wisconsin Commissioner of Immigration, *Statistics of Wisconsin* (Madison, 1870), 65. See also Wisconsin Board of Immigration, *Wisconsin, What It Offers the Immigrant* (Madison, 1883), 38–40.

[20] Wisconsin Commissioner of Immigration, *Wisconsin, Ein Bericht . . .* (Milwaukee, 1868), 19–20; *1870*, pp. 35–36; Wisconsin Board of Immigration, *Wisconsin, Ein Bericht . . .* (Milwaukee, 1881), 40; *1884*, pp. 34–38.

[21] Still, *Milwaukee*, 80; Wisconsin Commissioner of Immigration, *Ein Bericht, 1868*, pp. 19–20; Wisconsin Board of Immigration, *Ein Bericht, 1881*, p. 40; the *Germania*, a Lutheran weekly published in the city, complained on July 27, 1881, that there was not enough detailed information about sectarian schools, and insisted that German peasants and "wage workers" wanted such data.

[22] Still, *Milwaukee*, 73, 114.

[23] Wisconsin Commissioner of Immigration, *Report, 1871*, p. 10; James A. Becher to William E. Smith, April 3, 1879; Charles L. Colby to Becher, May 31, 1880, both in Executive Department, Immigration, 1852–1905, Series 1/1/1–4, in the Wisconsin State Archives.

Railroad persuaded the state to appoint to the agency K. K. Kennan, who was then in Europe trying to encourage emigration from Germany, Norway, and Sweden for the railroad company.[24] In addition to these groups, immigrants who already had settled in Milwaukee attracted fellow countrymen with their letters and remittances.

When they needed special skills, employers brought directly to Milwaukee the Europeans they wanted. The mobility of Europe's and America's population made the manufacturing centers of England and the continent a part of the labor market for the city's employers. When they could not find a skilled worker at home they turned elsewhere, and when they needed him urgently enough, but could not find him in this country, they turned to Europe.[25]

Eber B. Ward's Milwaukee Iron Company recruited such help from England. Ward had gained experience in recruiting activities before building his plants in Bay View, having brought iron and steel workers to his Detroit and North Chicago plants, and having supported the efforts of the American Emigrant Company, an organization which signed skilled Europeans to work contracts before they left for the United States.[26] Either through this organization or by some other means, he imported skilled iron and steel workers for building and operating his Milwaukee plant. He drew particularly on a region that had been visited by an agent of the emigrant

[24] Colby to Smith, June 5, 17, 1881; to Becher, May 31, 1880, *ibid.*, in the Wisconsin State Archives. For Kennan's activities abroad, see Wisconsin Board of Immigration, *Report, 1881*, pp. 12–13; *1882*, p. 11; Erickson, *American Industry and the European Immigrant*, 74. Kennan advertised in Germany and Sweden, offering "just as cordial and ready assistance to the mechanic bound for Milwaukee as to the farmer who proposes to buy lands . . ."; see Wisconsin Board of Immigration, *Report, 1882*, p. 11.

[25] On workmen who came to Milwaukee from beyond Wisconsin, see, for example, the biographical sketches in Flower, *History of Milwaukee*, 1293–1295, 1620; Wisconsin Bureau of Labor and Industrial Statistics, *Biennial Report, 1887–1888*, pp. 108–109; *1907–1908*, p. 1065.

[26] Bernard C. Korn, "Eber Brock Ward: Pathfinder of Industry," (unpublished Ph.D. dissertation, Marquette University, 1942), 149; Erickson, *American Industry and the European Immigrant*, 3–31, discusses the work of the American Emigrant Company.

company in 1864, the industrial cities of Staffordshire, then England's center for manufacturing iron and steel.[27] In 1868 that area was plagued by a wage dispute, during which the Iron Workers Association of Staffordshire encouraged emigration to prevent wage reductions.[28] Ward capitalized on the situation to bring a sizable number of skilled workers from there to Milwaukee. He also brought workers from Wales and Scotland. These men provided the skills necessary for producing railroad iron and Bessemer steel at Ward's Milwaukee works.[29]

Other manufacturers in the city followed Ward's lead. In 1872 E. P. Allis obtained the services of an expert pipe caster from Scotland.[30] In 1881 cigar manufacturers sent special agents to Bohemia to recruit craftsmen for breaking a strike of skilled cigar makers.[31] In 1884, when recruitment on contract of European glass blowers was common in the Middle West, the Window Glass Company, a firm founded in Bay View four years earlier, employed glass blowers from Belgium, Germany, France, and England.[32]

Recruitment of these small numbers of skilled workers did not mean, however, that the city's manufacturers made any serious efforts, consciously and systematically, to direct large-scale emigration from Europe. Between 1885 and 1906, only three companies and one individual in Wisconsin were suspected of violating the laws that prohibited bringing individual workers to the United States without signing them to a contract: the Wisconsin Central Railroad Company, the Wisconsin Southern Railroad Company, the Illinois Steel Company, and an anonymous individual in Fond du Lac. While

[27] Korn, "Bay View," 159–160.

[28] Erickson, *American Industry and the European Immigrant,* 17, 18, 39–40.

[29] *Ibid.,* 39–40; Korn, "Bay View," 159–160.

[30] *Milwaukee Sentinel,* May 16, 1872, in "Old Newspaper Stories of E. P. Allis," 56.

[31] Wisconsin Bureau of Labor and Industrial Statistics, *Biennial Reports, 1883–1884,* p. 141; Erickson, *American Industry and the European Immigrant,* 154.

[32] *Fortschritt der Zeit,* 13: 294 (October 10, 1884); Erickson, *American Industry and the European Immigrant,* 140–142.

it was relatively simple to circumvent the officials responsible for enforcing contract labor legislation, organized labor in Milwaukee and elsewhere in Wisconsin would have protested as vigorously as did the unions in other states if employers had recruited substantial numbers of immigrants.[33]

Milwaukee employers, in short, usually could obtain most of their workers from American labor pools which were fed from the streams of migration across the Atlantic. They did co-operate with other groups interested in attracting immigrants to the city and state, and they sometimes asked immigrant workers in their shops to write home asking fellow countrymen to emigrate. Normally, even when they wanted to replace a striking worker, Milwaukee employers usually found the replacement in the United States.[34] In 1872 the president of the Chamber of Commerce pleaded for efforts to bring "cheap labor" to the city, but such efforts proved unnecessary. The Panic of 1873 brought a sharp slump in

[33] United States Department of Justice, Record Group 60, Central Files 5053, 1885–1906, in the National Archives, Washington. The most recent analysis of contract labor legislation and recruitment of immigrants signed to contracts abroad may be found in Erickson, *American Industry and the European Immigrant*, 139–186. The Wisconsin legislature endorsed the Foran Bill; no petitions have been preserved. On the other hand, there are many petitions and remonstrances in the archives on the subjects of prison labor and paying wages by the week. Organized labor in Wisconsin appeared far more concerned with these issues than with contract labor legislation. See Secretary of State, General Records, Wisconsin Legislative Papers, Series 2/2/2 (1885–1890), in the Wisconsin State Archives.

[34] Still, *Milwaukee*, 114, note 12; Cudahy, *His Life*, 45; Ferdinand Vogel to Lucius Fairchild, March 15, 30, 1871, Executive Department, Immigration, 1852–1905, in the Wisconsin State Archives; Wisconsin Commissioner of Immigration, *Report, 1871*, pp. 1, 10; Erickson, *American Industry and the European Immigrant*, 86, 227–228, note 120. An Italian workman, Gaitano Balestriere, told the author in 1957 that many years earlier he had urged his relatives to come to Milwaukee to work for the International Harvester Company. For the replacement of strikers, see *Milwaukee Sentinel*, May 3, 9, 10, 1876; Wisconsin Bureau of Labor and Industrial Statistics, *Biennial Report, 1883–1884*, p. 141; *1891–1892*, p. 192; *Milwaukee Germania Abendpost*, September 29, 1897; Citizens Committee on Unemployment and the Milwaukee Free Employment Office, *Report, 1916*, p. 12; Daniel D. Hoan to Milwaukee County Council of Defense, March 13, 1918, in the Daniel D. Hoan Papers, in the Milwaukee County Historical Society.

manufacturing activities, and by the time the city recovered from the depression the mass migration of Germans and Poles was already under way. In the 1870's and especially in the 1880's thousands of these immigrants streamed into the city: Germans to join countrymen who had settled in large numbers in Milwaukee in earlier years; Poles to increase greatly the city's small Polish colony. Italians, Austrians, Greeks, Hungarians, Russians, and Bulgarians arrived later and augmented the numbers of Germans, Poles, Scandinavians, and Irish in the "cheap labor" force of the city.[35]

Doubtless some of them had been recruited from abroad, but probably not by the Milwaukee employers themselves. Agents in New York and Chicago recruited and distributed immigrants, particularly those from Scandinavia and Italy. These agents rarely acted upon orders from employers; instead, they depended on the immigrant traffic for their livelihood. They usually recruited immigrants before finding jobs for them, and then attempted in various ways to get work for their men in lumber camps, mines, railroad construction outfits, and factories.[36] Unquestionably some, and perhaps many, of the unskilled immigrants who flowed into Milwaukee were recruited by private agents. In the 1880's, for example, when Italians founded a small colony in Milwaukee near the yards of the Chicago and North Western Railroad, the Wisconsin Bureau of Labor and Industrial Statistics reported that a "New York Labor and Construction Company" had brought many of them from Europe to work on Wisconsin's railroads.[37]

---

[35] Milwaukee Chamber of Commerce, *Report, 1871,* p. 144. The extent of emigration of Germans and Poles from Germany in the early 1880's was widely discussed in the German press. Many such pieces were reprinted in the New York *Staats-Zeitung,* 1880–1883. For the other immigrant groups, see *L'Italia,* January 15, 1887; Wisconsin Bureau of Labor and Industrial Statistics, *Biennial Report, 1905–1906,* pp. 289, 305; G. La Piana, *The Italians in Milwaukee, Wisconsin* (Milwaukee, 1915), 5, 18; Manuscript Wisconsin Census, 1905, Wards 2–3, 5; Walter H. Houser, *Tabular Statement of the 1905 Census* (Madison, 1906), part 1: 172–173.

[36] Erickson, *American Industry and the European Immigrant,* 83–105.

[37] Wisconsin Bureau of Labor and Industrial Statistics, *Biennial Report, 1885–1886,* p. 426. In 1907 a special assistant to the Attorney General

That others ended up in Milwaukee was a matter of chance. One Jewish tailor from Poland recalled that when he had been laid off by a shop in New York's garment district, he had joined many other tailors milling about in a park on the Lower East Side. There on a park bench he fell into conversation with a stranger. The pair decided to go to Cleveland, where, they had been told, there were Jews and garment shops. They found work for a few weeks in Cleveland, but when they were again laid off they decided to try Milwaukee, where, they had learned, there were also both Jews and garment shops.[38]

In Milwaukee immigrants entered a labor market ruled by the laws of supply and demand. Competing with members of their own group and with native-born Americans, and encountering men who were often not of their own kind, workers found jobs in a variety of ways. Job tips were passed on from worker to worker, and most men made the rounds of the factory gates. The city's English- and foreign-language newspapers informed workers about employment opportunities, and agents of companies recruited workers when their plants needed more men. Immigrants who had become foremen often brought their countrymen into the shops, and immigrant aid societies functioned as clearing houses for jobs.

---

of the United States charged that the Peter McDonald Company of New York City dominated the recruitment and distribution of immigrants; see Mary Grace Quackenbos, typescript report on conditions at Delta Plantations, in the Numerical File, case number 6923/10/11, p. 11, United States Department of State, in the National Archives. In 1911 it was suspected that Greeks were being recruited for shipment to Milwaukee; typescript report of the meeting of a Board of Special Inquiry held at Ellis Island, April 9, 1911; Bloodgood, Kemper, and Bloodgood to the Commissioner General of Immigration, Milwaukee, April 11, 1911 [telegram]; typescript report of Decision of Deportation, April 27, 1911; Commissioner General of Immigration to Edward Haas, July 11, 1912, United States Bureau of Immigration and Naturalization, Record Group 85, case file 53246/206, in the National Archives. Mexicans may have been recruited for work in Milwaukee; see *Milwaukee Journal*, May 15, 1919; Milwaukee Y.M.C.A., *Annual Report, 1920*, p. 7.

[38] Interview with Sam Leshin, 1956.

Various individuals, independently and in concert, functioned as informal employment agents. In German and Polish neighborhoods, for example, the saloonkeepers often charged fees for finding employment for beer-drinking customers. Such operators were not licensed, posted no bonds, and did not register their addresses with governmental agencies. They charged as much as the traffic would bear for their services, and workers had little or no recourse to the courts in the event that agents took their fees but did not deliver the promised employment. Not until 1899 did the state legislature seek to prohibit the most flagrant practices of private employment agents, and even then the law did not provide adequate administrative and enforcement machinery. More than fifteen years elapsed before private employment agents were brought under effective governmental control. Finally in 1914, three years after its establishment, the state's free public employment office began to help immigrants find employment.[39]

Three kinds of more formal employment agencies flourished in the city's labor market: the general employment office, those specializing in female labor, and those handling immigrant labor. The Milwaukee Employment Agency handled positions for "attendants of machinery, janitors, foremen in tinware factories, delivery clerks, choremen, teamsters, hostlers, factory hands, choppers of cord wood," and farm hands.[40] The private United States Employment Office had positions for girls as well as for teamsters, general laborers, butchers, sausage makers, cabinet and wagon makers, blacksmiths, machinists, and for men who could make railroad ties and posts.[41] Mrs. J. Enders' "intelligence office" specialized in female help. She did not specify the kinds of

---

[39] William G. Bruce, *I Was Born in America* (Milwaukee, 1937), 8; interview with Leiserson; Wisconsin Bureau of Labor and Industrial Statistics, *Biennial Report, 1899–1900,* pp. 24–25; Erickson, *American Industry and the European Immigrant,* 88–105; Lescohier, *Labor Market,* 141–145.

[40] *Milwaukee Sentinel,* January 4, 1893.

[41] *Ibid.,* January 6, 1893.

positions she had available, but instead announced that she wanted a few "first class girls" and that persons needing girls would "do well to call" at her address.[42]

At least two agencies specialized in immigrant labor, particularly seeking unskilled laborers from eastern and southern Europe.[43] The C. W. St. John's agency served immigrant labor by supplying workers to railroad and lumber companies and to building contractors in and out of Milwaukee. The agency usually handled temporary help and supplied labor gangs. "Two hundred men for R.R. work in Wisconsin and northern Michigan. Highest wages paid. Free fare. Ship tonight," was a typical newspaper announcement for this agency.[44]

St. John's, like its counterparts in other industrial centers, customarily offered immigrants special services. Gangs of immigrants not speaking English required interpreters. They needed instructions for traveling. They usually wanted help in reading letters and other matter. Sometimes they wanted translations and help in sending money orders to relatives abroad. For these and other services, the employment agencies charged a price.[45]

[42] *Ibid.,* June 29, 1882. She was not located in the prostitution district of Milwaukee.

[43] William M. Leiserson was in charge of the free employment office, operated in Milwaukee after 1911 by the Wisconsin Industrial Commission. In his study *Adjusting Immigrant and Industry,* he did not name the agencies that handled immigrants, but shortly before his death he told the author that there were more than two agencies specializing in immigrant labor.

[44] The positions handled by the St. John's agency were usually filled by immigrants from eastern and southern Europe. Wisconsin Bureau of Labor and Industrial Statistics, *Biennial Report, 1885–1886,* pp. 425–426; Leiserson, *Adjusting Immigrant and Industry,* 61; Fred C. Lorenz to Robert M. La Follette, November 8, 1902, in the Robert M. La Follette Papers, in the State Historical Society of Wisconsin. For examples of advertisements placed in Milwaukee newspapers by the St. John's agency, see *Milwaukee Sentinel,* June 12, 1882; February 6, 1893; *Milwaukee Germania Abendpost,* October 14, 1897.

[45] For special services generally rendered by immigrant employment agencies or agents, see Erickson, *American Industry and the European Immigrant,* 178–179. The office of the industrial commission in Milwaukee was forced to supply some of these services when it attempted to serve immigrants. Leiserson, *Adjusting Immigrant and Industry,* 61; Wisconsin Industrial Commission, *Bulletin,* 2: 216 (1913); *Report on Allied Functions, 1914,* p. 41; Citi-

Factory owners occasionally sent some of their employees directly into the market to find workers.[46] One that regularly did so was the Bucyrus Company, a manufacturer of excavation equipment, which had learned to rely on a floating labor population. When production was at its peak, the company sent out its agents. They brought itinerant mechanics and unskilled laborers to South Milwaukee. Bucyrus also followed the practice, common in Milwaukee, of sending out agents to replace striking workers with non-union men in times of protracted strikes. During a strike in 1901, for example, Bucyrus set up a permanent recruiting office in a Milwaukee hotel where agents of the company interviewed applicants. The agents hired men for machine shop work and sent them to South Milwaukee under protective escort.[47]

Contractors and subcontractors were also important to the immigrant for obtaining employment. They had agreements with factory owners permitting them to hire their own immigrant workers and to pay them wages.[48] Contract systems of labor were common in the garment industry and in construction work, sectors of the economy employing immigrants from eastern and southern Europe. When Italians were employed as coal heavers or as construction workers, the practice usually was called the *padrone* system of contracting.[49]

---

zens Committee on Unemployment and the Milwaukee Free Employment Office, *Report, 1914*, p. 4.

[46] Wisconsin Industrial Commission, *Bulletin*, 2: 216, 217, 231 (1913); interview with Leiserson.

[47] Williamson and Myers, *Designed for Digging*, 128–129, 63; John M. Millman to Howard P. Eells, June 26, July 18, 1901, quoted in typescript draft 5, p. 134, of *ibid.*

[48] Wisconsin Bureau of Labor and Industrial Statistics, *Biennial Report, 1901–1902*, pp. 227–228. For contracting arrangements in the metal trades in Milwaukee, see the *Proceedings of the Iron Molders International Union of North America*, July 10, 1882, p. 67; *Milwaukee Germania Abendpost*, August 2, 1897.

[49] *Milwaukee Sentinel*, January 13, 1893; Wisconsin Bureau of Labor and Industrial Statistics, *Biennial Report, 1885–1886*, pp. 425–426; La Piana, *The Italians in Milwaukee*, 15; Angelo Cerminara to author, May 16, 1956. Cerminara was a consular agent of the Italian government in Milwaukee in the years preceding World War I. For many of the fundamental similarities between the padrone system and general contracting, see Erickson, *American Industry and the European Immigrant*, 85.

Private, non-profit organizations, though active as employment agencies, actually distributed relatively few workers within Milwaukee. The Young Men's Christian Association had an employment office to place applicants with Christian firms, and it helped workers find room and board in Christian homes. But its impact on the labor market was slight. In 1880, the "Y" secured only forty-four positions; in 1904 that number had not increased.[50] Much the same story was true of the *Deutsche Gesellschaft,* the leading immigrant aid society in Milwaukee. It, too, had an employment agency from the time of its establishment in 1880, but over the years it placed a surprisingly small number of workers. Like other immigrant societies, the *Gesellschaft* was more eager to locate newcomers outside rather than inside the city,[51] mainly because it wanted to lighten the burden on Milwaukee's German community and because it believed that other, smaller communities in Wisconsin could more readily assist the new arrivals.

Other private organizations provided similar services. Some of them were formed for specific purposes. The Russian Relief Committee was set up in 1882 to relocate Russian Jewish refugees unwanted in the city by leaders of the German and Bohemian Jewish community.[52] The committee found employment for a number of the newcomers within the city, on farms outside Milwaukee, and in various towns in Wisconsin, Iowa, and Minnesota.[53] The Hebrew Relief Association sought employment for Jews living in Milwaukee. After 1911 such agencies as the Associated Charities, the Home for the

[50] Milwaukee Y.M.C.A., *Annual Report, 1880,* pp. 16–17; *1904,* p. 26, in the Y.M.C.A. Archives.

[51] Deutsche Gesellschaft von Milwaukee, *Yearbooks,* 1881–1905. See also *Milwaukee Germania Abendpost,* March 5, June 9, July 12, August 6, 1897, for the number of Germans placed by the Gesellschaft. In the 1880's Christopher Reuter, the immigrant agent of the Gesellschaft, had an office in the immigrant's room of the depot of the Chicago, Milwaukee and St. Paul Railroad in Milwaukee; see *Milwaukee Sentinel,* January 6, 1893.

[52] For attitudes of German and Bohemian Jewish leaders of Milwaukee, see *ibid.,* June 1, 1882.

[53] *Ibid.,* September 1, 1882.

Friendless, the Volunteers of America, and the University Settlement House co-operated with the recently established state employment office to find work for immigrants as well as for native Americans.[54]

In times of serious unemployment and especially during periods of labor agitation, leading citizens of Milwaukee attempted to establish labor distribution centers.[55] In May of 1885, for example, such leading industrialists as Alexander Mitchell, D. N. Sanger, and David Adler informed the Milwaukee City Council that they intended to establish a "wood-yard" in Milwaukee which was to serve as a labor bureau "for the purpose of affording opportunity and means to intelligently deal with the evils of beggary and idleness that exist among the tramps and street loafers which infest our city." It was to be a non-profit organization intended "solely as a means of applying the labor test to the individual cases of tramps and beggars whereby those who [were] able but unwilling to work [might] be discovered and recognized and dealt with according to law." For men who passed the test the group proposed compensation by "giving them food and lodging before parting with them." In return "the beneficiary [was] to perform such manual labor as [might] be agreed upon." This proposal, termed "charitable" by the industrialists, was rejected by the city council.[56] It was not until after the turn of the century that employers established a permanent committee to deal with the problems of unemployment.

Employers attracted immigrants by advertising in the city's newspapers. The English-language press was used to recruit workers of all sorts, for employers knew that even those who could not read English would soon hear about the vacancies by word of mouth. The phrase "Poles wanted" commonly

---

[54] Citizens Committee on Unemployment and the Milwaukee Free Employment Office, *Report, 1916,* p. 12.

[55] Donald J. Berthrong, "Social Legislation in Wisconsin, 1836–1900," (doctoral thesis, typescript, University of Wisconsin, 1951), 238.

[56] Milwaukee Common Council, *Proceedings,* May 11, 1885, pp. 43, 91–92.

appeared in the *Kuryer Polski,* while advertisements in German-language newspapers were likely to attract German-Poles as well as Germans.[57]

Both the English- and German-language newspapers were used particularly to announce employment opportunities for skilled and semi-skilled workers, especially butchers, painters, bakers, machinists, tanners, cigar makers, tailors, wagon makers, sausage makers, furniture carpenters, and machine operators in the clothing, shoe, and leather industries. The garment industry advertised frequently for semi-skilled workers. "Fifty girls wanted for men's shirts, easy work, good pay," ran a typical advertisement. Some employers required experience in sewing particular garments; others advertised that the work was to be done on machines; still others announced that they wanted women to take sewing home, that the tools were supplied free of charge, and that complete instructions were available for one dollar. A few employers promised steady employment. One employer, seeking to tap the child labor market, advertised for a few girls to learn how to make vests. He asked specifically that girls bring their mothers so that working terms could be agreed on.[58]

Newspapers were less helpful to unskilled workers. Large employers, such as E. P. Allis, the Bradley and Metcalf Shoe Company, and the Ascherman cigar-making establishment did on occasion advertise in the *Kuryer,* but since its readers were primarily unskilled workers, it did not offer many positions, and, unlike other papers, it did not set aside a section

---

[57] The *Kuryer Polski* of Milwaukee was the successor to the *Krytyka* (1885–1888) and the *Dziennik Polski* (1887–1888). By 1893 it claimed to have 35,000 Polish readers in the city; see January 4, 1893. For examples of the use of the phrase "Poles wanted," see *ibid.,* May 11, June 2, 3, 1893. German newspapers rarely carried advertisements making a comparable appeal; however, newly arrived immigrants and those seeking domestics sometimes did advertise; see *Germania,* 1880–1883; *Herold,* 1886; *Milwaukee Abendpost,* January–May, 1897; *Milwaukee Germania Abendpost,* June–December, 1897, especially August 13, October 10, 1897.

[58] *Milwaukee Abendpost,* February 25, March 11, 12, April 5, 1897; *Milwaukee Germania Abendpost,* June 20, July 9, 15, August 22, September 22, 1897; see ads in the *Milwaukee Sentinel,* 1880, 1892.

for want ads.[59] From time to time, employers advertised in the German press for construction workers: ten men and five shovelers were wanted for a construction crew at Buffalo Street, between East Water Street and Broadway, and twenty shovel men could find work at Frederick and Bradford streets. But such announcements were not nearly so common as those calling for skilled and semi-skilled workers.[60] Most of Milwaukee's unskilled workers had to rely on informal tips and on the tedious method of going from factory to factory, from shop to shop, and from construction site to construction site.

Newly arrived immigrants particularly depended on temporary jobs, and their livelihoods often depended on the seasonal fluctuations in industrial activity. In the 1880's the commissioner of the Wisconsin Bureau of Labor and Industrial Statistics asserted that newcomers from Europe, mostly Germans and Poles, went first into such highly seasonal and unskilled work as sewer digging, hod carrying, and other outdoor labor. Then they found unskilled jobs in planing mills, bottling departments of breweries, tanneries, foundries, and trunk factories.[61] The United States Immigration Commission of 1910 found most of Milwaukee's Poles and Italians engaged as day laborers in factories, as track layers for the street railway, or as dockhands.[62]

Seasonal work was the best that many Milwaukeeans could obtain, for, with the possible exception of the brewing industry, almost all sectors of the economy had a yearly slack season.[63] Weather determined the employment seasons in outside construction work and ice harvesting. Cold winters provided employment for about 2,500 men in the ice fields,

[59] *Kuryer Polski,* April 24, May 11, June 5, 1893, including advertisements of the Rocky Mountain Oil Company and the Milwaukee Furniture Company.

[60] *Milwaukee Germania Abendpost,* July 2, August 26, October 5, 17, 25, November 17, 1897; *Milwaukee Abendpost,* April 19, 1897.

[61] Wisconsin Bureau of Labor and Industrial Statistics, *Biennial Report, 1885–1886,* pp. xxxvi–xxxviii, 269.

[62] United States Immigration Commission, *Immigrants in Cities: A Study of the Population of Selected Districts in New York, Chicago, Philadelphia, Boston, Cleveland and Milwaukee* (2 vols. Washington, 1911) 1: 732.

[63] Cochran, *Pabst,* 203, 402.

but with the thaw the harvesters had to look elsewhere for work. Construction workers knew that even in the best years a slack season would come between November and February.[64] The metal industries laid off many of their unskilled workers in the slow months of the summer.[65] The meat-packing industry, which gave employment to large numbers of German, Irish, and Polish immigrants, was a seasonal business until the middle of the 1890's, when the advent of economical mechanical refrigeration made it possible for this industry to operate throughout the year. Until then, meat-packing establishments operated during the winter by picking up workers from all over the city and laying them off in the early spring. In his youth the Irish immigrant Patrick Cudahy was a typical employee of meat-packing plants. He worked as a clerk, as an ice harvester, and at other odd jobs during the off-season until he finally learned to be a stone-cutter, a trade that served him in good stead when the meat-packing establishments were closed.[66]

During extended periods of high productivity, common laborers fared well. One such period occurred between 1916 and 1920, the years of World War I. In part because of the general cessation of immigration to the United States, and in part because of the maldistribution of labor in Milwaukee, skilled and unskilled laborers were scarce. Immigrants found jobs easily no matter what their nationality, and manufacturers even used female immigrants in traditionally masculine occupations. "A few foreign born women who cannot even speak English," reported the Citizens Committee on Unemployment in 1918, "working in local lumber yards, core

[64] Citizens Committee on Unemployment and the Milwaukee Free Employment Office, Report, 1912, p. 226; 1913, p. 3; 1914, p. 304; 1915, pp. 3–4; 1916, pp. 3–4; 1918, pp. 5–6.

[65] For seasonal changes in the labor force of the Milwaukee Harvester Company, see its payroll books, 1899–1901, in the McCormick Collection.

[66] Cudahy, His Life, 135; James E. Pooles, "Stories of Packingtowns: Plankinton of Milwaukee and the Four Cudahys," in Country Gentlemen, 93: 22–23, 119 (April, 1928).

rooms and machine shops [earned] twenty-five to thirty cents an hour for a nine-hour day, and in some cases [received] a bonus besides."[67]

The period of World War I was, however, exceptional. When the Civil War boom collapsed in 1873, none but the highly skilled had employment security. In normal years there were usually many applicants for each job, and in depressions, particularly those of 1893 and 1911, thousands were unemployed. Immigrants had little choice but to make the rounds of factory gates, where men by the hundreds congregated every day in hope that the foremen would pick them for a job. Frederick Heath, a Socialist and a member of the Federated Trades Council of Milwaukee, hardly exaggerated when he spoke of the "crowds of work-hungry men scrambling desperately for work in the knowledge that their families were anxiously waiting to learn of their successes or failures at the gates."[68]

In Milwaukee's competitive economy the number of men employed by a growing company increased irregularly. The E. P. Allis Company in 1879 employed an average of about 400 workers. In the "good years" of 1879 to 1883, the work force doubled, and by the end of the decade the company had some 1,500 men distributed among its three plants. In the 1890's, the number of men employed fluctuated between 1,100 and 1,700. The company had begun the decade with about 1,400 employees, but in 1893–1894, the first year of the depression, it reduced this number to about 1,100. In 1895–1896, its work force began to grow again. The company employed about 1,300 men that year; 1,400 in 1897; 1,700 in 1899; 2,800 in 1903; 3,535 in 1908; and 4,500 in 1909.

The size of a company's average work force, however, indicated little about the total number of men a firm hired during a year. Hundreds of men were taken on each year,

[67] Citizens Committee on Unemployment and the Milwaukee Free Employment Office, *Report, 1918,* p. 7.
[68] Wisconsin Industrial Commission, *Bulletin, 1913,* 2: 219.

some only to work a few hours a day or a few days a week. At the Allis firm in the 1890's, the number of new men taken on each year varied from about 200 to 800, and at the Bucyrus Company the rate of labor turnover in the early twentieth century annually varied from 200 to 350 per cent of average employment.

Fluctuations in the size of a company's work force occurred at irregular intervals. At the Milwaukee Harvester Company, between September and June, 1899–1900, the complement of workers in eight departments doubled at the peak of employment. In the machine shop, the wood shop, and the foundry, the number climbed from an average of seventy to an average of 155, but in three other departments—the blacksmith shop, the canvasroom, and the shipping department—the fluctuations were less marked.[69]

In most factories, wages varied among and within occupational groups. At the E. P. Allis works, for example, from 5 to 10 per cent of the workers were employed by the month, the remainder by the day. Wages averaged $538 annually in 1894–1895, and $610 in 1897–1898. Workers averaged from $1.83 to $1.99 for a ten-hour day; but one to two per cent of them earned $5.00 or more, and the daily rates for foremen, masons, draftsmen, molders of various types, and laboratory workers averaged between $2.70 and $4.00 daily, according to their particular skills. Such men as carpenters, molders on piecework, blacksmiths, and machinists earned between $2.00 and $2.70 a day. Unskilled laborers received from $1.34 to $1.47 daily; helpers and apprentices, still less. The relatively high proportion of unskilled to skilled workers in the

[69] Employment data for E. P. Allis may be found in the factory inspection reports of the Wisconsin Bureau of Labor and Industrial Statistics, *Biennial Report*, 1885 to 1910; E. P. Allis Company payroll books, 1889–1904, in the Allis-Chalmers Archives; Wisconsin Legislature, Committee on Industrial Insurance, typescript report and testimony, October 13, 1909, pp. 336–337, 344, in the Wisconsin Legislative Library, Madison. For the Bucyrus Company see Williamson and Myers, *Designed for Digging*, 128, and for the Milwaukee Harvester Company see its payroll books, 1899–1901.

Allis labor force held the average daily wage to the relatively low levels.

Occupational classifications were neither precise nor rigid. As late as 1918 no company in the metal trades subscribed to the practice of paying workmen according to occupational ratings.[70] Instead, each man was paid on the basis of an evaluation by his superiors. Thus two machinists in the same shop, who in theory might have had identical ratings, did not necessarily draw identical wages even if they worked the same number of hours or made the same number of pieces. At the E. P. Allis works, there were also wage differences within occupational groupings which were apparently related to the particular shops of the company. Thus in 1902–1903 machinists in six different shops earned six different wages, ranging from $2.14 to $2.71 a day. Not one of these machinists was listed as a pieceworker.

According to its payroll book, the E. P. Allis Company divided its work force into thirty to forty classifications, forming a wage hierarchy. The company also created an occupational hierarchy based on skills and the type of work within the various classifications. In 1902 there were carpenter laborers, yard laborers, machinist laborers, and foundry laborers. The daily wage rate in each group varied from about $1.50 to about $1.70. Machinist laborers received the lowest pay; yet work in the machine shop was considered to be cleaner and more desirable than work in the foundry.

Over the years, in companies employing thousands of immigrants and native Americans, many factors determined the worker's point of entry into, and his direction and rate of mobility within, the hierarchies. The factors included the labor needs of a manufacturing enterprise; a man's skills; his age and physical well-being; his length of service with a company; his participation in strikes; and his ethnic origin. This

---

[70] Typescript testimony of Otto Falk in "Brief of Employers," National War Labor Board, Record Group 2, case file no. 163, in the National Archives.

complex of considerations governed the decisions of the men
who hired and supervised Milwaukee's workers.[71]

[71] On August 1, 1901, J. M. J. Keogh wrote that he had been instructed
"to advance wages of the 92 machinists who stuck by us during the strike
and to have the advance date from May 20th . . . ." Keogh to J. A. Milne,
quoted in Alberta Price, "History of the Allis-Chalmers Company, 1866–
1900," 104, in the Allis-Chalmers Archives.

2

The Immigrants

ANY IMMIGRANTS who thought that moving to the Land of the Free made them masters of their own destinies—or even of their economic well-being—were in for a rude shock. In the America of the late nineteenth century, power flowed from above—more circuitously than it flowed in Europe, perhaps, but just as surely.

It could hardly have been otherwise, but two conditions in particular precluded other possibilities. Immigrants, like natives, accepted the working myth (like all working myths, partially true) that in the United States any individual could, through the magic of self-help, rise towards the source of power. The other was that above, at the levels of management and ownership of the burgeoning factories, power was becoming increasingly concentrated; while below, on the level of workers, both immigrant and native-born, there was division—division accentuated by almost everything in the steam-powered system.

Until the turn of the century, only one force was theoretically working otherwise: the weak trade unions, striving through collective bargaining to limit managerial power in the interest of their members and in the name of all workers. The doctrine of collective bargaining was clearly subversive for the emerging economic order. Accordingly, management tried to quash it, ruthlessly and efficiently.

Outside the factory, choice and chance combined to remind immigrants that each ethnic group was imprisoned in a stereotype that dictated where and how its members could work, live, worship, vote, or deal with members of other groups. Inside the factory, management accepted and chose to preserve both the stereotypes and the real characteristics that underlay them. Until management got caught up in a rationalization movement of its own making, but beyond its control, the system of ethnic stereotypes made the tasks of management easier.

The patterns of ethnic stereotypes in Milwaukee dictated a clear pecking order for immigrants from central, eastern, and southern Europe.[1] At the head of it stood the Germans. In 1871, the secretary of the Milwaukee Chamber of Commerce boasted that the city's Germans were "thrifty, frugal, industrious, and productive." They were a stable group: "Each owns a little land about his house, sports a pig or two, sends his troupe of children to school, and even saves on nine dollars a week." The image of stability, industriousness, and frugality did not change over the years.[2] Indeed, by the 1880's

[1] Apart from these immigrants were such influential immigrant groups as the Scots and the Irish. Alexander Mitchell made the Scots the most influential ethnic group in Milwaukee's economy, and for many years the Irish shared the control of politics with native Americans. For Mitchell, see Horace S. Merrill, *William Freeman Vilas: Doctrinaire Democrat* (Madison, 1954), 32, 175; *Dictionary of American Biography*, 13: 39–40; Andersen, *A Century of Banking in Wisconsin*, 7–13, 27, 39, 46, 56, 81, 82; Derleth, *The Milwaukee Road: Its First Hundred Years* (New York, 1948), 66–95. On the Irish and politics, see Still, *Milwaukee*, 75–77, 81, 105, 130, 134–135. The small number of German names appearing on the lists of postmasters and custom inspectors for the period 1843 to 1880 is striking. Flower, *History of Milwaukee*, 1052, 1062. The chairman of the Wisconsin Democratic State Central Committee complained to Senator William F. Vilas in 1888 that "The Irish are constant and persistent applicants for positions, and unless the class is closely watched will get much more than their proportion. No Milwaukee German has so far received any considerable appointment [and] the class of Germans who are pressing [for appointments] are important." Ellis P. Usher to Vilas, April 4, 1888, in the Ellis P. Usher Papers, in the State Historical Society of Wisconsin. In 1892 Edward C. Wall informed Vilas that there "had been a lot of bad nominations made here for Aldermen. The Catholics and Irish as usual, walked away with everything. . . ." Wall to Vilas, March 18, 1892, in the William F. Vilas Papers, in the State Historical Society of Wisconsin.

[2] Milwaukee Chamber of Commerce, *Report, 1871*, p. 16; Wisconsin Bureau of Labor and Industrial Statistics, *Biennial Report, 1905–1906*, pp. 315–316; Irene Osgood, in *ibid., 1907–1908*, p. 1079.

Germans were usually thought of as being separate from other immigrant groups—almost as if they had gained the stature of native Americans.

Thereafter, Germans moved with relative ease into most areas of the city's life. In the last two decades of the nineteenth century they could be found living in almost every section of Milwaukee; their churches, press, labor organizations, and cultural groups gave the city its distinctive German-American flavor; and Germans were influential, though not necessarily leaders, in Milwaukee's economic, political, religious, and social life. Germans belonged not only to an old well-established immigrant group, but also to that larger body of citizens who had transformed Milwaukee from a village into a city and who had defended the Union during the Civil War. To be sure, some Germans were social laborites and social democrats, but not enough to offset the influence of the majority who were committed to either Bourbon Democracy or Stalwart Republicanism. Moreover, too many Germans belonged to Lutheran churches to justify labeling the Germans a Catholic influence in the city, and opponents of radicalism and Catholicism could be found as readily among Germans as among native Americans. Indeed, on such issues Germans were often more vehement in their opposition than were American-born citizens. Until World War I, nativists had great difficulty in finding grounds for opposing the entire German immigrant community.[3]

Most Americans thought that immigrants were plodding and industrious, and that, because they had brought little cash from the old country, they had to work or starve. Immigrants, it was thought, would work in occupations which were spurned by non-immigrants. They were considered socially inferior. In times of serious labor disturbances, as in 1886,

[3] Wilhelm Hense-Jensen and Ernest Bruncken, *Wisconsin's Deutsch-Amerikaner bis Schluss des neunzehnten Jahrhunderts* (2 vols. Milwaukee, 1900–1902), 1: 183–210; 2: 67–68, 82, 83, 85, 88, 92–96, 106–107, 135–136, 175–181; Still, *Milwaukee,* 157–160, 259–262, 265, 420–421; Cochran, *Pabst,* 42, 68; Clark, *History of Manufactures,* 3: 465. See also membership and officer lists for the following associations: Association for the Advancement of Milwaukee, in Anderson and Blyer, *Milwaukee's Great Industries,* xiii–xx; *Milwaukee Industrial Exposition, 1882,* p. 1; *1901–1902,* p. 12; *Milwaukee Club, 1883,*

they were seen as a group that hated the military, and as an uneducated, helpless, ignorant mass, easily misled by labor agitators. Many immigrants were considered inherently unclean and unfit for the industrial discipline of the workshop.[4]

Each group, however, had its special image. Though sometimes thought of as ignorant newcomers, Poles were generally considered thrifty and industrious, somewhat less stable than the Germans, and, in times of unemployment, given to quarreling and pilfering. Too, both German- and native-born persons alike considered Polish immigrants to be subservient to Rome in political matters. Republicans utilized the Catholic affiliation of the Poles in denouncing local Democracy, especially when the American Protective Association made significant inroads into Milwaukee politics. In 1886, when violence broke out between forces of capital and labor, officials and other spokesmen blamed Poles for the disorders. The lone Polish alderman on the city council was held accountable for the actions of his countrymen; his critics left little doubt that they viewed him and his constitutents as second-class citizens.[5] Still, Poles were considered superior to Italians, Hungarians, and Greeks.

Almost from the beginning, Italians in America had been

---

p. 1; *1884*, pp. 33–36; *1898*, n.p. For anti-Catholicism among Milwaukee Germans, see, for example, Wall to Vilas, September 13, 1893; January 31, 1894; Reverend J. Schlerf to Vilas, February 10, 12, 1894; A. F. Ernst to Vilas, February 12, 1894, all in the Vilas Papers. For examples of Germans in Democratic and Republican politics, see Wall to Vilas, May 18, 26, August 25, 1891; January 27, September 13, October 12, 1894, in the Vilas Papers, and Zeno M. Host to Robert M. La Follette, November 22, 1902, in the La Follette Papers.

[4] *Milwaukee Sentinel,* June 2, 1882; Wisconsin Bureau of Labor and Industrial Statistics, *Biennial Report, 1883–1884,* pp. 111–112; *1885–1886,* pp. xxi, 416–421; *1899–1900,* pp. 283–284; *1901–1902,* pp. 228–231; *1903–1904,* pp. 157–158, 163; *1905–1906,* p. 333. For Governor Rusk's comments on the immigrants during the labor disturbances of 1886, see his draft of a speech to be given in Milwaukee in May of that year, in the Jeremiah Rusk Papers, in the State Historical Society of Wisconsin.

[5] *Herold,* May 4–7, 1886, April 6, 9, 1892; *Milwaukee Sentinel,* February 5, 1893; Wisconsin Bureau of Labor and Industrial Statistics, *Biennial Report, 1885–1886,* pp. xxi, lvi, 329, 330–332, 337; Milwaukee Common Council, *Proceedings,* May 10, 24, July 2, 1886.

categorized as itinerant laborers, moving with the seasons in their search for work with railroad construction gangs or on the levees of New Orleans. Long after they had settled in Milwaukee, this stereotype stayed with them: they were untidy in their habits, but not destructive; they were especially ignorant of the English language and did not comprehend American methods and technology. These factors and their presumed natural disposition to laziness made them fit only for common labor. They drank too much, indulged in hasty quarreling among themselves (though without coming into conflict with other nationality groups), and too often resorted to violence. In 1897, Italians were temporarily boycotted because of a revenge murder that had occurred in the third ward, the Italian section of Milwaukee.[6] "Very many of them," complained a German citizen of the third ward, "are supported by the city but this does not prevent them from consuming 5–6 pints of beer or more each day and disturbing the neighborhood as well as lowering the property value. *Raufereien* [rowdy brawls] are the order of the day, even murder does not bother them. . . . Can nothing be done?"

Hungarians were industrious and honest. Retailers considered them good customers. Hungarians, however, chose to live in wretched housing. Their habits of cleanliness, regardless of the environment or their personal means, left much to be desired. According to one investigator, they were just too interested in saving as much of their earnings as possible so that they could take their savings back to Hungary. The Greeks were considered more unstable than the Italians or Hungarians because "many Greeks [were] given to drinking and quarreling." They were considered less sober and less industrious than either Italians or Jews.[7] Patrick Cudahy of the Cudahy meat-packing company refused to hire Greeks after a small group of them became involved in a fight with

---

[6] Wisconsin Bureau of Labor and Industrial Statistics, *Biennial Report, 1905–1906,* pp. 297, 316–317; La Piana, *The Italians in Milwaukee,* 7–9. *Milwaukee Germania Abendpost,* July 12, 13, 16, 17, 18, 23, 1897.

[7] Wisconsin Bureau of Labor and Industrial Statistics, *Biennial Report, 1905–1906,* pp. 316–317.

some other workers. When the Greeks drew knives, Cudahy promptly fired them and never again hired Greeks. His image of Greek workers had been set: they were too volatile to accept industrial discipline.[8]

The attitude of William Powell, the emigration commissioner for the Chicago, Milwaukee and St. Paul Railroad, revealed how an image of an ethnic group was sometimes formed. In 1882, a group of 250 Jewish refugees from Russia reached Milwaukee. The local German and Bohemian Jews, offended by the newcomers' personal habits and by their strange garb, tried desperately to ship them out of the city. They turned to Powell, hoping that he would settle them on railroad land. Powell refused, partly because his knowledge of Russian life, derived from the novels of Turgenev and Tolstoi, had led him to conclude that the Russian Jewish refugees had no capacity for tilling the soil. In his view, the railroad company would derive little benefit from settling such immigrants on its lands.[9]

Residential patterns—who lived near whom—reflected ethnic images and immigrants' preferences to live with their own kind. Within the limits imposed by the physical features of the city, the existence of earlier settlements, and distribution of factory sites, the residential patterns of Milwaukee were established between 1870 and 1905.

Jews from eastern Europe, Greeks, Hungarians, and some Poles settled in the wards north of the Menomonee River and west of the Milwaukee River, where they gradually displaced the German residents who were then in the process of locating almost exclusively in the sections farther north and west. Poles usually came to the South Side, first living among Germans and Scandinavians in a sparsely settled neighbor-

---

[8] Cudahy, *His Life,* 145; interview with Cudahy.

[9] *Milwaukee Sentinel,* July 1, 1882. In 1914, H. J. Beckerle, the superintendent of the Wisconsin Free Employment Office in Milwaukee, also placed men on the basis of his image of nationality groups. Russians, he said, "are accustomed to hard manual labor. We place them if possible in street or railway construction work. The Jews are different. They are often not accustomed to hard work and often are unskilled. We find factory work, if possible, for them." *Milwaukee Journal,* January 4, 1914.

hood bounded by factory sites, railroad tracks, and unsettled marshland, then expanding in a southwesterly direction. By 1905 the South Side was predominantly Polish. The Italians who came in the 1880's settled the ward hemmed in by the Milwaukee River and Lake Michigan and, as the Irish moved elsewhere, gradually came to dominate the neighborhood.[10] Scandinavians were scattered. In 1905 they constituted almost a fifth of the foreign-born population in the third ward and were, next to the Italians and Irish, the largest single immigrant group there; but they were also found in relatively large numbers in six other neighborhoods near the factory sites on the rivers and on the southern lake front. Most Austrians settled in the fifth ward.[11]

Later, recruitment of immigrants helped give Cudahy and South Milwaukee their ethnic compositions. Patrick Cudahy did not leave this to chance. In 1893 he flooded the *Kuryer Polski* with advertisements telling readers that he wanted 1,000 Poles to live and work in the new suburb. He promised employment to every Pole who bought one of his parcels of land and assured them that they could build their own churches and schools. In addition, he gave land to the Catholic Church and strove to improve transportation facilities between Milwaukee and his suburb. In 1893 the Chicago and North Western Railroad was its only means of rapid transit. By the end of the decade a trolley line also connected the new community with Milwaukee. The results of these efforts were

[10] Manuscript United States Census, 1880, City of Milwaukee, especially wards 1–5, 12; Manuscript Wisconsin Census, 1905, Milwaukee, especially wards 2–3, 5, 12–14, 18. See also Houser, *Tabular Statement of the 1905 Census*, part 2: 172–173; *United States Census, 1870*, 1: 386–391; *1890*, 4, part 2: 259, 260–267; Wisconsin Bureau of Labor and Industrial Statistics, *Biennial Report, 1905–1906*, pp. 289, 305; *Milwaukee City Directory, 1880; 1905*; *Milwaukee Sentinel*, February 24, 1880; *Milwaukee Germania Abendpost*, September 19, 1897; *L'Italia,* January 15, 1887; Still, *Milwaukee*, 112; Cochran, *Pabst*, 254–255; Bruce, *I Was Born in America*, 1–2, 5–6; Laurence M. Larson, *The Log Book of a Young Immigrant* (Northfield, Minn., 1939), 284.

[11] *L'Italia,* January 15, 1887; Wisconsin Bureau of Labor and Industrial Statistics, *Biennial Report, 1905–1906*, pp. 289, 305; La Piana, *Italians in Milwaukee*, 5, 18; Manuscript Wisconsin Census, 1905, Milwaukee, wards 2, 3, 5; Houser, *Tabular Statement of the 1905 Census*, part 1: 172–173.

reflected in the census of 1905. Foreign-born residents made up 45 per cent of the population; more than a third of the immigrants were Poles, almost all of them from German and Russian Poland; a quarter of the immigrants were Germans.[12]

The South Milwaukee Improvement Company made similar efforts to settle its new suburb. It promoted the new townsite by advertising in the *Kuryer Polski* and other Milwaukee newspapers and by subsidizing manufacturers who located in the new community. The Bucyrus Company of Ohio was the first of a number of companies to relocate there. Beginning in 1893, Bucyrus brought in workers from Ohio and in later years recruited workers in Milwaukee and elsewhere. Bucyrus built company houses at a time when little housing was available, and in 1898 it established a home loan association to finance construction by new residents. In 1905, foreign-born residents formed almost a third of the population, with Germans and Austrian-Poles constituting nearly three-quarters of this total.[13]

Organized religion accentuated the stereotyped images and patterns of population distribution. Most Christian immigrants in Milwaukee were either Lutherans or Roman Catholics who worshipped in churches which had been established in ante-bellum days by the first German settlers. A close tie between language and religion, the steady Lutheran and Catholic immigration to the city, and the churches' educational institutions contributed to the hold these bodies retained over the offspring of European immigrants. The Lutheran churches recruited most of their members from the

---

[12] Cudahy, *His Life*, 115, 135, 138, 139–141, 146–147, 161–162; *Kuryer Polski*, June 1–3, 1893; Wisconsin Bank Examiner, *Annual Report of the Conditions of the Loan and Building Associations of Wisconsin, 1898*, p. 52; *1900*, pp. 4, 72; interview with Cudahy; *Milwaukee Sentinel*, March 20, 1893; Still, *Milwaukee*, 379; Houser, *Tabular Statement of the 1905 Census*, part 1: 170. The manuscript copy of the Cudahy census was inspected.

[13] Williamson and Myers, *Designed for Digging*, 44–45, 62–63, 72–73, 127–129; Wisconsin Bank Examiner, *Annual Report of Loan and Building Associations, 1898*, p. 28; *1901*, p. 140; *Kuryer Polski*, January 2, 3, June 17, 1893; Houser, *Tabular Statement of the 1905 Census*, part 1: 170, 172–173. The manuscript copy of the South Milwaukee census was inspected.

German element, so that few nationality conflicts disturbed internal Lutheran peace.[14]

The Roman Catholic Church faced much more complicated problems. Poles especially, but also Italians and other eastern and southern Europeans, joined native Americans and the Irish in opposing German control of the Catholic hierarchy. In their early years in Milwaukee, Poles were usually obliged to worship in churches founded by Germans and led by German priests. Later, after the turn of the century, when they had already established a number of large parishes and were receiving the sacraments from Polish priests, they continued to charge that they were inadequately represented in the Milwaukee hierarchy.[15]

In the 1880's and 1890's the Poles could not, however, join the Irish and native Americans in their successful struggle against the Germans to Americanize the Catholic Church. For Poles, as for Germans, nationalism and Catholicism were so intertwined that the one nourished the other, and the last thing that Poles wanted in America in their early years was to lose identity as a separate group. Thus they petitioned for, but did not obtain, national representation within the Roman Church. The stumbling block, at least as it appeared to the hierarchy, was that appointment of a Polish bishop would hamper rather than aid the unity of the church. As a former opponent of the Americanizers, the Swiss-German Archbishop of Milwaukee, Sebastian Messmer, explained to Archbishop James Gibbons in 1905: "The longer I think it over the more it seems to me a dangerous experiment to give the Polish people a bishop." The trouble, Messmer thought,

[14] Still, *Milwaukee*, 80, 90, 92, 269–272, 274, 275, 277, 419–420, 472–473; Hense-Jensen and Bruncken, *Wisconsin's Deutsch-Amerikaner*, 2: 172–181, for a discussion of the social and political conservatism of the Lutheran church, especially its opposition to socialism.

[15] Waclaw Kruszka, *Historya polski w ameryce* (13 volumes, Milwaukee, 1907), 7: 126–127; 8: 28–32; Thaddeus Borun, compiler, *We, the Milwaukee Poles* (Milwaukee, 1946), 3–28, 39, 54–55; Still, *Milwaukee*, 267–270; Colman J. Barry, *The Catholic Church and German Americans* (Milwaukee, 1953), 46–47, 128, 131–182; Hense-Jensen and Bruncken, *Wisconsin's Deutsch-Amerikaner*, 2: 170–171.

was that he would be considered "the bishop for *all the Poles* of the U.S."[16]

Milwaukee politicians also faced (and sometimes exploited) distinctions among immigrants, especially between Germans and Poles. In the competition for votes, all parties approached naturalized citizens on their own terms. Politicians spoke the language of their constituents and printed party propaganda in various languages.[17] The Social Democrats gained support in the Polish wards after the turn of the century by printing their pamphlets in Polish.[18] Before World War I, campaigners usually took care not to offend immigrants, but when it suited their purposes they played on ethnic animosities.[19] Prejudice in politics—as Edward C. Wall, the astute chairman of the Wisconsin Democratic State Central Committee in the 1890's, recognized—was a "far more potent factor than argument." Whenever possible, he strove "to have prejudice work against the other side."[20] To be sure, the immigrant expected to be rewarded for his support at the polls. Teaching of German, Polish, and Italian in the public school curriculum, the use of German as the second official language in municipal publications, the use of interpreters in local courts, the absence of state-wide temperance legislation, the failure of attacks on

[16] Messmer to Gibbons, January 19, 1905, quoted in Barry, *Catholic Church and German Americans,* 275, note 61.

[17] Gerd Korman, "Political Loyalties, Immigrant Traditions, and Reform: The Wisconsin German-American Press and Progressivism, 1909–1912," in the *Wisconsin Magazine of History,* 40: 161–168 (Spring, 1957).

[18] Marvin Wachman, *History of the Social-Democratic Party of Milwaukee, 1897–1910* (Urbana, 1945), 62–63, 71, 80.

[19] For examples of the use of campaign techniques tailored to immigrants, see R. H. Baker, chairman of the Republican State Central Committee, to E. Keyes, July 20, 1880, in the Elisha Keyes Papers, in the State Historical Society of Wisconsin; Usher to Calvin C. Brice, August 18, 31, 1888; Brice, chairman, Campaign Committee of the National Democratic Committee, to Usher, August 6, 1888; Andrew Simonson, secretary and treasurer of the Wisconsin Democratic Editorial Association, to Usher, October 11, 1888, all in the Usher Papers; La Follette to George E. Bryant, chairman, Republican State Central Committee, October 1, 1900; October 19, 1902, in the La Follette Papers; the *Milwaukee Wochenblatt* (Yiddish) to Paul O. Husting, August 22, 1914, in the Paul O. Husting Papers, in the State Historical Society of Wisconsin.

[20] Wall to Vilas, May 18, June 12, 1892, in the Vilas Papers.

immigrants' parochial schools, and, of course, the political appointments of Germans and particularly of Poles, were all direct results of the interplay between politicians and immigrants.[21]

Labor leaders, despite their commitment to the brotherhood of all workers, were not free of ethnic prejudice, particularly against Poles and Italians.[22] As early as 1876, when Poles refused to participate in a coal heavers' strike, they were labeled scabs, cheap laborers, and bad union material—labels that persisted for at least a decade. The fact that most unions denied membership to immigrants from eastern and southern Europe left its mark on the larger community, for, in the decades after the Civil War, craft unions were also social clubs. "After working for more than 12 years in this city," noted a craftsman belonging to the recently organized Milwaukee Trades Assembly of 1883, "I hardly knew any craftsmen except those working with me in the same shop. Today I am personally acquainted with four-fifths of the men engaged in my trade and everybody seems to know me. This

[21] Still, *Milwaukee*, 272, 465. For a brief Republican account of the increase in municipal appointments of Poles, see *Milwaukee Sentinel*, February 5, 1893. For a list of Milwaukee Poles in municipal affairs, see Wallace E. Mceiejewski, "Our Role in Municipal Affairs," in Borun, *We, the Milwaukee Poles*, 71–72. For Szymon Deptula's 1946 comments about his countrymen in Milwaukee, see *ibid.*, 150–151.

[22] Theodore Mueller, "Milwaukee Workers," in Milwaukee Writers' Project, *History of Milwaukee County* (Milwaukee, 1947), 232, 235–236, 237–238, 242; Wisconsin Bureau of Labor and Industrial Statistics, *Biennial Report, 1883–1884*, pp. 122–127, 129, 130; *1885–1886*, p. 383; *1887–1888*, p. 36; *Proceedings of the Knights of Labor, 1885*, p. 219; *1886*, pp. 195, 327; *1887*, pp. 1848–1849; Cochran, *Pabst*, 273–275, 277; *Proceedings of the Milwaukee Common Council*, May 10, 1886, p. 35; *Herold*, May 7, 1886; *Milwaukee Labor Review*, June 23, 1888. In the 1880's and 1890's the national Amalgamated Association of Iron and Steel Workers, whose local in Milwaukee was probably the strongest craft union in the city, refused to adopt policies to meet the demands of German immigrant workers. The union prohibited the establishment of locals on the basis of nationality and was reluctant to print union documents in the German language. This policy was also followed after the turn of the century by the much weaker Amalgamated Meat Cutters and Butcher Workmen of North America. Jesse S. Robinson, *The Amalgamated Association of Iron and Steel and Tin Workers* (Baltimore, 1920), 39–40, 44, 45; *Proceedings of the Amalgamated Meat Cutters and Butcher Workmen of North America, 1902*, p. 15; *1904*, pp. 51, 52.

fact I appreciate more than almost anything connected with my social position." The former consular agent of the Italian government recalled that before World War I Italians were excluded from all organized labor "for the usual reasons— ignorance of the language, or plain cussedness on the part of the bosses of the unions, who naturally preferred their own friends and members of their own race."[23]

Part of the continuing difficulty arose from the fact that, among non-English-speaking immigrants, Germans dominated the labor movement in Milwaukee from the outset and for many years thereafter. After 1887, most organized German skilled workers belonged to the Federated Trades Council, the parent body of local unions in the city. The FTC was bilingual until after the turn of the century. A number of its constitutent unions were almost exclusively German in membership. In addition, the United Brewery Workmen was a German-speaking organization with considerable strength in Milwaukee.[24] The national brewery union, the FTC affiliates, and the FTC itself were very much a part of the life of the German immigrant community. Not until 1905 did the FTC begin to consider organizing Poles, and when it finally made the effort the results were modest. During World War I, the FTC launched an enthusiastic drive to organize the unskilled, but the fruits of that campaign were spoiled by the depression of 1921.[25] Most English- and German-speaking union

[23] Thomas W. Gavett, *Development of the Labor Movement in Milwaukee* (Madison, University of Wisconsin Press, 1965), 25; *Milwaukee Sentinel*, May 3, 9, 10, 1876; Wisconsin Bureau of Labor and Industrial Statistics, *Biennial Report, 1883–1884*, p. 122; Angelo Cerminara to author, May 16, 1956.

[24] *The Milwaukee Germania Abendpost*, a stalwart Republican paper in the last years of the 1890's, regularly printed news about union activities in German circles. Announcements of meetings and rallies usually included the statement "English and German speakers will address the group"; for examples, see issues for February 24, April 29, July 2, July 29, 1897. See also, manuscript "Minutes of Proceedings of the Federated Trades Council," May 14, 1904; January 4, 1905, in the State Historical Society of Wisconsin; *Proceedings of the United Brewery Workmen, 1917;* Cochran, *Pabst*, 271–301; Wisconsin Bureau of Labor and Industrial Statistics, *Biennial Report, 1883–1884*, pp. 131–132.

[25] Manuscript "Minutes of Proceedings of the Federated Trades Council," October 4, 1905; October 4, 1907; March 17, 1909; *Social Democratic Herald,*

leaders probably agreed with John R. Commons when he declared that in general immigrants from southern and eastern Europe were incapable of sustained union activity. Union organizers in Milwaukee undoubtedly also felt that the Catholic Church was a serious obstacle to Polish unionism.[26] Despite these differences, prejudice was less an obstacle to unions mitigating social distinctions among immigrants than their lack of power. Unions had no real voice in the matter, for by the 1890's capital and labor had fought their battle, and capital had won.

Organized conflict between labor and capital had emerged in Milwaukee as factory production began to be centralized. Throughout the 1870's and 1880's contemporary observers recognized that mechanization and its logical consequences threatened the social order. The craftsman no longer held his revered position, claimed Milwaukee's *Fortschritt der Zeit*. Young men seemed reluctant to learn a trade. "Ladies" refused to eat in the same dining room as machinists. And in the public schools, with their emphasis on academic rather than vocational subjects, skilled labor declined in status. These conditions threatened the craftsman with extinction and boded ill for the community. In short, asserted the *Fortschritt der Zeit*, mechanization would destroy individualism, and the spiritual and social worth of the working class would sink into the pit of proletarianism.[27]

Those advocating the nineteenth-century notion of self-help advised the worker to seek his own salvation; for he could hardly expect employers to concern themselves with his future. "Thousands of artisans are inclined to drift with the tide to acquire mastery of only such mechanical details as are thrust upon them, in the special department in which

---

October 5, 1907; Borun, "Poles in Milwaukee Industry," in Borun, *We the Milwaukee Poles*, 63.

[26] Commons, *Races and Immigrants in America*, 1–7, 179; Gavett, *Development of the Labor Movement in Milwaukee*, 208.

[27] *Fortschritt der Zeit*, 10: 104, 232, 312 (April 10, August 10, October 25, 1881); 13: 232 (August 10, 1884); 15: 2, 120 (January 25, April 25, 1886); 18: 344, 360 (November 25, December 10, 1889); 19: 168 (June 10, 1890).

they chance to find employment," explained the *Milwaukee Journal of Commerce.* This was satisfactory to employers, for "it trained up a class of workers, each to perform a particular kind of mechanical manipulation, at common wages. . . ." But it should not, insisted the paper, "be satisfactory to an intelligent, industrious, and ambitious artisan because it restricts his advancement and material prosperity."[28] Many workers in Milwaukee factories rejected the notion of self-help. Instead they took up the weapons of the strike, of unionism, and of political radicalism.[29]

In time, Milwaukee's factory workers achieved some of their goals, but they did so only over the adamant opposition of their employers. Trade unionists and socialists committed to political action challenged two notions: that the care of society could be safely entrusted to industrial leaders, and that industrial leaders were acting in harmony with God's natural order. Labor unions demanded some control over the conditions of employment; Lassallean socialists challenged the power of political parties which, they charged, legislated on behalf of industrial leaders and other capitalists. In the midst of depression they convinced some 1,500 of the electorate to vote for socialism in the local election of 1877, with the result that the Milwaukee sections of the Workingmen's Party of the United States elected two aldermen, two supervisors, and two constables. Factionalism, loss of leadership, and the return of prosperity prevented the Socialists from nominating their own ticket in the next few years. But it was apparent that the conflict between labor and capital in Milwaukee had taken a serious turn, paralleling events throughout the nation.[30]

---

[28] *Milwaukee Journal of Commerce,* October 1, 1879.

[29] For unionism and radicalism in Milwaukee preceding the Civil War, see Wachman, *History of the Social Democratic Party of Milwaukee,* 11, 12; Still, *Milwaukee,* 287; for radicalism among Germans, see Robert Ernst, *Immigrant Life in New York City, 1825–1863* (New York, 1949), viii, 18–19, 119–120, 121; Carl Wittke, *The German-Language Press in America* (Lexington, 1957), 103–156.

[30] Milwaukee Chamber of Commerce, *Reports, 1885,* pp. 26, 28, 149, 187; Still, *Milwaukee,* 344–355, 353, note 65; *Proceedings of the Milwaukee Common Council, 1882–1883,* pp. 134–138, 157, 161; Hense-Jensen and Bruncken, *Wis-*

In November of 1877, a Lutheran clergyman looking at developments in Milwaukee recognized some of the fundamental aspects of the conflict. He was opposed to socialism, but he recognized that some of the socialists' demands, such as abolition of employment of women and children in factories, were justified. He counseled Christian harmony where strife threatened. "Labor ought not to be valued as a commodity, to be paid as a commodity. The employer is obligated to treat employees as his co-workers and as his brothers." The minister insisted that the employer had obligations beyond the payment of wages. "The worker on the other hand ought not to view the employer as an enemy. He too owes the employer a full measure of Christian love." The "labor question," explained the *Milwaukee Journal* in 1879, was not "a mere fiscal question, to be determined by statute, but it is a problem of the philosophy of life, deeply founded in the nature of man itself."[31]

In Milwaukee as in the nation, the decade of the 1880's was one of intense conflict between labor and capital. Membership in the Knights of Labor soared; the American Federation of Labor organized around growing national unions; and the movement for an eight-hour working day gained mass support. These emerging organizations collided headlong with employers over the basic principles of collective bargaining. Strikes, boycotts, and lockouts erupted across the industrial landscape. Some industrial leaders armed themselves, and in many communities state militia and constabularies stood guard over private property. The United States, warned the Chicago *Industrial World,* would escape the horrors of the French Revolution and the Paris Commune only by forcibly crushing labor uprisings before they gathered strength.[32]

consin's Deutsch-Amerikaner, 2: 68, 81–82, 83; Wittke, *German-Language Press,* 172.

[31] A. F. Ernst, quoted in Hense-Jensen and Bruncken, *Wisconsin's Deutsch-Amerikaner,* 2: 83–84; *Milwaukee Journal,* August 13, 20, 1879. See also *Milwaukee Journal of Commerce,* April 30, June 11, September 17, 1879; *Freie Presse,* January 3, 1880.

[32] *Iron Age,* 30: 14 (August 10, 1882); 37: 22 (May 6, 1886); *Industrial World,* 15: 5 (July 16, 1885); Cudahy, *His Life,* 104–105; John Higham,

In the first half of the decade, almost every sector of Milwaukee's economy was affected by strikes and boycotts. Management retaliated with strikebreakers and lockouts. Some of the conflicts lasted for many days and were bitterly fought. In the contests involving the cigar manufacturers, the printers, and the Chicago, Milwaukee and St. Paul Railroad, each side used whatever methods were at its disposal. In addition, labor turned to direct political action. In the local elections of 1882, trade unionists secured the endorsement of Democrats and captured control of the city government. Though the Republicans returned to power in 1884, labor had demonstrated its potential strength at the polls.[33]

In 1885 and 1886 labor made a concerted effort to improve conditions of employment. Self-appointed leaders, union organizers, and socialists recognized that the growing concentration of workers in the larger factories, which had been produced by the mechanization and centralization of production, gave them a potentially powerful nucleus for protesting against unsatisfactory working conditions. For the first time in Milwaukee, large groups of unskilled workers organized and participated in a mass struggle to achieve labor's goals. Men marched from factory to factory, gaining strength with each rally, and, by leaving their work benches en masse, temporarily halted the entire machinery of the industrial community.[34] That, however, was the limit of their economic power, for they did not have the coercive force of the city and state behind them. Employers had the police and

---

Strangers in the Land: Patterns of American Nativism, 1860–1925 (New Brunswick, 1955), 45–56; Charles King, "The Cream City," in *Cosmopolitan,* 10: 556 (March, 1891).

[33] *Milwaukee Sentinel,* February 10, 11, 18, 1880; *Milwaukee Journal of Commerce,* September 29, 1880; Wisconsin Bureau of Labor and Industrial Statistics, *Biennial Report, 1883–1884,* pp. 122–131; Mueller, "Milwaukee Workers," 235–238; Still, *Milwaukee,* 288–291; *Proceedings of the National Amalgamated Association of Iron and Steel Workers, 1885,* p. 1561.

[34] *Herold,* May 4–6, 1886; Wisconsin Bureau of Labor and Industrial Statistics, *Biennial Report, 1885–1886,* pp. lvi, 329–337.

militia at their beck and call to protect private property—and the status quo.

The mass movement against the terms of employment was spearheaded by the Knights of Labor, the organization which in these years first organized unskilled workers. Between 1885 and the early months of 1886, the Knights of Labor took the country by storm; in Milwaukee alone they recruited about 9,000 workers. Skilled and unskilled workers joined the Knights, among them brewery workers, the molders in the metal trades, and workers in the meat-packing plants. Many of the recruits had not belonged to labor organizations before, although some had worked together in relief and benefit societies. By the spring of 1886 between 10,000 and 12,000 Milwaukee Knights insisted on an eight-hour day without reduction in pay.[35]

Socialists also fought for this reform. About 2,000 men followed Paul Grottkau, the Lassallean socialist and the recognized leader of the Central Labor Union, which considered the national leadership of the Knights too conservative to cope with the decade's industrial problems. But in the spring of 1886 the Central Labor Union joined with the Knights and other unions in the fight for the eight-hour day, thereby confronting Milwaukee employers with their sharpest challenge since the beginnings of industrialization.[36]

To meet the challenge, leading employers turned to the police forces of city and state. In April of 1886, after numerous strikes had already taken place, E. P. Allis, Fred Pabst, and others alerted Governor Jeremiah Rusk that they would call on him for support in the event of trouble. As tension mounted, the state prepared for military action, and early in May, at the height of the conflict, state troops entered Milwaukee.

---

[35] *Proceedings of the Knights of Labor, Summary of Quarterly Reports, 1885,* pp. 210, 219, 224; *Proceedings of the Knights of Labor, 1886,* p. 327; Price, "Allis-Chalmers," 256; Cudahy, *His Life,* 104; Wisconsin Bureau of Labor and Industrial Statistics, *Biennial Report, 1885–1886,* p. 383; *1887–1888,* p. 36; Mueller, "Milwaukee Workers," 238; Cochran, *Pabst,* 273–275, 277.
[36] Mueller, "Milwaukee Workers," 238.

On May 4, workers and soldiers clashed in front of the rolling mills in Bay View. They fought again next day, and this time soldiers fired into a marching crowd, inflicting nine casualties.[37]

In the following months labor continued the battle on the political front. In the fall election of 1886, a labor party captured all county offices and elected one of its candidates to Congress. To counter labor's obvious strength in the city, industrialists and their supporters coalesced around a Citizens ticket. "Republicans and Democrats," wrote the *Milwaukee Sentinel*, "stood shoulder to shoulder in defense of the sacred rights of property, in defense of homes of thousands of working men as well as of capitalists, and against the building up of a class party." "If the working class organizes itself as a political party," wrote one prominent supporter of the Citizens ticket, "such a procedure must have a deadly effect upon the interest of our commonwealth. A popular government is wholly incompatible with class rule, and our citizenry cannot or dare not permit itself to be dictated to or [be] tyrannized over by any element of society." The Citizens ticket won the municipal election of 1888 by a slim margin of 945 votes out of a total of 31,975 ballots cast, in part because the opposition ranks were split by the refusal of Paul Grottkau to work with the dominant labor party.[38]

This defeat could not obscure the fact that trade unionism and direct political action had come to Milwaukee to stay. To be sure, after 1886 the Knights of Labor declined rapidly, trade union membership declined, the organization of unskilled workers proceeded slowly, and it was to be twenty years before a labor party secured comparable political support. Nevertheless, the Federated Trades Council, an outgrowth of

[37] *Proceedings of the Milwaukee Common Council*, May 24, 1886, pp. 49, 57; Cudahy, *His Life*, 105, 106; Jeremiah Rusk to Edward P. Allis; to Fred Pabst, both May 14, 1886; Frank R. Falk to Rusk, undated telegram, all in the Rusk Papers; *Herold*, May 4–7, 1886.

[38] *Milwaukee Sentinel*, quoted in Still, *Milwaukee*, 285–286; *ibid.*, 286, 288; Mueller, "Milwaukee Workers," 238, 243.

the Central Labor Union, was organized in 1887. It became the parent body of Milwaukee's trade unions and a member of the American Federation of Labor. In 1890 the council spearheaded the second drive for an eight-hour day and established itself as the major force among the unions of the city. By 1891 trade union membership was almost as high as it had been in 1886. Labor parties continued to compete with Republicans and Democrats throughout the 1890's, and at the end of the decade the Social Democrats began their steady climb to victory.[39]

By the middle of the 1880's some employers had come to recognize that unions were a fact of industrial life. "Since combinations and consolidations of capital are becoming more and more common," asked John Johnston, "is there any good reason why labor should not have its organizations and combinations?" The brewers of the city stated that a worker had a right "to organize and to promote his own interests, if the circumstances are oppressive and make the improvement of living conditions advisable. We have therefore never denied anyone the privilege of belonging to any order or any lodge, and regard it as a rank injustice to dictate to anyone on this matter."[40]

Recognition of the right to organize did not mean, however, that these employers felt obligated to deal with a union as the bargaining agent for all workers. Nor did the right to organize mean that all matters pertaining to employment were subject to collective bargaining. Employers then, and for many years to come, insisted on the open shop. With few exceptions, they refused to discuss their right to govern the conditions of employment. To employers in Milwaukee, as well as in the nation at large, the right to organize merely meant that organized labor had the right to fight for its de-

---

[39] *Proceedings of the Knights of Labor, 1887,* pp. 1848–1849; Mueller, "Milwaukee Workers," 238, 242–243; Cochran, *Pabst,* 290; Wisconsin Bureau of Labor and Industrial Statistics, *Biennial Report, 1891–1892,* p. 116.

[40] Johnston is quoted in the Milwaukee Chamber of Commerce, *Report, 1885,* pp. 26–27; Cochran, *Pabst,* 277.

mands within the same competitive economy in which the employer found himself.[41]

There remained one other possible force that might have altered the lot of immigrants entering the factories: the government. But government failed them by default. In the late nineteenth century neither state nor federal government used its power to interfere in Milwaukee's industrial life, save to defend entrepreneurial liberty. The United States Supreme Court's interpretation of the Fourteenth Amendment precluded federal involvement in the industrial affairs of the city. The Wisconsin courts likewise insisted that government had no right to interfere in the conditions of employment, so that the state's safety and sanitation legislation was haphazard and poorly enforced. Municipal health commissioners usually pleaded in vain for ordinances to correct the most obvious sanitation deficiencies. In short, government on all levels left industrial relations in the hands of employers and to the natural laws which allegedly governed labor, production, and the market place.

[41] For an excellent discussion of this problem, see Edward C. Kirkland, "You Can't Win," in the *Journal of Economic History,* 14: 321–332 (Fall, 1954).

3

The Factory Masters

SO IT WAS from the vantage point of the employer that the fate of the immigrant worker in Milwaukee would be viewed and decided. Yet that fate was not so clear-cut as it might seem, for the view from management went through several distinct phases in the decades between the Civil War and World War I. At first the factory masters were just like workers, except for the combination of luck and brains and skill and circumstance that had made them bosses. Thus they handled their men in crude, casual, and personal ways. As the gap between capitalists and workers widened, employers, committed to production growth in an expanding and highly competitive market, responded to their consciences, to unions, and to the pressure exerted by moralists in and out of government. Consequently they adopted measures—often vague and ineffectual—designed to better the lot of their employees. And finally, as control of industry passed from Milwaukee to Chicago and New York and control of government passed from "safe" politicians in Milwaukee to reformers in Madison and Washington, the factory masters were caught up in a rationalization movement which they had helped to create but which was suddenly larger than themselves. As a result, they began to rationalize their relations with their workers.

In the beginning, when most employers were not many years removed from the status of workmen, they governed their men by the rough-and-tumble methods they had learned in the shops. Typical of managers in these early years was Patrick Cudahy, an Irish immigrant who rose from common laborer to foreman and ultimately to president of a large meat-packing company. In 1873, Cudahy, still in his early twenties, had just been promoted to general foreman in command of 200 men in a Milwaukee meat-packing house. The young man from Ireland made "the best bluff [he] knew how and ran up and downstairs, two steps at a time, shouting and hollering everywhere [he] went." "Got along fairly well, organized different gangs to do the work, principally from green . . . Irishmen," he claimed in later years.[1]

As steam moved machines, so the foreman moved men. For all practical purposes, he was the decisive figure for all blue-collar workers. Day after day he implemented the production schedule of a company and executed whatever wage and disciplinary policy it had. He was usually master of his particular shop, and he represented the blue-collar workers' superior whether in the shop or elsewhere. He hired men at the factory gates, at his home, or wherever he happened to be. In his shop he raised or lowered wages, appointed assistant foremen or straw bosses, moved men about, promoted them, demoted them, and dismissed them. He inspired loyalty or hatred, but rarely indifference.[2]

Each day the foreman made innumerable decisions involving his estimation of man, the social animal, at a time when he and his employer considered their rules to be law. The factory whistle blew, and the men were expected to be at their places of work. If they did not come, if the timekeeper did not

---

[1] Cudahy, *His Life,* 73–74.

[2] For examples of foremen hiring workers at their homes, see *Milwaukee Sentinel,* February 6, 1880; *Milwaukee Leader,* May 12, 1914; Price, "History of Allis-Chalmers," 58, 102–104, 120, 151; interview with A. F. Leidel, Milwaukee, 1956. The information about foremen in the shop was obtained through interviews with pensioners of International Harvester. They are named in the bibliography. See also *Foundry,* 23: *passim* (1903–1904). In 1919 International Harvester appointed an employment manager who prevented foremen from hiring directly. They were sent workers hired by the employment manager. Interview with Elmer Kreutzer, Milwaukee, 1959.

find their attendance tags on his rack, then their wages were docked. At the end of the workday the lights went out, often without warning, and workers had to stumble out in the dark. If a man, particularly an unskilled laborer, worked too slowly he was likely to spurred by his foreman with harsh four-letter words. If he did not obey he was likely to be dismissed.[3] A foreman's word was law.

On the rare occasions when unions established themselves, they had no share in administering shop discipline. Cudahy's example was again instructive. In the winter of 1899 his employees wanted to join the Amalgamated Meat Cutters and Butcher Workmen of North America. "I opposed the men and in a loud voice told them I would not stand for a union in our plant," Cudahy claimed later. "I stated that I would discharge any man that joined it. But they paid no attention to me. They went on. They gave a . . . dance, and I had one of my friends attend . . . and report the fellows who wore rosettes." In April, 1906, recalled Cudahy, at a season "when we are always obliged to cut down and lay men off . . . it was the rosette men [the members of Local 64] that had to go."[4]

The union demanded that Cudahy dismiss non-unionists instead and threatened to boycott his firm if he refused.[5] This he positively refused to do, and Cudahy was boycotted by all the union men of Milwaukee. "I anticipated it," recalled Cudahy, "and told all our salesmen to prepare for it, be extra nice to the women, give a piece of sausage to little ones, etc., etc. Then I went off to Europe and let them fight it out. The result was, if they had not informed us we would never have known that we were being boycotted." After he returned—the boycott had been in effect for about a year—the president of the butcher's union "came up from Chicago,

---

[3] *Foundry*, 23: 272–273 (February, 1904); interview with Leidel; Cudahy, *His Life*, 4–5; Price, "History of Allis-Chalmers," 124.
[4] Cudahy, *His Life*, 135; *Proceedings of the Amalgamated Meat Cutters and Butcher Workmen of North America, 1899*, p. 30.
[5] *Ibid., 1906*, pp. 5–6.

sent in his card with a request to see me," Cudahy wrote. "I was too busy and that was the last of it, and our plant has been an open shop ever since."[6]

Decisions were usually arbitrary, little thought being given to the systematic handling of workers. For many years most Milwaukee firms kept only meager employment records. This was true even of the E. P. Allis Company which by the mid-1880's was already employing hundreds of workers. Foremen and timekeepers simply noted the number of hours worked, rates of wages, and prices for piecework, often keeping no formal records at all. Indeed, the company made no effort to pay by check during its early years, preferring to refer to its Polish workers as "Mike 1," "Mike 2," or "Mike 3." This seemed much easier than trying to master Polish names.[7]

The same kind of informality prevailed in many other phases of factory life. According to J. M. J. Keogh of E. P. Allis: "When I was timekeeper [in the 1880's] the workmen were given no work tickets. They obtained the number of the casting or forging verbally from the foreman and gave their job to the timekeeper who posted it on a sheet which covered the entire labor cost on the order. . . . There were no time clocks and no production boards to assist the foremen in knowing the next job to give the workers. The result being that the foreman would let his men run out of work and the men would have to call at the foreman's desk or trail him around the shop to see what the next job would be." Highly skilled pieceworkers haggled with foremen over prices for particular jobs, partly in their own interests, but also because foremen, not the company, paid the helpers.[8]

Eventually, in 1886, the Allis company began to pay its workers by check and it gradually began to keep payroll books and other production records.[9] But this was only a small

[6] Cudahy, *His Life*, 135.

[7] Price, "History of Allis-Chalmers," 6, 9, 148–149.

[8] *Ibid.*; interview with James Bremmer, Milwaukee, 1957; Milwaukee Harvester Company payroll books, 1899–1900; *Proceedings of the Iron Molders Union of North America, 1882*, p. 67; *Milwaukee Germania Abendpost*, August 2, 1897.

[9] Price, "History of Allis-Chalmers," 9.

step towards making industrial affairs more rational, and most firms kept only the most elementary records until World War I.

Methods to handle labor systematically developed slowly because of the prevailing belief that existing methods were both efficient and well-adapted to conditions of the day, especially those relating to the employment of immigrant workers. From experience, employers and foremen came to prefer certain immigrants over others. The knitting industry relied heavily on German and Polish girls, for they "appeared to have a peculiar aptitude to the work."[10] An employer who had been in the ice business for about twenty-five years told a *Milwaukee Sentinel* reporter of his preferences: "The Polacks are the best workers we have here and the Swedes are also good men. A great many of them we hire, however, are unreliable. They work a day or two and then make some excuse for drawing their pay, and we never see them again. I don't know who these men are but I think they are tramps." Railroad bosses who employed Greeks, Italians, Bulgarians, Austrians, and Hungarians claimed to prefer hoboes, whom, they insisted, were the "best of railroad labor. . . . They can do four or five times the work a gang of Greeks or Bulgarians can do."[11]

Employers, jealous of their prerogatives in this as in other areas, expressed their prejudices but often did not allow workers to do the same. The various nationality groups in Milwaukee were not permitted to carry their antagonisms into the shop, for workers who argued among themselves posed a threat to industrial discipline. One new manager of a shop employing about 500 girls, for example, was surprised that German and Polish girls had difficulty in working together. He claimed that in the East, from where he had just come, such antagonisms did not exist. There, he said, Negroes and whites, Irish and Germans worked peacefully side by side. He was determined that national antagonisms should

---

[10] Anderson and Bleyer, *Milwaukee's Great Industries*, 154.

[11] *Milwaukee Sentinel*, January 15, 1893; William M. Leiserson, quoted in the *Milwaukee Leader*, January 8, 1914.

not be allowed between the two groups that made up the largest proportion of the unskilled labor force of Milwaukee. In fact, in most shops in the city it was already the rule that workers had to bury their ethnic hostilities while on the job.[12] Not once during the period from 1883 to 1914 did the Wisconsin Bureau of Labor and Industrial Statistics comment that employers or foremen fostered such antagonisms.[13]

Peace in the shop was obtained, at least in part, either by preserving the stereotyped ethnic pecking order or by allowing ethnic connections to govern employment practices. The Pabst Brewing Company staffed most of its departments with Germans, and hired non-Germans (usually Polish girls) only for the most unskilled tasks—in the bottling department.[14] In other companies, the assistant foreman or the straw boss was usually responsible for preserving ethnic employment patterns. Commonly, he interpreted for the foreman and supervisor, provided the most direct link to immigrant groups within the city, and sought to bring relatives and friends into his shop.[15]

The activities of an Italian assistant foreman in the chipping room of the International Harvester Company's foundry in the early twentieth century reflected this informal recruiting system. He had come to America at the prompting of an uncle who worked in the foundry of International Harvester, and he boarded with him in Milwaukee's Italian sec-

---

[12] Wisconsin Bureau of Labor and Industrial Statistics, *Biennial Report, 1901–1902*, pp. 729–730; interviews with pensioners of the International Harvester Company.

[13] William R. Jones, one of Carnegie's superintendents, claimed that he followed such a policy; see Erickson, *American Industry and the European Immigrant*, 62. For the meatpacking industry, see John R. Commons, "Labor Conditions in Slaughtering and Meatpacking," in the *Quarterly Journal of Economics*, 19: 28 (January, 1904); Amalgamated Meat Cutters and Butcher Workmen of North America, *50 Progressive Years* (n.p., 1948). Employers sometimes fostered ethnic antagonism as a device to discourage unionization, though such techniques may not have been necessary in Milwaukee.

[14] Cochran, *Pabst*, 91–92.

[15] Interviews with pensioners of the International Harvester Company; Leiserson, quoted in the *Milwaukee Leader*, January 8, 1914.

tion. The uncle promptly obtained employment for him in the chipping room of the foundry. He shortly became the company's informal labor agent for the third ward, and when he became an assistant foreman he interpreted for the Italians he brought to the firm. His methods were simple. He was, after all, in charge of the chipping room work force. When he needed workers, he informed other Italians in his neighborhood that he wanted help and then took their names. The men were hired and sent to him in the chipping room. During World War I, when the company badly needed unskilled labor, the Italian turned his home into a neighborhood employment office by placing a sign in his window informing passersby that he could hire workers for International Harvester. Because of these methods the chipping room remained an Italian-speaking section of the plant from about the turn of the century until well into the 1920's.[16]

Workers themselves had some influence in the hiring and placement of employees. Since Poles constituted such a large proportion of the unskilled labor force, they made it particularly difficult for large employers to exercise freedom of choice about whom they hired. Whether the supervisors liked it or not, Poles sometimes so harassed German workers that the Germans felt compelled to leave.[17]

Ethnic connections occasionally affected employment practices in another way. A Scottish-born foreman who had worked for about fifty years in International Harvester's foundry believed that Poles made the best workers in the foundry, even better than his own countrymen. He lived with Scots, belonged to Scottish organizations, and considered himself a Scottish-American, but he was also a foreman who took great pride in his craft and his responsibilities, and for whom productivity was paramount. Accordingly, he hired Poles in preference to Scots, claiming that his countrymen usually wanted to take advantage of their ethnic connections with him.[18]

[16] Interview with Balestriere.
[17] Interview with Bremmer.
[18] *Ibid.*

These employment practices shaped occupational patterns among immigrants, especially among the Poles. In the decades following the 1870's, Milwaukee considered Poles good workers, but workers best fitted for "dirty" tasks. In their neighborhoods and in large factories, Poles were almost always to be found as common laborers or as blacksmiths and molders working in foundries.

Supervisory positions above straw boss or assistant foreman seem to have been closed to Poles, perhaps because Poles did not become factory masters. By 1905, thirty-four years after industrialization had begun and about twenty-five years after Poles had begun to arrive in large numbers, most Milwaukee foremen were native Americans or Germans, English, Irish, and Scandinavians, ethnic groups which had established themselves before Milwaukee industrialized.[19] Similarly, native Americans, Germans, Englishmen, or Irishmen owned or controlled industrial organizations in Milwaukee, particularly the city's large enterprises in the metal trades, tanning, brewing, and meat packing.

English and German were the prestige languages in Milwaukee's large factories, but supervisors did not force workers to speak in either of these tongues. Neither did they attempt to learn more than a smattering of the languages of their workers. A foreman usually learned sufficient words to give simple orders; he knew the names of tools and such commands as "Hurry up!" Likewise, immigrants learned the essential English or German equivalents used by their foremen. If detailed instructions or explanations were needed, straw bosses, assistant foremen, or knowledgeable workers usually could interpret. But if an immigrant spoke a lan-

---

[19] I am completing a systematic study of the occupational patterns among Milwaukee's immigrants from 1850–1905. For occupational data, see the ward figures for foremen published in the *Tabular Statement of the 1905 Wisconsin Census;* Manuscript Wisconsin Census, Milwaukee, 1905, especially wards 12 (precincts 2–4), 14, 17, 18 (precincts 1–2); Allis-Chalmers Club, "Minute Book, 1911," 63, in the Allis-Chalmers Archives; Cudahy Brothers Company, *Thirty Years of Progress, 1892–1922* (Milwaukee, 1922), unpaged.

guage unknown to his fellow workers, gestures and screams became the foreman's working language.[20]

Because manufacturers were unsystematic in handling their workers did not mean, however, that they ignored human relations. Guided by a gospel of work rooted in the Bible and an older agrarian economy, they concerned themselves, albeit haphazardly, with the social problems of the workshop. With variations in kind and intent they rendered services to their workers, foreign-born as well as native, over and above the payment of wages.

Some of the services in the Milwaukee area grew out of townsite developments at Bay View, Cudahy, and South Milwaukee. In the late 1860's and the 1870's the Milwaukee Iron Company concerned itself with the religious and social welfare of its workers. When first founded, the company made its offices available to members of the Methodist Episcopal Church. Then it donated one lot of its property for a church site and helped raise funds for the building. The company gave similar assistance to both Catholics and Lutherans, built tenements and cottages especially for imported English workers, and sold building lots to workmen in the new village of Bay View.[21] The company also attempted to limit the amount of alcohol consumed by its workers. Each of its property deeds stipulated that the "manufacture and sale of intoxicating liquor be prohibited on any lots sold by the company as long as the company or its successors operated its works."[22] Patrick Cudahy gave lots to the Catholic

[20] Interviews with pensioners of the International Harvester Company; Cudahy, *His Life*, 138–139; Mike Magda *vs* Plankinton Packing Company, in Wisconsin Industrial Commission, *Workmen's Compensation Report, 1912–1913*, pp. 62–63.

[21] Flower, *History of Milwaukee*, 1616–1617, 1627–1629; *Milwaukee Germania Abendpost*, October 16, 1897; Korn, "Bay View," 187, 264–265; Manuscript United States Census, Village of Bay View, 1870; 1880, microfilm copies in the State Historical Society of Wisconsin.

[22] Flower, *History of Milwaukee*, 161. This was characteristic of all deeds covering Ward's industrial property. After he died the prohibition on the manufacture and sale of liquor was relaxed. See Korn, "Eber Brock Ward," 120–121.

Church when he founded Cudahy in 1893. He also established the Cudahy Building and Loan Association, which lent money to potential workers so that they could buy lots and build homes. The promoters of the South Milwaukee Improvement Company and the managers of the Bucyrus Steam Shovel and Dredge Company also followed these practices.[23]

Other services were common among Milwaukee's employers. They conducted raffles on company premises to raise relief funds for the employees' countrymen abroad. Brewery workers received free mugs of beer while on the job. When the Milwaukee Industrial Exposition opened in 1881, many employers purchased admission tickets for their workers. Celebrations for shop openings or for anniversaries of establishments were not unusual. In 1888, the E. P. Allis Company celebrated the opening of its South Foundry with a ball and supper. A "vast army of employees," wrote the *Milwaukee Sentinel,* "with their wives and sweethearts gathered for an evening of enjoyment" that did not end until midnight. Allis also closed his shops once a year for a company outing and provided special trains to carry his workers to and from the picnic sites. In the clothing industry the A. W. Rich Company marked its silver anniversary with a banquet on Thanksgiving Day in 1889 for its 250 employees.[24]

Relatively large employers such as the Allis firm and the Pabst and Schlitz brewing companies usually handled major injuries to their workers directly and on an individual basis. In the 1870's, when common-law rules still governed employer liability, Allis paid the medical and general family expenses of any regular employee who was seriously injured

[23] Cudahy, *His Life,* 146–147; interview with Cudahy; Williamson and Myers, *Designed for Digging,* 44–45, 62–63, 72–73, 127–129; Still, *Milwaukee,* 379; Wisconsin Bank Examiner, *Annual Report of the Conditions of the Loan and Building Associations of Wisconsin, 1898,* pp. 52, 98; *1900,* pp. 4, 72; *1901,* p. 140.

[24] *Milwaukee Sentinel,* February 3, 13, 1880; Cochran, *Pabst,* 253; Wisconsin Bureau of Labor and Industrial Statistics, *Biennial Report, 1883–1884,* p. 117; *Milwaukee Labor Review,* November 2, 1887; *Milwaukee Sentinel,* August 19, September 16, 1888.

at work. As late as 1909, the Schlitz Brewing Company dealt directly with its injured workers because it thought this method to be cheaper than carrying liability insurance, and because it preferred not to have an insurance company standing between it and its employees. Pabst executives continued to review serious accident cases even after the state introduced workmen's compensation in 1911, and at times the company supplemented the state benefits.[25]

Some employers also helped their workers by contributing to benevolent aid societies. These organizations operated in a variety of ways. Whether sponsored or merely subsidized by employers, they served not only as social clubs but also aided those who were disabled in the shop and helped pay the medical and funeral expenses of those who were killed in industrial accidents. Most members were recruited from among a company's steady employees. Membership was sometimes voluntary, sometimes compulsory.[26]

Some benevolent societies were formed when employers became weary of passing the hat for injured employees, a common form of aid before the introduction of workmen's compensation. But, as Thomas J. Neacy, an owner of Filer and Stowell, complained, "the high priced men" who were sure of keeping their jobs "put me off with 10 cents," while their helpers would contribute as much as one or two days' wages, depending on how scared they were of losing their jobs. In disgust, the firm formed a benevolent association and

---

[25] *Milwaukee Sentinel,* October 9, 1874; June 30, 1876; testimony of Richard H. Norris, a general agent for the London Guarantee and Accident Company, in the "Proceedings of the Committee on Industrial Insurance," October 7, 1909, p. 319, in Wisconsin Legislative Reference Library, Madison; Wisconsin Industrial Commission, *Annual Report of Workmen's Compensation, 1912,* p. 109; Cochran, *Pabst,* 253.

[26] For the names of Milwaukee companies that had benevolent societies, see Wisconsin Bureau of Labor and Industrial Statistics, *Biennial Report, 1883–1884,* pp. 4, 134; *1887–1888,* p. 291; *Milwaukee Labor Review,* November 7, 1887; "Proceedings of the Committee on Industrial Insurance," October 5, 1909, pp. 128, 139; October 13, 1909, pp. 342, 382; Wisconsin Industrial Commission, *Annual Report on Workmen's Compensation, 1912,* p. 105.

asked each worker to make a voluntary contribution of twenty-five cents a month. When this system did not work out satisfactorily, the company made membership and contributions compulsory.[27]

Employers commonly aided benevolent associations. In 1883 workers organized the Allis Mutual Aid Society, which became the instrument through which Edward Allis assisted his employees, matching annual membership fees and providing rooms for society meetings. By 1889, the year Allis died, the society's facilities included a dining room, a reading room, and a social hall, open to all company employees.[28] In later years, the society increasingly concerned itself with matters of safety. Following the explosion of an emery wheel and the death of a worker, the company set up a sick bay in a part of the shipping room. It also obtained a horsedrawn ambulance, distributed dustproof first-aid boxes throughout the plant, and, after the turn of the century, sponsored lectures on infection and accidents. These and other services made the mutual aid society the chief instrument by which a growing company maintained personal contact with employees. In the spring of 1900 the *Milwaukee Journal* claimed that the E. P. Allis Company "probably keeps in closer contact with [its] employees than any other establishment in the country."[29]

Until the turn of the century, employers did not consider themselves obliged to increase services for employees, though concern about working conditions had been voiced for some years. Individuals and groups outside the ranks of labor felt that employers should deny Cain's dictum about the welfare

[27] Testimony of Thomas J. Neacy, in the "Proceedings of the Committee on Industrial Insurance," October 5, 1909, pp. 122, 128–129.

[28] Wisconsin Bureau of Labor and Industrial Statistics, *Biennial Report, 1883–1884*, pp. 138–139; *1887–1888*, p. 291; *Milwaukee Sentinel*, April 2, 1889; Price, "History of Allis-Chalmers," 25.

[29] *Ibid.*, 211–213, 222–224, 229–230; *Milwaukee Journal*, March 31, 1900. For the testimony of Max W. Babb of the Allis-Chalmers Company, see "Proceedings of the Committee on Industrial Insurance," October 13, 1909, pp. 342, 349, 364–365.

of his brother Abel. Those affiliated with the Young Men's Christian Association eagerly sought to furnish workers "with an effective wholesome substitute for sinful amusement," and to help them "avoid temptation."[30] The Wisconsin Bureau of Labor and Industrial Statistics, established in 1883 in response to a growing concern for the well-being of the worker, encouraged employers to improve factory conditions.[31] Conservative German-language newspaper editors urged employers to emulate the paternalism of Gustav Krupp, the German iron and steel manufacturer. Krupp's pension system, according to the daily *Milwaukee Germania Abendpost,* recognized "the worth of the worker as well as his work." This recognition, the paper claimed, had never come to such men as George M. Pullman.[32] But these nineteenth-century protests did not result in effective legislation.

Toward the end of the century, concern for working conditions became more intense. In 1900, after eight years of energetic campaigning, Robert M. La Follette captured the governorship of Wisconsin. He and his followers were committed to the proposition that government was responsible for the social and economic well-being of the people, in part by exercising greater supervision over industrial life. Too, in Milwaukee the Social Democratic party steadily increased its strength until it gained control of the city's government in

[30] "Religious Work of the Y.M.C.A.," an unsigned typescript work sheet, dated November, 1903, in the Y.M.C.A. Archives. For the earlier activities of the Milwaukee branch of the association, see its *Annual Reports,* 1880–1883, 1892, 1894. On December 3, 1879, the *Milwaukee Journal of Commerce,* a paper that advocated "co-operation," urged employers to take a personal interest in the character and habits of their workers. In particular, they should attend to "their employees' frivolousness," declared the editor.

[31] Wisconsin Bureau of Labor and Industrial Statistics, *Biennial Report, 1883–1884,* pp. 115–117. For employer support of a proposal to enlarge and strengthen the Bureau of Labor, see manuscript Assembly Petitions, 200–399, 401–439; manuscript Senate Petitions, 8–159, both in Wisconsin Legislative Papers, Office of the Secretary of State, 1885, Series 2/2/2, in the Wisconsin State Archives.

[32] *Milwaukee Germania Abendpost,* February 12, October 20, 1897. See also *Fortschritt der Zeit,* 10: 24 (January 25, 1881); 11: 5 (January 10, 1882); 18: 168, 376 (June 10, December 25, 1889); *Germania,* August 29, 1881.

1910. An alliance between the Milwaukee Federated Trades Council and the Social Democrats was perhaps more significant for intensifying concern about working conditions. With La Follette and his followers in control of the state's political machinery and with socialists rapidly gaining control of the city, critics of economic conditions quickly forced industrial leaders to the defensive.[33]

Some of the city's mild ameliorators—such groups as the Young Men's Christian Association and the Young Women's Christian Association—were welcomed by employers. Railroad companies had used the Y.M.C.A. for years, and a number of railroad executives had regularly served on the advisory board of the Milwaukee Y.M.C.A.[34] Toward the end of the century, just as "Y" workers were turning their zeal from missionary work to social services, more companies began to permit them to enter industrial shops. The Y.M.C.A. held noonday meetings and managed the lunchroom and outdoor eating places which various companies provided for their workers.[35] After 1897, the Y.W.C.A. inaugurated an extension service for women in Milwaukee factories. This work was done by a special secretary who visited factories in various parts of the city, establishing a number of small classes for younger women to gain their "confidence and respect . . . in order to bring higher thoughts and practical ideas into their lives."[36] Such thoughts and ideas encompassed every

[33] La Follette, *La Follette's Autobiography*, *passim*; Robert S. Maxwell, *La Follette and the Rise of the Progressives in Wisconsin* (Madison, 1956), 1–73, 128–130, 153–172; *The Blue Book of the State of Wisconsin* (Madison, 1911), 670–672; Wisconsin Industrial Commission, *Bulletin*, 1: 168 (December, 1912); Still, *Milwaukee*, 356–395, 515–518. See also the remarks of the Reverend Frederick Edwards of Milwaukee's St. James Episcopal Church, in *Merchants and Manufacturers Bulletin* (Milwaukee), February, 1907, 64–68.

[34] Milwaukee Y.M.C.A., *Annual Report, 1881*, p. 35; *1883*, p. 11; *1892*, p. 31.

[35] *Ibid., 1904*, p. 19. One plant manager at Allis-Chalmers later recalled that after the strike of 1905 the company set up "a sort of lunchroom service." The kitchen and dining room was managed by the South Side Y.M.C.A., but the workmen "refused to eat there because they felt that the service was started by the company to house and feed strikebreakers in the event of another strike." Quoted in Price, "Allis-Chalmers Company," 162–163.

[36] Milwaukee Y.M.C.A., *Annual Report, 1897*, pp. 12–13.

manner of activity for the uplift of workmen. Some crusading ameliorators, for example, believed that their highest duty was to teach employees, native- or foreign-born, the rudiments of cleanliness, particularly the art of taking baths.[37] Others, convinced that the nation's general welfare required the proper education of young workers, turned their efforts to industrial education.[38]

These pressures from government and private organizations partly explain why some companies expanded their service work after the turn of the century. Throughout the Milwaukee area, firms embarked on programs which one Milwaukee executive called an attempt to "help workers help themselves." His firm provided overalls and laundry facilities, a lunchroom for female employees, and a library service. It also formed a fire brigade and a "Query Club" where workers could discuss topics of mutual interest.[39] In 1902, Samuel L. G. Knox, the new general manager of the Bucyrus firm and a veteran of work with Frederick W. Taylor, inaugurated

---

[37] Gertrude Beeks, typescript notes on American welfare programs, pages 10, 29, 33, in a folder marked "Gertrude Beeks," 1901–1902, in the McCormick Collection (hereafter cited as Beeks, "Notes"). For examples of Y workers in welfare programs, see *ibid.*, 3, 7, 16, 18. The religious character of the Y made some companies reluctant to give Y workers a leading role in welfare work; see, for example, *ibid.*, 3, 18. The issue was also discussed at the National Civic Federation, *Conference on Welfare Work*, March 16, 1904, pp. 72–94.

[38] John Dewey to Madam [Nettie F.] McCormick, February 20, 1904, in a folder marked "John Dewey, 1904"; Henry Bruére, typescript, "Recommendations . . . at the Reaper Works," June, 1903, pp. 2, 10, in a folder marked "Henry Bruére, 1903," both in the McCormick Collection. This response, of course, was not a novel one. There had been national and local interest in industrial education by businessmen and others throughout most of the period after 1865. For examples, see Edward C. Kirkland, *Dream and Thought in the Business Community, 1860–1900* (Ithaca, 1956), 51–82; C. H. Haskins to Elisha Keyes, June 18, 1884, in the Keyes Papers. For early interest by the Milwaukee school board, see its *Proceedings*, April 4, 1884, p. 173; May 6, 1884, p. 177; December 22, 1884, p. 56; May 15, 1885, p. 89. See *Merchants and Manufacturers Bulletin*, December, 1906, p. 8; October, 1907, p. 24, for data on the beginnings of Milwaukee's Trade School; see also Maxwell, *La Follette*, 135.

[39] O. F. Humphreys, in the National Civic Federation, *Conference on Welfare Work*, 54–60.

programs to improve the morale of his work force in the wake of a strike by machinists. He instituted practices designed to identify foremen with management, and he improved facilities for handling accidents, began sending doctors to workers who had suffered injuries on the job, sponsored an annual company picnic, and built an employees' "dining pavilion." At the same time he advocated high wages and, except as a last resort in times of trouble, opposed wage cuts on the ground that they "would seriously interfere with the excellent morale which . . . now exists in the shops."[40] In 1905 the Allis-Chalmers Company, facing the prospect of a machinists' strike, instituted a club to facilitate understanding between officers and employees.[41] Membership was open only to managerial personnel (including foremen) and the general office staff, though the club's lunchroom facilities were open to all workers.[42]

The day of casual, unsystematic managerial response to random suggestions was doomed by the time the nineteenth century came to a close. Enthusiasm for a more rational approach to the human side of the manufacturing process soon began to take hold, and a major change in the relations between management and worker was in the offing. This is not to say that the adoption of a new order was immediate and universal. It began around 1900 when a number of firms, employing something over 10 per cent of the nation's urban and nonprofessional work force, began the conscious development of rational welfare programs.[43] The evolution of in-

[40] Williamson and Myers, *Designed for Digging,* 67, 70, 71; Allis-Chalmers payroll books, 1889–1904; Milwaukee Harvester Company payroll books, 1899–1901.

[41] Allis-Chalmers Club, "Minute Book," August 7, 1905, p. 1.

[42] Whiteside Memorandum, September 29, 1905, in President's Letters, 1904–1907, in the Allis-Chalmers Archives. See also *Milwaukee Free Press,* October 27, 1907, in "Newspaper Clippings, Allis-Chalmers, 1907," in the Allis-Chalmers Archives; *Foundry,* 22: 219–222 (July, 1903).

[43] In 1900 a total of 25,035,727 white workers were gainfully employed; 8,183,813 of them were in agricultural pursuits, 1,215,291 were in professional services, 4,279,277 were in domestic and personal service, 4,548,151 were in trade and transportation, and 6,809,195 were in manufacturing and mechanical pursuits; see Edward P. Hutchinson, *Immigrants and Their Children 1850–1950* (New York, 1956), 159.

dividual programs differed markedly, and the majority of American employers did not practice elaborate welfare work until after World War I. Those who did develop early welfare programs, however, became the pacemakers for other firms, and they laid the groundwork for the later growth of personnel management. At the same time they experimented with policies intended to make all workers identify themselves with the interests of a company.

The early advocates of the new approach were at first unable to agree even on what to call what they were doing. Frederick W. Taylor and his followers insisted that they were engaged in "scientific management," some years after Taylor had begun publishing his papers on time-and-motion studies. William H. Tolman, who concerned himself with other aspects of internal shop management, in 1898 designated his work "industrial betterment," a term used later by John R. Commons and other members of the National Civic Federation. Because "industrial betterment" was often used interchangeably with another phrase, "welfare work," Tolman turned to still another term. In 1909 he wrote a book about the "record of things done by American industrialists employing upwards of one and one-half million people," and called it *Social Engineering*.

The confusion also applied to the individuals engaged by employers to apply the new techniques. Some employers called them social workers; other referred to them as social secretaries; still others called them welfare workers.[44] But if they could not agree on terminology they did agree on the spirit of the new movement. As Thomas Edison put it, American business civilization was raw and crude, "pretty wasteful, pretty cruel, which often comes to the same thing. . . . Our production, our factory laws, our charities, our relations between capital and labor [are] all wrong, out of gear. We've

---

[44] Commons, *History of Labor*, 3: 303–335; William H. Tolman, *Social Engineering: A Record of Things Done by American Industrialists Employing Upwards of One and One-half Million People* (New York, 1909), iii–iv, 1–59; John R. Commons, " 'Welfare Work' in a Great Industrial Plant," in the *American Monthly Review of Reviews*, July, 1903, pp. 79–81.

stumbled along for a while trying to run a new civilization in old ways, but we've got to start to make this world over."[45]

The reasons for launching elaborate new welfare programs were varied, but underlying many of them was the growing complexity of industrial life, a complexity well demonstrated by developments in Milwaukee. The history of changes of ownership of the Milwaukee Iron Company in Bay View reflected the increasing integration of Milwaukee's establishments with organizations outside of the city. In 1876, a year after the death of Eber Brock Ward, its founder, the company was sold to the North Chicago Rolling Mill Company, another Ward enterprise. Thirteen years later this company consolidated with Union Steel and Joliet Steel to form the Illinois Steel Company and in another nine years it became a subsidiary of the Federal Steel Company, owned by J. P. Morgan and Company. When Federal Steel became a part of the United States Steel Corporation in 1901, Illinois Steel became a subsidiary and operated the Bay View works with about 2,000 men until 1929.[46]

The E. P. Allis Company, the Milwaukee Harvester Company, and the Bucyrus Company followed a similar pattern of integration with other corporations. In 1901, E. P. Allis joined three outside firms to form the Allis-Chalmers Manufacturing Company. By 1907 its board of directors read like a *Who's Who* of industrial America. The most notable member was Judge Elbert Gary, its chairman, who was simultaneously chairman of the board of United State Steel and a director of thirteen other leading American corporations. Herman Falk, head of the Falk Manufacturing Company and director of numerous other Milwaukee firms, also sat on the board. Shortly after 1913, Otto Falk, Herman's brother and a former vice-president of the Falk organization, became president of Allis-Chalmers.[47]

---

[45] Quoted in Nevins and Hill, *Ford,* 1: 531–532.

[46] Clark, *History of Manufactures,* 3: 54–55, 57; *Milwaukee Germania Abendpost,* March 13, 1897; Korn, "Bay View," 124–125, 170–171, 327.

[47] W. H. Whiteside to district managers, October 14, 1907; Otto Falk, Circular Letter, April, 1913, both in President's Letters, 1904–1907, 1911–1915, in the

The Milwaukee Harvester Company, whose directors were Wisconsinites living outside Milwaukee, joined four other firms in 1902 to form the International Harvester Company. The board of the new organization also included numerous leading figures in America's industrial world, most notably Judge Gary and Cyrus McCormick, Jr. International Harvester quickly became one of the city's most important employers. Before World War I the city's plant employed between 2,000 and 3,000 men; by 1918 the number had risen to between 5,000 and 6,000 men. In Milwaukee only Allis-Chalmers employed as many metalworkers.[48]

Bucyrus, a firm employing less than 1,000 men before World War I, followed the pattern of the E. P. Allis and Milwaukee Harvester companies. In 1911, the South Milwaukee firm joined with two companies to form the Bucyrus Company, with a banking affiliate of Morgan underwriting a new security issue. In characteristic fashion, this led to a new board of directors controlled by the underwriting syndicate. At the same time Bucyrus eagerly sought board members connected with Milwaukee's important financial and industrial organizations. Thus William Bigelow of the First National Bank served on the board for a year, and when he left Fred Vogel, Jr., president of the bank, replaced him. In addition, Bucyrus recruited for its board Frank R. Bacon, president and principal owner of Milwaukee's Cutler-Hammer Manufacturing Company and, like Bigelow and Vogel, a part owner and director of several companies in the city.[49]

Another and related trend was centralization of production. In 1905, 415 corporations, or 27 per cent of Milwaukee's manufacturing establishments, produced almost 90 per cent of the dollar value of manufactured products and employed about 78 per cent of the work force. In 1914, forty-five companies, or 2.4 per cent of the manufacturing estab-

---

Allis-Chalmers Archives; *Milwaukee Journal,* October 24, 1907; *House Report* no. 1127, 62 Congress, 2 session, p. 2; *Wisconsin Necrology,* 43: 45–47.

[48] *Milwaukee Germania Abendpost,* February 25, 1897; *Harvester World,* 3: 13 (July, 1912).

[49] Williamson and Myers, *Designed for Digging,* 109–113.

lishments, employed almost half of Milwaukee's workers and produced nearly three fifths of the dollar value of manufactured products. More than half the city's industrial work force worked in factories employing more than 250 men. Each of seven establishments employed more than 1,000 men; together, these seven firms employed about 13,000 men, or about one fifth of the labor force.[50]

These developments were an integral part of a change in the competitive character of the national economy. The notion that market demands were the measure of all practices in industry was slowly being eroded, now that such corporate giants as United States Steel dominated output. Among such influential men as Judge Gary and George W. Perkins, rationalization of the means of production brought with it the realization that U.S. Steel's competitive position had become secure, and as soon as company officers deemed profit margins adequate they began to consider new criteria for determining the firm's industrial relations.[51]

The more-or-less simultaneous integration of management and centralization of production posed serious problems in industry. Managerial integration was sometimes abetted by marriages among Milwaukee's leading industrial families, and it centralized the decision-making process for setting prices and for dealing with such problems as market distribution, allocation of raw materials, and relations with unions. Trade associations facilitated the process. In Milwaukee, members of the National Metal Trades Association joined forces after 1900, effectively breaking strikes and maintaining the "open shop."[52]

Centralization of production, however, involved both in-

[50] *United States Census Bulletin,* 56: 22 (1905); *United States Census of Manufacture, 1914,* 1: 1641, 1644, 1645.

[51] David Brody, *Steelworkers in America: The Nonunion Era* (Cambridge, 1960), 148–158.

[52] Williamson and Myers, *Designed for Digging,* 73, 127. A study of the obituary notices in the first forty-nine volumes of *Wisconsin Necrology* reveals that managerial relationships were strengthened by marriages between a number of families which owned factories in Milwaukee.

dustrial specialization and the diffusion of power among administrators, trends which weakened the loyalty of production workers. With a labor force sometimes numbering in the tens of thousands, presidents, chairmen, and even factory managers lost direct and continuous contact with their employees. The precarious tenure and rapid turnover of corporation officials and supervisors hampered working relationships still further. Though smaller corporations had an easier administrative task, even they often found it difficult to maintain employee loyalty, in part because their specialties, a wide range of very complicated products, required a highly specialized labor force and made it difficult for company executives to maintain familiarity with all phases of the manufacturing process.[53]

To hope to inculcate employee loyalty to a board chairman or to a company under these conditions was simply daydreaming. Loyalties were more likely to go to foremen or possibly to superintendents—the men in the lower echelon of administrators. These loyalties had little to do with attachments to the company, for superintendents and foremen also were hired employees, who could be dismissed, transferred, or demoted.[54] Thus large industrial organizations and some small companies sought to discover means by which they could inculcate loyalty in their workers. Some organizations turned to what the president of International Harvester called "benevolent despotism over the human side of manufacture."[55]

The search for methods to obtain workers' loyalty was

[53] Cochran and Miller, *The Age of Enterprise*, 230, and, for an enlightening discussion of structural changes in the economy and in welfare work, 229.

[54] This conclusion is based on interviews with pensioners of the International Harvester Company in Milwaukee, several of whom recalled transferring with their foremen to the Allis-Chalmers Company. In many firms loyalty to foremen mainly reflected their power to hire and fire. In the First World War, foremen often raided other companies for workers. See, for example, Willits Pollock, "Weekly Report," July 14, 1917, typescript, Series 76/1/2, in the Wisconsin State Archives. For managerial changes in a small firm, see Williamson and Myers, *Designed for Digging*, 103–104.

[55] Cyrus McCormick, Jr., "Co-operation and Industrial Progress," in the *Harvester World*, 10: 2–3 (December, 1919).

stimulated by the growth of unionism, radicalism, and progressivism, and by the introduction of "scientific" methods in handling men. Employers believed the growth of unionism threatened their industrial control. It especially endangered their rationalizing endeavors because unions demanded the right to help set wages and hours, important components in the cost of production. At the turn of the century, national unions still commanded only a relatively small following, but their membership was increasing. Welfare programs, some employers thought, at best would prevent the unionization of shops, and at least would temper the amount of control unions had over the workers.[56]

In the first decades of the twentieth century, many employers came under steady attack from radicals and urban reformers who were trying to limit employer authority and seeking to change conditions of employment. The Socialist party steadily increased its strength. In 1905, the Industrial Workers of the World, an American syndicalist labor union, was organized. Theodore Roosevelt clamored for reform from the White House. In a number of states, particularly in Wisconsin, industry found itself spotlighted by adverse publicity and subjected increasingly to governmental regulation.[57] Under these circumstances, some companies viewed welfare programs as a corrective to offset muckracking articles and bad publicity stemming from social surveys of industrial communities, and as an asset during strikes when a company

---

[56] Beeks, "Notes," 1–4, 12–13, 25, 32, 41. The attitudes attributed to employers or their welfare workers are based largely on private conversations between them and Miss Beeks. In 1901 she investigated welfare programs in eighteen firms in eleven eastern and midwestern cities before introducing such programs at the McCormick Works in Chicago. Compare Tolman, *Social Engineering, passim.* See also Commons, *History of Labor,* 3: 316.

[57] Cochran and Miller, *The Age of Enterprise,* 273–297; Ira Kipnis, *The American Socialist Movement, 1897–1912* (New York, 1952), 334–369; Paul F. Brissenden, *The I.W.W.: A Study of American Syndicalism* (New York, 1919), 57–108; Commons, *History of Labor,* 4: 262–286; C. C. Regier, *The Era of the Muckrakers* (Chapel Hill, 1932), *passim;* Steffens, *Autobiography,* 357–621.

could obtain public sympathy by pointing to its welfare activities.[58]

The increasing concern about social conditions in industry was related to efforts to systematize and organize industrial life. At the time, progressivism gained many followers, and the scientific approach to handling men gained momentum. In Wisconsin, John R. Commons studied ways to involve government in employment conditions and to improve relations between management and organized labor. In these years, Frederick W. Taylor was publishing his papers on the pioneer experiments he had conducted on time and motion, functional foremanship, and other scientific adjustments of industrial relations. In 1909, the federal government utilized features of Taylor's scientific management principles in its arsenal at Watertown, Massachusetts. In 1910, the Eastern Rate Case gave national publicity to scientific management. By 1914, thirty-five plants had put one or more of Taylor's programs into practice.[59]

Few who administered welfare programs were familiar with the work of Taylor, but all agreed with the ultimate aims of the scientific approach to handling men.[60] First and foremost they viewed their program as a means of bringing harmony between labor and management—on the company's terms. It was hoped that a loyal and happy work force would increase productivity, improve the quality of the product, and reduce the cost of manufacture. Welfare programs were also expected to reduce labor turnover, which was high in many firms. In short, without having used the systematic methods

[58] Beeks, "Notes," 44; Commons, *History of Labor,* 3: 316. According to Andrew Carnegie, "It is by efforts of individual firms that the right solution to the problem will be furnished; and not through socialism, which can only talk speculatively while individuals can work practically, curing evils that Socialists point out." See his introduction to Tolman, *Social Engineering,* v.

[59] Commons, *History of Labor,* 3: 303–315; Cochran and Miller, *The Age of Enterprise,* 244; Jean T. McKelvey, *AFL Attitudes Toward Production, 1900–1932* (Ithaca, 1952), 12–26.

[60] Williamson and Myers, *Designed for Digging,* 71; Robert F. Hoxie, *Scientific Management and Labor* (New York, 1915), *passim.*

worked out by the school of scientific management, welfare workers arrived at the same conclusions as Taylor and his followers. They all expected to make a factory's industrial relations harmonious and peaceful and to increase the stability of the work force.[61]

[61] Commons, *History of Labor*, 3: 331; Tolman, *Social Engineering*, 1–47, 132–182.

PART TWO

THE LARGER CONTEXT

4

The Web of Welfare Work

THE PARENT COMPANY of one of Milwaukee's large factories, the International Harvester Company, pioneered in developing a comprehensive welfare program. In doing so, it helped to shape for many years to come the pattern of welfare work in Milwaukee, though the origins and most of the immediate impact of its program were centered in Chicago.

International Harvester's program was initiated by welfare workers who shared many of the attitudes of their colleagues in other firms, but who differed from most of them on one important point: they realized that welfare work was no substitute for higher wages, for lower hours, or for recognizing trade unions as bona fide agents of collective bargaining. John R. Commons, who supported organized labor and collective bargaining and who was then working for the National Civic Federation seeking methods to improve industrial relations systematically, believed that this difference in attitude made International Harvester distinctive. It had one of the most enlightened welfare programs in the nation, and was part "of the labor movement for better treatment, better conditions, and greater opportunities."[1]

The program was of direct significance to Milwaukee because it applied to the International plant there, but, more

---

[1] Commons, "Welfare Work," in the *American Monthly Review of Reviews,* July, 1903, p. 79.

importantly, because it influenced the relationship between the Wisconsin Industrial Commission and the state's employers. In 1912, Commons asked Charles W. Price of International Harvester to launch the state's welfare and safety program because Price had become a self-taught expert in his company's welfare and safety program, and therefore knew how to work within a framework set by plant managers. His selection assured Wisconsin employers that the state's industrial reforms would be overseen by a practical man who understood and sympathized with management's needs and interests.

International Harvester's welfare program began in the Chicago area, where diverse groups, ranging from socialists and labor leaders to upper-class women and leaders of the business community, sought to cope with the social and economic problems of an urban population then in the throes of industrialization.[2] The program was actually started by the McCormick family in 1901, a year before the formation of the International Harvester Company. It continued in 1902, when Cyrus H. McCormick, Jr., and his brothers Harold and Stanley became the chief executive officers in the new enterprise.[3]

The McCormicks belonged to Chicago's social and business elite, and some of them actively supported social improvement efforts there. Stanley and his sister, Mrs. Emmons

---

[2] Ray Ginger, *Altgeld's America: The Lincoln Ideal versus Changing Realities* (New York, 1958), 113–167, 242–248. Almont Lindsey, *The Pullman Strike: The Story of a Unique Experiment and of a Great Labor Upheaval* (Chicago, 1942), *passim*.

[3] Nettie Fowler McCormick was still influential in the affairs of the company, especially in matters pertaining to welfare work, but by this time her interests and views were usually subordinated to those of her sons. This judgment, and the comment in the text about the McCormicks, is based on a study of "Welfare File" in the Harold F. McCormick Papers and of the few Nettie F. McCormick letters, both in the McCormick Collection, and on conversations with Mrs. Lucile Kellar, formerly co-ordinator of the McCormick Collection. In 1940, Harold claimed that his mother did not take much interest in the affairs of the company after the formation of International Harvester. Typescript of interview with Harold F. McCormick, August 21, 28, 30, 1940, in the Harold F. McCormick Papers.

Blaine, were close to the circles of Jane Addams' Hull House, Graham Taylor's Chicago Commons, and Francis Parker's experimental school (later the University of Chicago's School of Education).[4] Cyrus and his mother, Nettie F. McCormick, did not move in these circles, though they knew Miss Addams and Taylor. Rather, they supported the Y.M.C.A. and charity organizations.[5] Harold and his wife, Edith Rockefeller, had still other interests, particularly opera, but Edith did concern herself with the social needs of Chicago's businesswomen.[6]

The varied interests of the McCormicks brought them in touch with Gertrude Beeks, the president of the National Association of Women Stenographers, in part because Edith McCormick became interested in her plan to establish clubrooms in Chicago for businesswomen "where we may have luncheon served and carry on our work generally." In the fall of 1900, when Miss Beeks was working for the Civic Federation in Chicago, the McCormick brothers, apparently prodded by Stanley McCormick, offered her a position with the McCormick Harvesting Machine Company. Within a few months she joined the firm to launch a program of industrial betterment work for the many women employed in the McCormick's twining mill. Though she left after three years, Miss Beeks served International Harvester as a consultant throughout much of the decade.[7]

[4] Stanley McCormick to Graham Taylor, September 8, 1899; March 12, 1904; Katherine D. McCormick to Taylor, December 17, 1913, in the Graham Taylor Papers, in the Newberry Library, Chicago. Beginning in 1899 the Stanley McCormicks each year sent Taylor $1,000. They continued this annual gift until 1935.

[5] *Harvester World*, 28: 14, 30–31 (July, 1936); *Chicago Tribune*, September 26, 1902; Graham Taylor, Diary, June 15, 1901; October 28, 1902, in the Taylor Papers; Cyrus McCormick, Jr., to Joseph M. Field, April 16, 1910, in the private letters in the Cyrus McCormick, Jr., Papers, in the McCormick Collection.

[6] Ginger, *Altgeld's America*, 190, 193, 307. Chicago's influential men concerned with the city's industrial conditions worked increasingly through the Civic Federation of Chicago, an organization trying to bridge the gap between Chicago's social elite and her industrial workers. The National Civic Federation, founded in 1900, grew out of the Chicago group. *Ibid.,* 248–253.

[7] Gertrude Beeks to Edith McCormick, April 14, 1899; to Harold F. McCor-

She began by surveying welfare activities in Cleveland, Pittsburgh, New York City, San Francisco, and the towns of New England, studying all aspects of existing programs in order to find the right combination for the McCormicks. She was interested in why employers and their welfare workers introduced welfare work and what they thought of its value, in the kinds of reactions workers had to the entire program and to its various parts, and in the differences in reaction between native-born and immigrant workers. She wanted to know how companies explained to workers what they were trying to do in their welfare work, and, when a company had difficulties in reaching immigrant workers, she wanted to know if that company had made a special effort to explain its intentions and purposes to men who could not understand English. She sought data on the physical details of the programs: whether washrooms were available, how they were furnished, and even what kind and what number of towels were supplied. She was concerned about the space provided in washrooms, lunchrooms, and entertainment centers. If lunches were served, she wanted to know what foods were served and how much was charged. Finally, she asked questions about the relationships of unions, wages, and hours to a successful welfare program.[8]

When she completed her survey, Miss Beeks thought she knew what was necessary to make a welfare program succeed. She insisted that physical welfare comprised the "first letters" of the welfare work alphabet. Her ABC's included general cleanliness, pure drinking water, adequate toilet facilities, good ventilation and lighting, separate lockers for outdoor clothing, dressing rooms, relief periods for men whose work demanded it, free laundry facilities for washing work clothes,

---

mick, April 25, 1899; to John R. Hoagland, May 9, 1899; October 10, 1900; to Cyrus McCormick, Jr., July 24, 1903; September 12, 1904; April 13, 1907; Cyrus McCormick to Beeks, June 20, 1906, all in the Harold F. McCormick Papers. Miss Beeks became an associate of Ralph Easely of the Civic Federation of Chicago and later the National Civic Federation. She went to New York City, and in time became Mrs. Ralph Easely.

[8] Beeks, "Notes," in the McCormick Collection.

baths, cooling equipment for hot working areas, adequate medical care for the sick and injured, and safety devices for dangerous machinery. She also called for recreational and educational facilities, and for improving the home environment of workers.[9]

Such a program had to rest on certain fundamentals, she maintained, or it would certainly fail. First she insisted on the separation of the question of wages and hours from that of welfare activities, arguing that welfare work would flounder if the workers feared it would impede wage increases, prevent a reduction of hours, and discourage unions.[10] Second, "the spirit of welfare work," Miss Beeks contended, should not "be that of condescension, nor have the appearance of thrusting benefits upon subordinates nor rob the worker of his self-respect." Any welfare work, she recognized, "may be regarded as more or less paternalistic," but direct paternalism should be avoided with all workers except those recently arrived from Europe. For these, direct paternalism was essential because "in their native lands [they] have been accustomed to the guardianship of superior authority."[11] Third, though Miss Beeks encouraged the use of employee committees in operating a welfare program, she insisted that "the so-called democratic idea" should be avoided. "The chief purpose of committees of employees," she maintained, "is advisory and to enlist [the employees'] interest rather than to initiate or execute welfare plans." Committee work was "also valuable in developing among . . . employees a spirit of helping one another," though too much committee work at intermission time or at the end of a working day could frustrate the worker's desire for relaxation and "the mutual impulse homeward."[12]

In the early stage of developing a program, Miss Beeks worked closely with Henry Bruère. Bruère, a recent graduate

[9] Gertrude Beeks, in National Civic Federation, *Conference on Welfare Work,* v.

[10] *Ibid.,* ix.

[11] *Ibid.*

[12] *Ibid.,* x.

of the University of Chicago and a friend of Stanley McCormick, came from Boston with newly acquired experiences as a "social worker" in factories.[13] The McCormicks, through the efforts of Stanley and Nettie, first made Bruère a timekeeper so that he might study working conditions in one of their plants, and then, in August of 1903, engaged him to develop "a welfare institution for the employees . . . at the McCormick works."[14] He was highly recommended by John Dewey, then director of the School of Education at the University of Chicago, and acquainted with Jane Addams and with the sociologist Charles Zueblin.[15] Bruère consulted all three while he was employed by the International Harvester Company.[16]

He approached welfare work by analyzing the effects of occupations on workers. He concluded that machine-tending "stultified" men. The "lowering of a lever and the occasional adjustment of a jig" was a necessary but undesirable class of work that made workers believe that they could never escape from their occupations. Trade unions did not improve the situation, Bruère thought, for they sought only to limit hours and increase wages. Unionists made "no effort to . . . lift themselves into a higher grade of employment," and tended to accept routine work as "a necessary evil."[17]

Convinced that the division of labor had stifled the educational aspirations of most workers, Bruère wanted especially to enhance the opportunities available to boys and young men. For them Bruère proposed industrial education as the fundamental method for promoting "self-culture," combating "industrial warfare," and preserving American democracy.[18]

[13] Henry Bruère to John G. Wood, general superintendent, McCormick Works, March 9, 1904, in the McCormick Collection; interview with Miss Frances Perkins, a life-long friend of Bruère, Ithaca, N.Y., 1964. Technically speaking there were then no professional social workers.

[14] Bruère to John G. Wood, March 9, 1904; Bruère, "Recommendations . . . at the Reaper Works," 10–11, in the McCormick Collection.

[15] John Dewey to Madam McCormick, February 20, 1904, in *ibid.*

[16] Bruère, "Recommendations . . . at the Reaper Works," 10.

[17] *Ibid.*, 1. On the same page he also said that machine tending should be relegated as a permanent occupation to men incapable of self-development, or performed by potentially skilled workmen during their years of preparation for positions requiring skill.

[18] *Ibid.*, 2, 8.

The rest of the workers were beyond the reach of industrial education, for they constituted "the large class of married workmen whose method of life had become unalterably *fixed.*" They had "lost interest in everything except the gratification of [their] grosser appetites." For them Bruère recommended "physical opportunities."[19]

By the time that Bruère began to collaborate with Miss Beeks, she had begun to implement some of her own ideas. Early in the fall of 1902, she started welfare work for the female employees in the twine mill.[20] As its chief social secretary, Miss Beeks convinced the company that a workday longer than ten hours was harmful to employees and did not increase output. She provided women's dressing rooms with mirrors, improved the ventilation system to remove excessive dust, established a lunchroom (maintained by a committee of employees in co-operation with the company), and secured for the workers rest rooms, hot water, towels and soap, clothing lockers, and a dancing platform equipped with a piano.[21] She also organized a recreation club and an employee opera company, and she recommended that the company lend money at nominal interest to worthy workers to combat the evil of "money sharks." She improved the medical services offered by the company, and extended her personal contacts to the families of employees.[22]

Bruère and Miss Beeks recommended a number of improvements for laborers in the Reaper Works. There were no bathing facilities in the blacksmith shops, and Miss Beeks had learned from the superintendent of a company in East Watertown, Massachusetts, that individual baths for the molders seemed to have an "uplifting" value. She suggested, with Bruère, that International Harvester provide the baths. They also recommended conveniently located lunchrooms big

[19] *Ibid.,* 2.

[20] *Chicago Tribune,* September 25, 1902.

[21] *Ibid.,* September 25, 1902; Commons, "Welfare Work," 79–80. Beeks to Stanley McCormick, December 2, 1902, in the McCormick Collection, including a proposed budget for 1903, with specific recommendations.

[22] Commons, "Welfare Work," 80; Beeks to Stanley McCormick, December 2, 1902, in the McCormick Collection.

enough to be divided into restaurants serving hot food and into locker rooms equipped with washing facilities and benches, where the men "might come to smoke after eating." Bruère also wanted to put "a large phonograph into this [locker] room to enliven things." With the same motives as Samuel Knox at the Bucyrus plant in Milwaukee, Bruère gave foremen special status by putting sinks in their offices.[23]

Bruère's primary concern, however, was industrial education, an area in which he had the support and advice of John Dewey, but which dramatized the limitations of idealistic welfare work and eventually proved Bruère's undoing. After Bruère had talked to Dewey about his plans on two occasions, the educator inspected the Reaper Works. Dewey thought Bruère's ideas "thoroughly sound and feasible," and wrote Nettie F. McCormick that his "purposes and methods are wholly in the right direction and I am sure that his temperament and executive abilities fit him unusually well to carry them out." Dewey agreed with Bruère that manual training for boys and home economics for girls were "the points at which to begin this education work."[24]

Bruère wanted to establish a McCormick technical school to train seventy-five to a hundred skilled workers for the Chicago firm. The course of instruction would be on an elementary level to meet the primary needs of the men, and would consist of arithmetic, English, and technical drawing. Using carefully selected students, Bruère proposed to build an institute that had something of "college life as its predominating spirit." This elite corps, protected against the influx of the "undesirable elements" among employees, would develop the "inspiring principle" of educational motivation.

[23] Beeks, "Notes," 40; Bruère, "Recommendations . . . at the Reaper Works," 11–12. When told of the "up-lift" value of individual baths, Beeks noted that it was "a point well worth considering especially for young apprentices." Beeks, "Notes," 40.

[24] In the same letter Dewey said that he felt "like congratulating all concerned upon their having Mr. Bruère to undertake this sort of work." Dewey to Madam McCormick, February 20, 1904; Bruère to Wood, March 9, 1904, both in the McCormick Collection.

"The education work will give the Institute stability and dignity, while it will serve to justify its existence as nothing else will. Let it be primarily an educational institute and its motives will not be impinged." This system of industrial education for carefully selected students would give the institute its strength.[25]

Bruère, viewing things as a social worker and not as a businessman, had great hopes that his institute would do more than merely serve the needs of McCormick. Although he planned to begin the institute with McCormick personnel, he aimed at ultimately serving the entire industrial community of Chicago. He strongly recommended establishing the institute as an organization separate from the firm, though one that would work closely with officials to meet the company's economic needs. Bruère realized that such a plan precluded using the institute as a means of cultivating company loyalty, but he argued that loyalty so cultivated might "stand in the way of the healthiest development of the employees." Idealistically, he proclaimed that workers "remain loyal to companies only so long as the physical conditions of their employment, and their wage scale are satisfactory. By developing a wholesome community life on one side, and by means of establishing responsibility for and interest in the company (profit sharing, stock owning, etc.), employees of the company will become valuable servants and the right kind of citizens."[26]

Bruère's project for an independent institute had the approval of Miss Beeks and Dewey, but it was rejected by the production managers of the firm, who understandably put the loyalty of their men and the economic needs of their company ahead of serving the entire industrial community and ahead of uplifting workers in general.[27] They thought

---

[25] Bruère, "Recommendations . . . at the Reaper Works," 1–2, 4–5.

[26] *Ibid.*, 4–5, 7–8.

[27] *Ibid.*, 10. Given Miss Beeks' opposition to the "democratic idea" for paternalistic practices, her support of Bruère's Institute must have been qualified. National Civic Federation, *Conference on Welfare Work*, x; Cyrus McCormick, Jr., "The Advantage of a Superintendent of Labor," in the *Harvester World*, 9: 4 (April, 1918).

Bruère should concentrate on something immediately useful, such as becoming the leader of an employee organization,
particularly a men's club, or a benevolent association. Bruère
objected that employee organizations of that kind were "at
best quixotic" because meaningful social clubs for workers
required adherence to a "suitable, inspiring principle"; and
such a principle was simply not forthcoming from the men
at the company.[28] The production managers had their way.
Bruère's project for a college-like independent institute was
vetoed, and he was put in charge of the McCormick Works
Club.[29]

Bruère and Miss Beeks soon ran into another obstacle, one
that deprived them of all real authority. Production men
looked on them as outsiders who tended to undermine the
authority of managers, superintendents, and foremen. E. A.
S. Clark, general manager of the manufacturing department
of McCormick in 1903 and 1904, moved to counter this
threat early in the development of welfare work at the company. He wrote to Harold McCormick that "it would be
unwise to consider employing an outsider—a special expert
in this line—who would be given authority and freedom that
such a man would expect." Such an outsider would upset
"the authority of the superintendents at their plants (possibly)
causing them . . . to lack interest in the scheme." Clark, after
consulting with his superintendents and heads of divisions,
proposed an alternate plan. The superintendent of each
works should appoint his own "assistant and representative
in this welfare work, . . . who might perhaps be termed the
Social, or Welfare Secretary." Social secretaries hired by the
company, as well as representatives from city organizations
interested in welfare work (such as the Y.M.C.A.), should
help to set up and maintain welfare activities, Clark said, but
their plans would have to be approved by plant managers,
and, if necessary, by Cyrus McCormick himself. The social

[28] Bruère to Wood, March 9, 1904, in the McCormick Collection.
[29] *Ibid.*, G. F. Steele to Harold F. McCormick, January 2, 1904, in the
Harold F. McCormick Papers.

secretaries thus would be under the authority of the superintendent, who would "have the interest of all their foremen . . . and work through them." "In that way," Clark wrote, "the best men could be selected from each department."[30]

Welfare work at International Harvester was implemented within the framework of Clark's proposals, for his views accurately reflected the sentiments of the managers of production and of Cyrus and Harold McCormick. Harold offered to consult with Clark about the composition of the welfare committee, but assured him that it was understood that "the appointment of men rests with yourself."[31] Clearly, the program and its staff had to be subordinated to the needs of production and, as the McCormicks indicated, to the profits of the company.[32] Anyone who failed to appreciate this was bound to have difficulty implementing his ideas.

The McCormicks and their production managers assumed that welfare work required little training and experience. Any intelligent individual could understand the character of the worker, they thought, for success required little more than selecting "sensible" persons who would inspire confidence by mixing well with the workers.[33] These views precluded a serious search for the few men and women in America who were professionally equipped to deal with the problems of industrial welfare work.

Thus the administration of the program fell into the hands of untrained individuals, recruited from the company's own ranks. Except for Bruère, the social secretaries appointed to the welfare committee (called the Sociological Committee) had neither training nor experience. S. M. Darling, who actually directed the affairs of the committee in 1904, was

---

[30] E. A. S. Clark to Harold F. McCormick, April 26, 1904, in *ibid.*

[31] Harold F. McCormick to Clark, May 28, 1904, in *ibid.*

[32] Cyrus McCormick to Harold F. McCormick, January 3, 1905; Harold to F. W. Stewart, June 29, 1906; B. A. Kennedy to Harold, June 27, 1906; Harold to Beeks, June 20, 1906, all in *ibid.*

[33] Cyrus McCormick to Harold F. McCormick, January 3, 1905; Wood to Steele, May 2, 1905; Steele to Harold, January 2, 1905 (three letters); Steele to Bruère, April 4, 1905; Harold to Steele, January 9, 1905, all in *ibid.*

Cyrus McCormick's personal secretary. His staff consisted of "sensible" men who more than anything else solicited and distributed information about welfare work. As late as 1908 the company's chief social secretary was a woman originally trained as a bookkeeper. She entered the program as a consequence of changes in the Chicago office's auditing department.[34]

The assumptions of the McCormicks and their production managers also accounted in part for keeping the welfare program under the supervision of company men directly responsible to production men, and for the delays in choosing a general supervisor. Executive changes at the McCormick works made it essential for incoming general managers to have adequate opportunity to familiarize themselves with the program before becoming involved in major policy decisions.[35] Delays of this nature, however, were only temporary, for the men who filled the position of general manager expressed sentiments in general agreement with the views of the owners and of John G. Wood, the general superintendent of manufacturing. They agreed on the need for a general supervisor of welfare work, for subordinating welfare workers to the production personnel, and for minimizing the costs of the program.[36]

In 1905, when Bruère's club became an integral part of

[34] Darling to American Institute of Social Service, July 18, 1904; Darling to N. O. Nelson, July 27, August 1, 22, 1904; Nelson to Darling, July 30, 1904; Darling to U.S. Department of Commerce and Labor, November 17, 1904; Darling to W. E. C. Nazro, April 22, 1904; G. F. Holmes to Darling, April 27, 1904; Darling to Clark, May 23, 1904; Frank A. Ericsson to Darling, June 22, July 1, 1904; Ericsson to A. C. Funk, June 22, 1904; W. H. Tolman to Darling, October 18, 1904; Darling to The Chicago Commons, October 31, 1904; Graham Taylor to Darling, November 1, 1904; Mary Goss to Cyrus McCormick, March 19, April 2, 1907, all in the Harold F. McCormick Papers. The Chicago Institute of Social Science sent its "Announcement of Conferences on Welfare Work, 1907," to Miss Mary Goss in the Auditing Department.

[35] Steele to Harold F. McCormick, January 2, 1905, in the Harold F. McCormick Papers.

[36] Steele to Harold F. McCormick, April 18, 1905; B. A. Kennedy to Harold, June 27, 1906, both in *ibid*. See also the letters about a picnic at the Milwaukee Works that had not been authorized by the Chicago office. Kennedy to Harold, July 3, 1907; Harold to Kennedy, July 6, 1907, both in *ibid*.

the welfare program under a general supervisor, the company considered a number of persons before filling the position. Gertrude Beeks recommended C. U. Carpenter of the National Cash Register Company, a prominent man in the field, but Cyrus McCormick rejected him on the ground that bringing in a prominent outsider would raise the cost of the program. Instead, Cyrus preferred that his personal secretary, Darling, work on a part-time basis with Bruère.[37] "Mr. Darling," Cyrus told Harold, "is very enthusiastic about this sociological and welfare work, and this is one of the requisites." Cyrus thought that Bruère had the organizational ability for the position, but he felt too that he needed Darling as his subordinate co-worker to provide the necessary personal enthusiasm.[38]

Though Bruère was the logical choice for the position of general supervisor, his candidacy was vigorously opposed. The production managers insisted that he could not win the confidence of the "laboring men because he did not mix well with them."[39] Beyond that they disagreed with Bruère's fundamental postulates: an institute separate from the company, composed of and governed by an elite corps of talented young employees. The general managers wanted a McCormick Works Club organized along lines to which Bruère specifically objected. The "better class men" to whom Bruère was addressing himself did not, they felt, need diversions. "It is the ones of narrow confines," those "who have little light and joy in them," that needed to be diverted.[40] They also thought that his requests for personnel and his expectations about the use of a lunchroom connected with the club were

[37] Cyrus to Harold F. McCormick, January 3, 1905; Steele to Harold, January 3, 1905; Beeks to Cyrus McCormick, April 10, 1905. All in *ibid*. Miss Beeks had recommended Carpenter as early as December, 1902, when she became too ill to continue her work with International Harvester. Beeks to Stanley McCormick, December 2, 1902, in *ibid*.

[38] Cyrus McCormick to Harold F. McCormick, January 3, 1905, in *ibid*.

[39] Wood to Steele, May 2, 1905; Steele to Harold F. McCormick, April 18, 1905, in *ibid*.

[40] Steele to Harold F. McCormick, April 14, 1905, in *ibid*.

unrealistic.[41] Some of their criticisms may have been valid, but the lack of support for Bruère really stemmed from his being an outsider and, in all probability, from disagreements about using welfare as a device for making more acceptable to workers the company's policies towards wages, hours, and organized labor.[42]

As a "professional," Bruère was more interested in industrial welfare than in the company. He was backed by Stanley and Nettie Fowler McCormick, and he had the advice of experts at Hull House and the University of Chicago. But he did not have the support of Cyrus and Harold McCormick and the others who mattered. They thought that welfare should be subordinated to production needs, though they did not necessarily agree with the "sensible" social secretary who considered his position "somewhat of a sinecure."[43] G. F. Steele, then general manager of manufacturing at the McCormick works, and Wood told Bruère that he and his ideas were on trial and that he would be considered for the position of welfare manager only if he made good in the McCormick factory. Shortly afterwards, early in the summer of 1905, the problem was resolved by making Charles W. Price the general supervisor of the company's welfare program, a position he held until he became International Harvester's "Inspector of Protection and Sanitation" in 1909.[44]

An insider, Price apparently became involved in welfare work through his close association with Darling. Along with

[41] Steele to Bruère, April 5, 1905, in *ibid.*

[42] In 1904 the conflict about welfare and its relationship to wages, hours, and unions probably came to a head. Beeks had to plead with Cyrus not to cut wages or increase hours while building a $40,000 club house; it was also the year that International Harvester became an open shop. In 1903, on the other hand, Bruère had consulted with Samuel Gompers and the officers of the International Machinists about his ideas for technical education. Beeks to Cyrus, September 12, 1904; Bruère to Wood, March 15, 1905, both in *ibid.*

[43] H. J. Montgomery to Darling, June 28, 1904, in *ibid.*

[44] Stanley McCormick to Cyrus McCormick, March 18, 1904; Bruère to Wood, April 18, 1904; March 15, 1905, Harold F. McCormick to Steele, January 9, 1905; Wood to Steele, May 2, 1905; Steele to Harold, May 15, 1905, all in *ibid.* Bruère left for New York City in 1905, but I have not been able to determine the date of Bruère's departure or of Price's appointment.

some others connected with the Sociological Committee, they seem to have constituted a clique which worked with Bruère but which implied privately that they, not he, had the right approach to welfare work.[45] They really meant that their views coincided with those of the men who controlled and managed the company.

Price educated himself in the ways of welfare by reading materials from other companies and from the American Social Science Association in New York. In this way he familiarized himself with welfare and safety practices in many parts of the country. Unlike most insiders, however, he worked systematically and persistently; he became a familiar figure at Hull House, where he heard and participated in discussion on welfare and safety and their relationship to trade unionism, workers' needs, efficiency, and industrial democracy.[46]

Price never lost sight of the production environment in which he carried on his welfare work, and he always applied his knowledge and ideas for the benefit of the company. In April, 1905, for example, when Steele asked him to comment on Bruère's views about the club, Price replied that a club organized along democratic lines required strong leadership, such as only "skilled men," not "humble foreigners," could give. No matter how the club was organized, Price thought, it would be patronized primarily by the brighter young men of the factory, such as clerks and skilled mechanics. Two winters of experience had shown that it was "the brighter and more ambitious men, with very few of the humble Poles and Bohemians," who attended the club's classes. "Judging from what I know of the men in the factory," Price told Steele, "I think it will require a great deal of genuine personal ef-

---

[45] Price to Darling, July 6, 1904, in *ibid.*

[46] Price to George F. Russell, May 1, 1905; typescript minutes of the fourth, fifth, and seventh meetings (April 24–May 15, 1906) for the Conference on Welfare Work at Chicago Commons, all in *ibid.* See also *Record Herald* (Chicago), April 4, 1906. For examples of Price's efforts to obtain information about welfare and safety work, see Steele to Wood, April 17, 1905; Price to Steele, March 21, April 7, 1905; Price to E. A. Atkins and Co., August 17, 1905, all in the Harold F. McCormick Papers.

fort to induce our humblest men to avail themselves of the opportunities of the club."[47]

Price knew how to work within the operational framework of the company. Always sensitive to the kinds of problems Clark had stressed, he sought to keep welfare costs to a minimum. In addition, Price had the personality so highly prized by production personnel: he mixed well with and inspired confidence among workers. He also knew that most of the company's social secretaries were ignorant in the field of welfare. By disseminating information, he sought to overcome their ignorance in the same way that he was overcoming his own.[48] In short, Price became the practical man of knowledge, the kind of man whom John R. Commons so greatly admired.

Between 1903 and 1905, welfare work at International Harvester became, to use Bruère's phrase, "a distinct company activity," within the framework of which Bruère laid the foundations for industrial education. He consulted with the company's managerial personnel, and with Price he organized a group of twenty-six employees into a general council which sent notices in five different languages to all departments of the Chicago company, announcing the education program.[49]

Courses were offered along the lines of Bruère's original scheme, namely, in mechanical drawing and English, but provision also was made for teaching any subject for which five or more men applied. The fee was twenty dollars for a twenty-lesson course. Classes were open to all nationality groups. During the first term, seventy-nine employees of sixteen different nationalities enrolled. The English class was tailored to meet the needs of European immigrants and was taught by Price and a Bohemian engineer. Skilled employees gave vocational instruction. Because of their status in the company, these men, Bruère wrote Wood, "gave substantial

---

[47] Price to Steele, April 10, 1905, in *ibid.*
[48] Price to Social Secretaries, Superintendents, etc., semi-monthly "newsletter," April 4, 1905, in *ibid.*
[49] Bruère to Wood, March 9, 1904, in *ibid.*

evidence of their authority to the members of the school."
An expert from the experimental department and two drafts-
men from the tool design department taught mechanical
drawing; a graduate of Purdue University, employed in the
tool design department, taught arithmetic.[50]

Bruère felt that even in this program he did not have the
full co-operation of management. He complained to general
superintendent Wood that enrollment in the classes had taken
place in spite of the company, and he asserted that the company had made no "great effort" to interest the boys. Bruère
also encountered opposition to his domestic science program.
The institute began by instructing women in sewing and
cooking. Bruère proposed to expand it by teaching various
phases of domestic science in a cottage that Stanley McCormick had made available to the institute as a "model work-
ingman's home." But Wood made it plain to Bruère that
the education work for women had to be sharply limited and
that the company was reluctant to provide women with educational facilities similar to those offered to men.[51]

Even so, Bruère believed that educational work could be
conducted "in connection with an industrial plant," and this
general principle remained a part of the company's policy
after he left the firm in 1905.[52] In 1908, the International
Harvester Company organized a school for apprentices, and
four years later the Milwaukee branch of the company added
a University of Wisconsin Extension Division course on gaso-
line engines.[53] By 1914, educational activities had become an
integral part of the company's welfare activities, and a special
committee of the advisory board of welfare, composed en-

[50] *Ibid.*
[51] *Ibid.* Bruère to Mrs. Nettie McCormick, December 17, 1904, in the
McCormick Collection.
[52] Bruère to Wood, March 9, 1904, in the Harold F. McCormick Papers.
[53] *Harvester World,* 3: 23 (December, 1912); Clarence Hicks, "International
Harvester Shop Schools," in *ibid.,* 5: 29 (July, 1914). The company had shown
an interest in apprenticeship training since 1902. F. A. Flather to Browne
and Sharpe Manufacturing Co., February 14, 1903, in the Harold F. McCormick
Papers. See also Louis E. Reber, in *Merchants and Manufacturers Bulletin,* 16:
25–26 (April, 1908).

tirely of superintendents, had jurisdiction over industrial education at three major plants, the McCormick, the Deering, and the Milwaukee works.[54]

By the eve of World War I, the company's schools had several purposes. They supplemented the education of their young male employees, many of whom came from immigrant families and had little or no formal schooling. The schools were open to all young men with a speaking knowledge of English, but only apprentices were required to attend. The curriculum stressed technical subjects taught in close relationship to actual production. Mechanical training was given in the shops and was supervised by foremen. The schools provided a "real opportunity for moulding character and influencing life," claimed a company spokesman. They promoted responsible citizenship by giving instruction in hygiene, history, and civics. The company maintained that every "effort is being made to stimulate the ambition" of the students "and to develop in them an interest in their work and to fit them for most of the responsible positions in the company's employ."[55]

The shop schools, as well as all other parts of the welfare program, operated under the direction of an advisory board which was created by the officers of the company in 1909. The board consisted of the plant superintendents and was responsible for organizing, promoting, and supervising all welfare work. The board appointed an executive committee to give day-to-day supervision and welfare specialists to investigate working conditions, make recommendations, and keep International Harvester informed of developments in other firms.[56] Thus, the company continued the system of requiring welfare specialists to work closely with superintendents and of involving superintendents and foremen in welfare activities.

[54] Hicks, "International Harvester Shop Schools," 29.
[55] *Harvester World*, 5: 29–30 (July, 1914); 5: 20 (August, 1914); 5: 29 (May, 1914); 3: 28–29 (January, 1912).
[56] *Ibid.*, 1: 22–23 (October, 1909).

After 1909, the welfare work of International Harvester expanded in step with the firm's growing concern for the well-being of its employees. Its program included protection against injury, sanitation improvements, an employee benefit association, rest rooms, lunchrooms, and coffee stations, health education, evening classes in English, charity work, recreation, lessons in civics, and savings and loan plans.[57] The company also added a profit-sharing plan "to increase the industry and ability of the employees by teaching them the principles of sound living and by demonstrating to them that the company's interest and theirs was identical." International Harvester urged its employees, particularly native-born ones, to "get the savings habit so that they could become financially independent and strengthen their will and character."[58]

Because International Harvester was so large, there were variations in the speed with which elements of the welfare program were introduced. Important decisions had to be cleared with the Chicago office, and, because conditions differed from plant to plant, welfare activities had to be adjusted to the needs of each factory and its superintendent. In Chicago, there were large numbers of "foreign workmen and workwomen, largely ignorant and unmoral," while in Springfield, Ohio, the firm employed only American, Irish, and Scottish workers. In Auburn, New York, the company employed many women, but in Milwaukee and in its mining and lumber camps, it had to contend with only masculine employees. "In one place it was a moral problem," explained the chief social secretary, "in another purely corporeal, and in a third . . . more educational than either. Here it was the black threat of clustering saloons, there it was the dearth of sanitation."[59]

[57] *Ibid.*, 1: 23 (October, 1909); 7: 23–24 (February, 1916).

[58] *Ibid.*, 1: 12, 23–24 (October, 1909); 7: 14–15 (January, 1916); 7: 12 (April, 1916); 8: 14 (March, 1917).

[59] Kimberly J. Mumford, "This Land of Opportunity: The Heart of a 'Soulless Corporation'," in *Harper's Weekly*, 52: 23 (July 18, 1908). By January, 1910, Miss Goss was secretary to the executive committee on welfare and all welfare work passed through her hands. Price had been put in charge of

Clubhouses were established at most installations. The Deering clubhouse in Chicago, for example, became the gathering place of office boys, foundrymen, mechanics, and foremen, of Slavs, Celts, Norwegians, and Anglo-Saxons. Its library served "employees of every walk of life." It was in these clubhouses that employees of various nationalities celebrated Christmas in their own ways, and it was there that both native- and foreign-born employees presented plays.[60] After one performance by Polish employees at Deering, the company's house organ remarked that "we American citizens do not realize what it means to our foreign-born citizens to have their own clubhouse used for their own plays. But after such a demonstration of their appreciation, there is no reason why we should ever forget it again."[61]

At the Milwaukee works, where the ethnic make-up of the work force was mixed, welfare activities tended to follow the pattern laid in Chicago, but they also were affected by established practices in the Milwaukee area. Foundrymen and chippers were furnished with individual washbowls and lockers, and medical care was provided on company premises. In 1908, an employee benefit association was established. Soup and coffee counters were instituted around 1910; a few years later Milwaukee had a lunchroom equipped to serve about 150 employees. By 1912, officers of the plant were working closely with the city's vocational schools and the Extension Division of the University of Wisconsin. In the following year the company expanded recreational facilities for workers and founded a company band, composed of fifty Italian musicians. By 1915, Thanksgiving banquets had become a regular event. In November of that year, the Milwaukee Harvester Works Club, open to all white male employees, was organized to serve as a social center in much the same

---

safety work. Serious friction had developed between Miss Goss and Price necessitating these changes. F. W. Stewart to Gertrude Beeks, January 28, 1910, in the Harold F. McCormick Papers.

[60] *Harvester World*, 5: 30–31 (September, 1914); 6: 21 (June, 1915).

[61] *Ibid.*, 6: 24 (January, 1915).

way that the Deering Club served Chicago workers. In 1917, the Milwaukee group began publishing *Pep,* a house organ, and a year later it formed an employees' mutual aid organization, similar to the one operating at Allis-Chalmers.[62]

These components of welfare work were the consequences of policies adopted by the company after the turn of the century. The McCormick family, like the Bucyrus firm in Milwaukee, embarked on a welfare program under the aegis of benevolence. With notable exceptions, the McCormicks developed their program with inexperienced personnel, in part because so few experienced practitioners were available, in part because the McCormicks did not want to pay the high salaries that experienced men commanded. They accepted the view that welfare workers had to subordinate themselves to production managers. By 1905, they had demonstrated that men like Bruère had no place in the program because they were too independent, and because they insisted that factory-sponsored education should serve the needs of employees and their community, rather than the exclusive interest of the company.

Using production personnel for welfare work was in keeping with the ideas of Cyrus McCormick and other company spokesmen, who repeatedly stressed the need for creating an industrial family. Throughout the second decade of the twentieth century, they spoke of welfare activities as a means of harmonizing the relations between capital and labor, but always on company terms. All phases of the program were designed to win the loyalty of its workers, for its officers knew that the tradition of worker loyalty to the individual employer belonged to another era.[63] The company wished to

[62] *Ibid.,* 3: 23 (December, 1912); 5: 23 (February, 1914); 5: 23 (October, 1914); 7: 21 (February, 1916); 7: 6–7, 9 (June, 1916); 7: 22 (December, 1916); 8: 2 (August, 1917); 9: 9–10 (March, 1918); 9: 8 (May, 1918); 13: 72 (September, October, 1922); Harvester Works Club of Milwaukee, Constitution and By-laws, 1915, Employee's Benefit Association International Harvester Company, Identification Card, 1908, in the possession of A. F. Leidel, pensioner of the International Harvester Milwaukee Works.

[63] Cyrus H. McCormick, Jr., quoted in Mumford, "This Land of Opportunity," 22–24; George W. Perkins, "The Underlying Principle of the Profit

impress employees and its public with the fact that it had a "soul" or a "conscience," but fundamentally welfare was intended to achieve harmony, loyalty, and greater efficiency.[64] "If profit-sharing means anything, if providing for old age means anything, if caring for those who become ill or injured means anything," one company spokesman insisted, "it should mean the fostering of the interest of men in their work, whether that work be sweeping out the office, shoveling coal, or presiding over a great company." Welfare work would "so knit its vast organization together, would so stimulate initiative, would so strengthen and develop the *esprit de corps* of the organization, as to make it possible for the company to increase its business and its earnings."[65]

As a result, Charles W. Price and practitioners like him dominated the welfare program. They accepted roles subordinate to production managers, and in that position they became the educators of workers employed by the company. However, they also became educators of the production manager himself, for by drawing managers into welfare work, they obliged superintendents and foremen to concern themselves with the human factor in the manufacturing process. Indeed, they served as liaison officers between the company's welfare practitioners and its workers—immigrants or native-born Americans. Thus, a practitioner like Charles Price was ideally suited for persuading employers to introduce welfare programs, particularly if and when governments began to spread the gospel of welfare work.

Before 1912, one other important result had emerged from

Sharing, Benefits, and Pension Plans of the International Harvester Company," in the *Harvester World*, 1: 27–28 (December, 1909); A. B. Keller, "A Review of Harvester Profit Sharing," in *ibid.*, 7: 4 (September, 1916); Philip S. Post, "Welfare Work—Its Deeper Reason and Meaning," in *ibid.*, 7: 2–3 (December, 1916); Cyrus McCormick, Jr., "The Advantage of a Superintendent of Labor," in *ibid.*, 9: 4 (April, 1918); Cyrus McCormick, Jr., "Cooperation and Industrial Progress," in *ibid.*, 9: 2–4 (December, 1919).

[64] Mumford, "This Land of Opportunity," 23; Post, "Welfare Work," 3.

[65] Perkins, "Underlying Principles of Profit Sharing," 27–28.

the evolution of welfare work at International Harvester. The industrial safety movement showed that the firm had developed a program with the absorptive and expansive qualities of a sponge. When safety in the factory became a national issue, International Harvester had little difficulty adopting innovations recommended by private groups or complying with legal requirements imposed by state governments.

5

Industrial Safety and Benevolent Despotism

SOON AFTER the turn of the century, a new and external force, the industrial safety movement, lent an element of compulsion to industrial welfare programs. Until that time, the state and federal governments had made little effort to enforce legislation regulating job safety. Unguarded machinery took a regular toll of life and limb; few workers were protected from the hazards of poor lighting, improper ventilation, dangerous fumes, and excessive dust; adequate standards of sanitation were the exception not the rule; and payments compensating workers and their families for industrial accidents were rarely adequate. All this was about to change, at least legally, and so remarkably would it change that management was soon convinced that safety programs, like other welfare activities, were in the interest of efficiency of production.

But until the change was wrought, until agencies of government effectively began to control the conditions of industrial employment, employers judged for themselves what, if any, services they ought to provide. They were at liberty to extend their "benevolent despotism" in any fashion they chose, or not to extend it at all. When they did, welfare work for employees was invariably subordinate to production, as Henry Bruère's experience at International Harvester had clearly shown.

Voluntarily, but impelled by the complex internal forces of industrial development, a sizable minority of industrial firms was turning to elaborate welfare activity. Before World

War I, three million employees worked for companies with comprehensive welfare programs of the type in operation at International Harvester and at two other major Milwaukee firms, Allis-Chalmers and Bucyrus. Undoubtedly many more workers were employed by other firms engaged in some aspects of welfare work.

But freedom of action in this sphere meant that employers could—and often did—ignore certain groups of workers under their jurisdiction, particularly immigrants and "floaters." Immigrants posed special problems because of language barriers. Floaters were a problem because of the nature of their employment: they were temporary workmen hired for a few hours or a few days. In a meat-packing house, for example, they shoveled accumulated fertilizer;[1] in the metal trades they often moved and stored such raw materials as pig iron, scrap, coke, sand, brick, stone, and lumber.[2] Little if any effort was made to deal with their welfare.[3] As A. T. Van Scoy, general manager of the International Harvester Works in Milwaukee, explained in 1909, his firm had "a floating element all the time coming and going," and when it employed a laborer on only a temporary basis, it did not even request that he join the benefit association.[4]

As long as welfare work was voluntary, it was possible for companies to ignore temporary and immigrant workers even in matters concerning industrial safety, sanitation, and com-

---

[1] F. C. Gross and Brothers Co. *vs.* Industrial Commission, 167 *Wisconsin Reports* 612 (1918).

[2] A. L. Clark in the *Proceedings of the National Safety Council, 1915*, pp. 686–687. For the sake of clarity all citations to the work of the council before 1916 follow this form. The full citations are as follows: *Proceedings of the First Co-operative Safety Congress, Milwaukee, Wisconsin, September 30 to October 5, 1912; Proceedings of the National Council for Industrial Safety, Second Safety Congress, New York City, September 23–25, 1913; Proceedings of the National Safety Council, Third Annual Safety Congress, Chicago, October 13–15, 1914; Proceedings of the National Safety Council, Fourth Annual Congress, Philadelphia, October 19, 20, 21, 1915.* After 1915, the name of the organization and the titles of its proceedings stabilized.

[3] *Proceedings of the National Safety Council, 1915*, pp. 686–687.

[4] "Proceedings of the Committee on Industrial Insurance," October 5, 1909, p. 69.

pensation for industrial accidents. By 1905 or so, welfare work was beginning to include such matters, but policy in this area as well as others was controlled by management. Testifying for Milwaukee's employers before a committee of the Wisconsin legislature, Thomas J. Neacy, owner of Filer and Stowell, recalled that in 1905 "there was a team ran away in the yard and turned over a cart and killed a man, and there was no liability on both of us, and we done quite a little for the family."[5] Van Scoy pointed out that International Harvester differentiated between old and new employees. The company "naturally" thought more of its old hands than of its new ones and claimed to know the families of the old workers.[6] Max W. Babb, who represented Allis-Chalmers, said that "not occasionally, but frequently, we contribute something to a person that is hurt where there is no liability . . . and if it is a worthy cause." He added: "We discriminate between what is a worthy case and where it is not. A man who has been in our service a long time and hurt and his family left destitute, we help him."[7]

Effective legislation governing industrial safety, sanitation, and compensation fundamentally altered the relationship between employer and employee. Protective labor legislation removed certain practices from the realm of benevolence by requiring employers to protect employees and to teach all workers the fundamentals of safety and sanitation. When accidents happened to uninstructed workers, whether floaters or immigrants, an employer was legally liable. Effective gov-

[5] *Ibid.,* 132. Some companies used welfare work to foster friction among immigrant groups to block unionizing efforts. In the mill towns of the steel industry employers tended to ignore the immigrant in their welfare work. Beeks, "Notes," 22, 44; Commons, *History of Labor,* 3: 319–320; Leiserson, *Adjusting Immigrants and Industry,* 140–141. Chicago meatpackers particularly kept the work force divided by regularly changing the nationality composition of work groups. John R. Commons, "Labor Conditions in Slaughtering and Meat Packing," in the *Quarterly Journal of Economics,* 19: 1–32 (January, 1904).

[6] "Proceedings of the Committee on Industrial Insurance," April 14, 1910, p. 955.

[7] *Ibid.,* October 14, 1909, pp. 345–346.

ernment regulation made it too risky, both legally and financially, for employers to ignore the welfare of their employees.

Wisconsin pioneered in developing protective labor legislation. After the Civil War, safety and sanitation legislation was passed haphazardly and enforced inadequately. The Wisconsin Bureau of Labor and Industrial Statistics was established in 1883, but it had only two factory inspectors. Even after 1899, when the inspection force was increased to seven, the bureau found it difficult to improve working conditions. The state's "factory inspection system is only of recent development," explained J. D. Beck, State Commissioner of Labor, in 1910. "We . . . have been up against a stone wall in thousands of different places in getting safety appliances, and nearly every law that we have introduced into the legislature to give us a little more power to correct this and the other thing, has met with strenuous opposition."[8] This opposition rested largely on the notion, legitimized by court decisions, that the state had no right to interfere with conditions of employment.[9]

In Milwaukee, the state's largest city, industrial working conditions were closely bound to the general health of the urban population. Health commissioners pleaded for ordinances requiring improved sanitation in workshops as well as in the city at large, but their efforts brought few results in the nineteenth century.[10] In the mid-1880's Milwaukee began to divert sewage into Lake Michigan, but alleys were still "covered with slop and manure and the contents of privy vaults [were still] suffered to run into the streets and alleys."[11]

---

[8] *Ibid.,* November 23, 1909, p. 450. See also Arthur J. Altmeyer, *The Industrial Commission of Wisconsin: A Case Study in Labor Law Administration* (Madison, 1932), 10–11; Wisconsin Industrial Commission, *Bulletin,* 1: 188 (December, 1912); Edwin Witte, in Gordon M. Haferbecker, *The Wisconsin Idea in Industrial Safety,* bound mimeographed pamphlet (Madison, 1953), iv; Commons, *History of Labor,* 3: 399.

[9] Altmeyer, *Industrial Commission,* 11–12.

[10] *Milwaukee Sentinel,* February 17, 1880; *Milwaukee Germania Abendpost,* August 2, 1897; "Annual Message of Emil Wallber, Mayor," in *Proceedings of the Milwaukee Common Council,* April 21, 1885, p. 4.

[11] *Ibid.*

In breweries, where working conditions were usually better than in meat-packing houses or the metal trades, men worked despite poor lighting, ventilation, and oppressively warm and damp conditions.[12] At the E. P. Allis Company, drinking water protected by a little oatmeal floating on top was kept in barrels, and workers drank from a common cup. Workmen who tended their injured fellows often applied tobacco, dirty cobwebs, shavings, or shellac to the wounds.[13] Enforcement of safety and sanitation ordinances was usually difficult, partly because employers disclaimed responsibility for individual accidents and diseases, and partly because the inspection system was ineffective. Neacy blamed the workers for accidents. In rush times, he insisted, the men sometimes would come "with a jag on or throw something or do something and someone gets hurt, but in dull times when they are scared of their job there are no accidents. I know absolutely that it is so."[14] In 1900 an employee of the Wisconsin Bureau of Labor charged that the city's district attorney did not prosecute many violators of protective labor legislation.[15]

Robert M. La Follette and his followers gained political ascendancy in Wisconsin in the early years of the twentieth century, and with the aid of John R. Commons and others at the University of Wisconsin they planned and enacted a series of laws which by 1911 made the state a progressive model and made its representatives the leading spokesmen for national economic and political reform.[16] In Milwaukee

[12] Factory inspection report, in Wisconsin Bureau of Labor and Industrial Statistics, *Biennial Report, 1887–1888,* p. 303.

[13] *Milwaukee Journal,* March 31, 1900. See also Price, "History of Allis-Chalmers," 215; "Leadership among Wage-earning Boys," manuscript copy of statement delivered at a Boy's Conference, Lake Geneva, July 24–August 4 [1903?], n.p., in the Milwaukee Y.M.C.A. Archives.

[14] "Proceedings of the Committee on Industrial Insurance," October 5, 1909, p. 12.

[15] A. C. Backus to Robert M. La Follette, November [?], 1900, in the La Follette Papers. See also *Proceedings of the Milwaukee Common Council,* October 16, 1882, p. 222; November 13, 1882, p. 247; December 11, 1882, pp. 268–269.

[16] The Wisconsin Republican convention of 1904 dramatically demonstrated that La Follette's organization had broken the back of stalwart opposition

in those years, the Social Democrats gradually became the dominant force in local politics. They secured representation on the city council and held important positions in the Federated Trades Council, and, after 1905, in the Wisconsin Federation of Labor.[17] Basing their efforts on scientific findings about the cause and prevention of communicable diseases, such as smallpox, diphtheria, and tuberculosis, the Social Democrats helped pass a number of health measures. These new ordinances provided for the distribution of diphtheria antitoxin to poor families, made food inspection more effective, licensed milk vendors, and prohibited spitting in public places. By 1910, the city owned a garbage incinerator, maintained tuberculosis hospitals, required tuberculin tests for cows supplying milk to Milwaukee, employed school nurses, and provided school children with regular medical examinations.[18]

Meanwhile, publicists alerted the nation to the high accident rate in industry. Between 1903 and 1907, journalists began demanding measures to reduce industrial accidents. Scholars disseminated information about European methods of protecting workmen. In liability cases, some judges became more sympathetic to the plight of injured workers, and more and more states modified the common-law defense against liability. Urban reformers, notably Frances Perkins in New York and Dr. Alice Hamilton in Chicago, enlisted in the crusade for safety and health.[19]

---

in the party. Maxwell, *La Follette*, 56–73. For economic and political legislation during this period, see *ibid.*, 128–172. See also La Follette, *La Follette's Autobiography, passim*; Benjamin Parker De Witt, *The Progressive Movement: A Non-Partisan Comprehensive Discussion of Current Tendencies in American Politics* (New York, 1915), 54–88; George E. Mowry, *Theodore Roosevelt and the Progressive Movement* (Madison, 1946), 36–64, 88–118. It should be noted that Wisconsin was a model for northern states, not for southern states. C. Vann Woodward, *Origins of the New South, 1877–1913* (Baton Rouge, 1951), 371.

[17] Wachman, *History of the Social-Democratic Party of Milwaukee*, 52–53.

[18] Still, *Milwaukee*, 362–365, 384–395, 515–517.

[19] Commons, *History of Labor*, 367; *Proceedings of the National Safety Council, 1913*, p. 67; *1914*, pp. 170–171.

At the same time, industry itself joined the campaign. Large corporations, including United States Steel, International Harvester, and the Chicago and North Western Railroad, already having some kind of welfare programs, now launched into safety work, partly in response to mounting criticism and partly to cope with the increasing cost of accidents. In 1907, the industry-sponsored American Institute of Social Science opened the American Museum of Safety in New York City; in the same year the Association of Iron and Steel Engineers established a safety committee, probably the first of its kind to be formed by a technical organization. In 1911, the year of the terrible fire at New York's Triangle shirtwaist factory, the association called a national conference devoted exclusively to safety, and the next year in Milwaukee the association joined with other organizations to establish the National Safety Council. For the next few years the Safety Council concentrated on problems of industrial safety and hygiene.[20]

It was in such a context that the Wisconsin legislature in 1911 replaced the Bureau of Labor with the Industrial Commission, which was responsible initially for industrial safety and sanitation and, later the same year, for enforcing the newly enacted workmen's compensation law, one of the first such laws to be declared constitutional by the courts. The commission enjoyed broad powers to interpret and enforce a statute which obliged employers to furnish and use safety devices and to do "every other thing" as was "reasonably necessary to protect the health, life, safety and welfare of their employees." In short, the commission's experts, not the legislature, formulated in detail the minimum acceptable standards of industrial safety in Wisconsin.[21]

The workmen's compensation act gave the Wisconsin Industrial Commission an effective instrument with which to compel improvements in safety and sanitation. The law re-

[20] Lucian W. Chaney and Hugh S. Hanna, *The Safety Movement in the Iron and Steel Industry,* in the *Bulletin of the Bureau of Labor Statistics,* no. 234 (Washington, 1918), *passim;* Tolman, *Social Engineering,* 113–122.

[21] Maxwell, *La Follette,* 153–172; Altmeyer, *Industrial Commission,* 16–18, 26–30; Haferbecker, *Industrial Safety,* 4–5.

moved the doctrines of "negligence," "contributory negligence," and the "assumption of risk" as issues between employer and employee by abolishing them as employer defenses. A worker no longer had to prove the extent of his employer's negligence in order to receive compensation; nor did he have to show that he himself had been totally free of negligence; nor did he have to prove the negligence of a fellow worker; nor did he have to convince the court that he had not assumed all the risks when he entered his employment. In practical terms, the law obliged employers to pay compensation for almost all job-connected injuries. The commission set the scale of benefits and acted as arbiter in most disputes between workers and employees. Punitive provisions required employers to pay up to 15 per cent compensation if their failure to comply with the commission's safety orders resulted in injuries to workers. Since insurance companies could assume the general liability an employer might incur under the new act, they were not permitted to assume this special liability.[22] As amended in 1913, the law applied to all employers of four or more workers, but any company could place itself outside the system simply by notifying the commission and taking its chances under the common-law rules of employer liability as amended by statutes. Actually, few companies chose this course of action.[23]

Industrialists as well as administrators recognized the coercive influence of workmen's compensation laws.[24] Almost

---

[22] Commons, *History of Labor*, 3: 565–569; Altmeyer, *Industrial Commission*, 27, 64; George P. Hambrecht, "What Wisconsin is Doing to Prevent Industrial Accidents," mimeographed copy of address given at the meeting of the Industrial Accident Board at Madison, January 1, 1918, p. 7.

[23] Altmeyer, *Industrial Commission*, 26–27; Commons, *History of Labor*, 3: 578. In 1912 the following companies in Milwaukee were already among those covered by the new law: Illinois Steel, International Harvester, Milwaukee Coke and Gas, Milwaukee Electric Railway and Light, Pfister and Vogel Leather, Fuller and Warren, Harley Davidson Motor, Wisconsin Iron and Bridge, Keystone Glue, and Kearny and Trecker. See *Civics and Commerce* (Milwaukee), January, 1912, p. 15.

[24] By the end of 1911 ten states had adopted workmen's compensation laws; by 1913, seventeen; by 1916, twenty-six; and by 1919, thirty-four. Commons, *History of Labor*, 3: 575–576.

immediately the chairman of the Wisconsin Industrial Commission noted that they already had stimulated "more real safety work in the United States than in any ten years preceding."[25] Charles W. Price, speaking out of his Wisconsin experience, observed in 1913 that compensation legislation added "a tremendous incentive for the promotion of safety as a business proposition." He had found that the statutes made it "easy for the officers of the state to meet the manufacturer on a common ground."[26] The "club of the law" made manufacturers more aware of the "wasteful cost of industrial accidents."[27]

Throughout Wisconsin, but particularly in Milwaukee, employers generally co-operated with the Industrial Commission.[28] For one thing, they had become aware of the rising cost of accidents. For another, they were quick to comprehend the commission's expert knowledge and understanding of safety problems. In the past, legislators and factory inspectors usually had not been so knowledgeable, and employers often had been dissatisfied with the detailed regulation by statute and the wide discretionary power enjoyed by inspectors. Finally, the common-law remedy, involving as it did the cumbersome process of litigation, had proved time consuming, occasionally indecisive, and always expensive.[29] To be sure, employers fought hard to require workers to share the financial burden of workmen's compensation; they gave up their

[25] Charles H. Crownhart, in the *Proceedings of the National Safety Council, 1912*, p. 60.

[26] *Ibid., 1913*, p. 113.

[27] *Ibid., 1912*, pp. 253–254; see also *ibid., 1913*, pp. 186–187, for a discussion of the cost of accidents when a company was covered by workmen's compensation.

[28] The state's supreme court fully endorsed workmen's compensation. In 1911 the court upheld the law on the grounds that the legislature had sought to "remedy a great economic and social problem which modern industrialsm had forced upon us, namely, the problem of who shall make pecuniary recompense for the toll of suffering and death which that industrialism levies and must continue to levy upon the civilized world." Borgnis *v.* Falk Co., 147 *Wisconsin Reports,* 327 (1911).

[29] Haferbecker, *Industrial Safety,* v, 2–3; Altmeyer, *Industrial Commission,* 105–107.

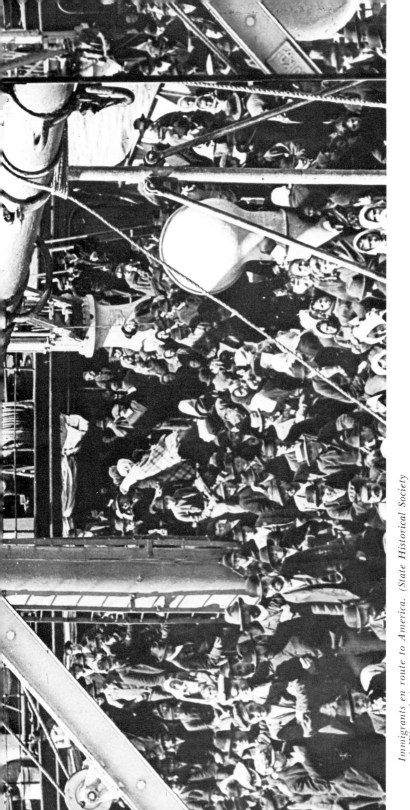

Immigrants en route to America. (State Historical Society of Wisconsin.)

Quitting time at the McCormick works. (State Historical

Illinois Steel Company works, Milwaukee, 1892. (State Historical Society of Wisconsin.)

Molding floor at the McCormick reaper works, 1885. (State Historical Society of Wisconsin.)

Reliance Works of the Edward P. Allis Company, Milwau-

Factory interior, International Harvester. (State Historical Society of Wisconsin.)

Dining room at an International Harvester factory. (State Historical Society of Wisconsin.)

Dr. Peter Roberts. (Y.M.C.A. Historical Library.)

May Wood Simons. (State Historical Society of Wisconsin.)

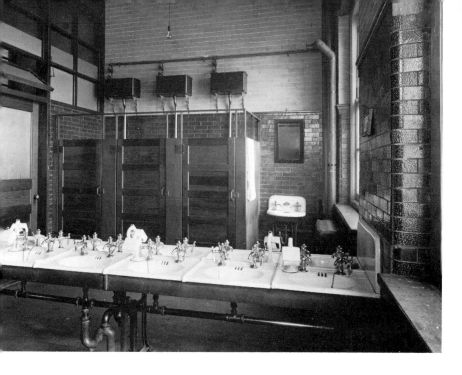

Interior views of the workers' lavatory and lounge at an
International Harvester factory. (State Historical Society
of Wisconsin.)

Loyalty parade, Madison, Wisconsin, 1917. (State Historical Society of Wisconsin.)

common-law defenses with the greatest reluctance; and they opposed bills establishing maximum hours and minimum wages. But they appreciated the determination of La Follette, his followers, and of the socialists to regulate the economy, and they realized in the long run that the system of workmen's compensation and the work of the Industrial Commission were beneficial. Hence, employers supported them out of self-interest.[30]

Among the commission's strongest advocates were a number of government and university experts, some of whom had worked earlier with employers on industrial and managerial problems. Once established, the commission capitalized on this good will. It worked closely with and vigorously supported the National Safety Council, and it took account of, and learned from, the welfare and safety programs of firms in Milwaukee and elsewhere.[31] More significant still, it created the Advisory Committee on Safety and Sanitation Standards, which greatly facilitated consultation among government specialists and manufacturing interests when drafting safety rules.

Employers readily accepted the advice of the experts and the rules which they drafted, in part because the commission's approach was often similar to their own. True, government experts usually started with premises different from those of management, particularly in their sympathy for organized labor. But the men of the commission, and especially its guiding spirit, John R. Commons, also wanted to harmonize relations between capital and labor, and their industrial safety

[30] Wisconsin Industrial Commission, *Annual Report on Workmen's Compensation, 1912*, pp. 104–105; William G. Bruce, in the *Proceedings of the National Safety Council, 1912*, p. 72; *Merchants and Manufacturers Bulletin*, October, 1907, p. 14; "Proceedings of the Committee on Industrial Insurance," October 5, 1909, pp. 65–66, 133, 135, 137, 140–141; *Civics and Commerce*, February, 1911, p. 11; January, 1914, p. 15; Gertrude Schmidt, "History of Labor Legislation in Wisconsin," (doctoral thesis, typescript, University of Wisconsin, 1933), 36, 68–69, 72–75.

[31] Wisconsin Bureau of Labor and Industrial Statistics, *Biennial Report, 1911–1912*, pp. 98–101; John R. Commons, quoted in Altmeyer, *Industrial Commission*, 116, 117–121; Witte, in Haferbecker, *Industrial Safety*, v; George P. Hambrecht, "Industrial Accidents," 5–6.

and sanitation work complemented existing programs. Indeed, Commons' choice of Charles W. Price of International Harvester to promote safety and sanitation work showed how closely the commission and industry could co-operate.[32]

When Price joined the commission, he had a national reputation as an expert on industrial safety, sanitation, and welfare. According to William H. Cameron, general manager of the National Safety Council between 1912 and 1919, Price was the most knowledgeable man in his field. Commons agreed, for he considered the welfare program at International Harvester to be one of the most enlightened in the nation, and considered Price to be a man who knew how to get technicians and committees to work for both safety and welfare.[33]

Price's recognition of the intimate relationship between these two goals was shared by many company executives and welfare practitioners. One firm began welfare work solely to bring "home the safety movement to the men."[34] "Under the beneficient influence of up-to-date safety organizations," said Stephen W. Tener of American Steel and Wire, "the vision of the employer, the man who formerly took personal interest in the welfare of his employees, is again appearing on the industrial horizon, principally through the work of interlocking and overlapping safety committees organized through all departments of the manufacturing establishments." These committees, Tener noted, were "called to-

[32] This point is developed below, but one may note here that Price was most influential in determining the safety policies of the commission. Interview with Don D. Lescohier, Madison, Wisconsin, 1958; Altmeyer, *Industrial Commission,* 151, 153.

[33] Charles W. Price, in the *Proceedings of the National Safety Council, 1913,* pp. 180–181; *Harvester World,* 1: 27 (November, 1909); 2: 26 (June, 1910); 3: 32 (October, 1911); interview with William H. Cameron, Evanston, Ill., 1959. Price would not leave the International Harvester Company for a "political job." He was lent to the commission at $25 a day for three days a week. John R. Commons, *Myself* (New York, 1934), 161.

[34] J. Schelling, Jr., in the *Proceedings of the National Safety Council, 1915,* pp. 754–755.

gether for an interchange of views and to consider suggestions, looking toward an elimination or reduction in the accident hazard." This type of work, explained Arthur T. Morey of Commonwealth Steel, was not done in the spirit of charity, but in the spirit of partners and associates joining together to promote efficiency and pride. Charles M. McChord of the Interstate Commerce Commission held similar views. The safety committees, he argued, "are also bound to be an important factor in reawakening in employees that old-time feeling of personal interest and pride in the record of 'our road' that has been so largely dissipated by modern development." A spokesman for International Harvester showed how easy it was for a company with a welfare program to incorporate safety work into the aims of a firm's program. He went so far as to say that the effectiveness of safety organizations served as an excellent barometer for the general morale of the work force because the safety committees required the co-operation of foremen.[35]

Administrators of welfare and safety work insisted that safety, sanitation, and welfare were interdependent. "There can be no clear-cut division between safety and welfare," insisted L. H. Burnett of the Carnegie Steel Company.[36] Thomas Darlington, secretary of the American Iron and Steel Institute's welfare committee, stressed the relationship between the health of a community and conditions in its workshops. Safety and welfare matters "bear upon the question of what we shall place in the mill of the [workmen's] environment."

---

[35] *Ibid., 1912,* pp. 35, 254–258; *1915,* p. 110; *Harvester World,* 5: statement on the inside of the front cover (October, 1914). Pages 22–23, the welfare pages of the house organ of the International Harvester Company, carried safety, sanitation, and health features in almost every issue from 1909–1917. A. T. Van Scoy on the basis of about thirty years of industrial experience viewed the concern about safety and workmen's compensation as an outgrowth of welfare-work experiments that had been only moderately successful. The experiments he referred to were those of George M. Pullman, A. T. Stewart of Garden City, New York, and the National Cash Register Company of Dayton, Ohio. "Proceedings of the Committee of Industrial Insurance," April 14, 1910, pp. 945–946.

[36] *Proceedings of the National Safety Council, 1913,* p. 126.

He thought that the "individual must be taught certain things. Those things which are under his control and which he should do for himself are the regulation of his meals, the amount, the character and the mastication of them, the amount and character of drink, the hours of rest and sleep, the ventilation of rooms, personal cleanliness (cleanliness of body lessens the chance of disease in case of accident), washing of hands before meals, daily washing of feet, proper fitting of shoes, amount and kind of clothing, care of the eye, ear and nose, brushing of the teeth, and regularity of the bowels. Cultivation of the cheerful thoughts has much to do with the body, especially digestion. . . . Another thing that the workmen should be taught is that the first condition of health is fruitful toil. We are made to labor."[37]

This kind of thinking called for physicians, and companies used medical examinations for a number of reasons: to improve the health of the work force and thus improve sanitary conditions in the shop; to eliminate sick workers and thus reduce accidents and the costs of workmen's compensation; and to assign the right men to the right job and thus increase the efficiency and stability of the work force. According to Price, physical examinations were a "boon . . . to the working man," for they protected his and his family's health.[38]

But the interlacing of safety and welfare made labor suspicious. These doubts were voiced in 1915 by Dr. Alice Hamilton, an authority on industrial lead poisoning and a member of the staff of Hull House. Physical examinations, she declared, were being used to eliminate "agitators" by the simple device of having company doctors declare them unfit for work. Moreover, examinations often prevented the hiring of older men, even though the worker himself "thinks he has many years of work left," and employers refused to hire ailing workers for fear of increasing the risks under workmen's

---

[37] *Ibid., 1912,* p. 308. See also *ibid., 1912,* p. 309; *1914,* pp. 133, 166.
[38] *Ibid., 1912,* p. 271; *1914,* p. 166; *1915,* pp. 431–432; *Harvester World,* 5: 32 (June, 1914); 7: 23 (May, 1916). See also Commons, *History of Labor,* 3: 364–365.

compensation. Workers were willing to undergo examinations to detect communicable diseases which might endanger the general public, asserted Dr. Hamilton, but they preferred to be examined by "impartial" rather than "company" doctors, and they wanted safeguards which would protect an employee "who was thrown out of work because of age, injury or illness."[39]

According to Price, these fears were groundless. He claimed that "laboring men [had] not got at the facts." They, as well as employers, had to be educated about safety and sanitation, and as special assistant to the state industrial commission he sought to do just that.[40]

In 1912, when Price began his work for the commission, safety education was considered "tremendously novel and progressive" by all but a few administrators. Most industrialists, superintendents, foremen, and workers knew little about the theory or practice of safety programs. From time to time in Wisconsin, as in other states, manufacturers had guarded their workers from this or that piece of machinery, but they had not made safety part of a general education program. Price was an ideal educator, combining his knowledge of welfare and factory production with an inspiring evangelical spirit.[41]

Price immediately helped organize an Advisory Committee on Safety and Sanitation Standards similar to the one established in 1910 by the old Wisconsin Bureau of Labor and Industrial Statistics, and similar to the advisory committees

[39] *Ibid.*, 321, 361–363; Alice Hamilton, "Some of the Objections to Health Supervision," in the *Proceedings of the National Safety Council, 1915*, pp. 424–427.

[40] *Ibid.*, 431.

[41] Altmeyer, *Industrial Commission*, 178–179. Interview with Selig Perlman, 1959. Don D. Lescohier, like Altmeyer and Perlman, was a contemporary of Price. In 1958, Lescohier remembered Price as a "high-class gentleman," who was "quiet and gentle," but who "had drive." Price, said Lescohier, always insisted that co-operation would go much further with manufacturers than coercion. Thus he stressed meeting manufacturers in small groups and supplying them with information. He opposed coercive legislation. Interview with Lescohier, Madison, 1958.

used at International Harvester. Drawing its members from all interested groups, the committee included representatives of the Wisconsin State Federation of Labor, the Milwaukee Merchants and Manufacturers Association, the Wisconsin Manufacturers Association, the Milwaukee Health Department, a number of workmen's compensation insurance companies, and the commission. Two of the commission's four representatives were safety engineers from private firms, and Price and four factory inspectors were the committee's safety experts. In 1913, the work of the committee was augmented by monthly round tables conducted for Milwaukee's large industries by the Merchants and Manufacturers Association.[42]

Price held safety meetings throughout Wisconsin at which he and other members of the commission demonstrated safety equipment, explained how safety work could be made effective, and discussed the administration of workmen's compensation. What "impresses the foremen most," Price said, "is a direct statement that a man lost his hand, or that an employee was killed, 'on that set screw.'" Employers learned that time lost through industrial accidents could be reduced by more than one half, though only partly through the installation of mechanical safeguards. Commission spokesmen argued that the best programs stressed rigid inspection by foremen and workmen, careful instruction—especially of new men—proper supervision and discipline, and booster meetings to promote interest and enthusiasm.[43]

Most large Wisconsin manufacturers (those employing 500 or more men) received Price cordially and were eager to learn about safety methods. From experience, Price found that the most effective safety programs were those which started with the enthusiastic support of company executives. The

[42] Commons, *History of Labor,* 3: 653; Altmeyer, *Industrial Commission,* 123–124; *Proceedings of the National Safety Council, 1913,* p. 111. The journal of the association, *Civics and Commerce,* printed the summaries of the round tables. See, for example, *ibid.,* April, 1913, p. 11; December, 1913, p. 12; February, 1914, p. 15; January, 1915, p. 16.
[43] *Proceedings of the National Safety Council, 1912,* pp. 63–64; *1913,* pp. 111–112, 170.

usual plan was to form a committee composed of the superintendent of the factory as chairman, and the safety inspector
and three or four "high grade men," such as master mechanics,
as members. Then the committee arranged for a meeting
(often a banquet) of superintendents, foremen, and sub-fore-
men to discuss a draft safety plan. A representative of the
commission was generally present to give advice and to out-
line the experiences of companies which had achieved the
largest reduction in accidents.[44] Price felt that the banquet
meetings convinced superintendents and foremen that safety
had become company policy, thereby infusing the work force
with a new spirit. By 1913, some Milwaukee companies had
adopted safety programs similar to those in the various plants
of the United States Steel Corporation, and there seemed
every reason to believe that others would soon follow suit.[45]

With local variations, most Wisconsin programs stressed
safety education for the entire work force, including foremen, and emphasized the use of shop committees and safety
inspectors. The most successful programs secured the enthusiastic support of foremen because a successful welfare
program necessarily had to enlist the aid of these shop com-
manders. They had to learn about safety devices, to co-
operate with safety experts, and to enlist the good will of
their men.

This was no easy task. As one authority explained, a foreman usually had advanced from the ranks "through individual effort," and had "probably stepped upon men under him
in consolidating his . . . power." A "czar in his domain," he
often resented outside interference.[46] His co-operation usually
was secured in a number of ways. He was introduced to safety

[44] *Ibid.*, 109–111.

[45] *Ibid.*, 109–110; *1914*, p. 227; *Civics and Commerce*, November, 1913, p. 17;
Wisconsin Industrial Commission, *Bulletin*, 1: 3, 4, 5, 160, 161 (1912);
2: 4, 75 (1913–1914); *Report, 1911–1912*, pp. 99, 100, 101; *1913–1914*, pp. 3, 4,
31; *Report on Allied Functions, 1915*, pp. 4, 5; *1917*, p. 7; *Harvester World*,
6: 23 (December, 1912). For a brief summary of Price's work in the state,
see Altmeyer, *Industrial Commission*, 151–156.

[46] Richard Moldenke, in the *Proceedings of the National Safety Council,
1915*, p. 679.

work in the convivial atmosphere of a banquet, and this preliminary effort was followed by regular discussions. Foremen received special safety booklets and bulletins. Some companies even held a foreman personally responsible for accidents in his domain if safety rules had not been followed. Most safety administrators, however, carefully avoided coercion.[47]

Most safety programs utilized inspection and education committees composed of workmen. Members sometimes were selected by management, sometimes by their fellow workers. In 1915, leading companies rotated membership regularly by changing one or two men every three months.[48] In addition to investigating and reporting on safety matters, these committees also had an important educational function—encouraging workers to report dangerous conditions, and enlisting their support as contributors to the safety effort.[49]

In 1912, the Illinois Steel Company, a subsidiary of United States Steel and the parent organization of the iron and steel works at Bay View in Milwaukee, had one of the most elaborate safety programs in the nation.[50] Besides using some ordinary safety techniques, the company utilized a number of other methods. Safety promotion began at the factory gate in the form of an illuminated safety sign. If the newcomer missed the sign, it was called to his attention, and he was told "that he must be willing to look out for his own and other's safety or 'move on.' " Within ten days of being hired, the worker had to sign an instruction card stating that he had received a copy of the company's safety rules and that his foreman had told him "how to perform the duties of his

[47] *Ibid., 1912*, pp. 158–159; *1913*, pp. 153–171; *1914*, p. 301.
[48] Industrial Commission, *Bulletin*, 2: 86 (February 20, 1913); *Civics and Commerce*, November, 1913, p. 17; *Proceedings of the National Safety Council, 1912*, pp. 35, 228; *1914*, p. 227; *1915*, p. 735.
[49] *Ibid., 1912*, pp. 35, 228; *1914*, p. 227; *1915*, p. 735.
[50] The Illinois Steel Company consisted of the following plants: South Works, South Chicago, 8,000–10,000 men; Gary Works, Gary, 8,000–10,000 men; Joliet Works, Joliet, 4,000–5,000 men; Milwaukee Works, Milwaukee, 2,000–3,000 men; North Works, North Chicago, 1,100–2,000 men. See R. W. Campbell, in the *Proceedings of the National Safety Council, 1912*, pp. 282–283.

particular job." The foreman had also to go on record as having warned the men of particular dangers, as having given each a safety rule book, and as having satisfied himself that each man understood the requirements. Constant supervision then ensured that each new worker conducted himself with due regard for his own as well as his fellows' safety.[51]

Illinois Steel utilized some additional methods. Safety bulletin boards, posted at the entrance to every plant and department, carried newspaper accounts of accidents. Alongside, photographs of safety devices and copies of the safety rules drove home the lessons of accident prevention. The company also stimulated competitive spirit by publicizing the safety record of each plant and department. Special bulletins, often illustrated with pictures of effective safety committees, carried a "monthly score card," setting out performances in baseball reporting style. The company found the technique "rather catchy with the men."[52]

In Wisconsin shops, as in most American factories, the success of these efforts presupposed effective communication between the employers who preached safety and the workers who were expected to practice it. But the large number of immigrant employees—and the babel of many tongues—constituted a major impediment. Most companies devised simple techniques to teach these workers. Demonstrations in pantomime often sufficed to explain how to use safety equipment and techniques. Sometimes it was sufficient to translate laconic signs into the language of the immigrant.[53]

As safety education became more complex, however, these simple methods no longer were enough. This was particularly true in relation to the complex details of common-law liability and the system of workmen's compensation insurance. As A. T. Van Scoy of the International Harvester Com-

---

[51] *Ibid., 1912*, pp. 303–304. See also the comments of Joseph A. Holmes, in *ibid.*, 17; Wisconsin Industrial Commission, *Bulletin*, 2: 80 (February 20, 1913).

[52] *Proceedings of the National Safety Council, 1912*, pp. 304–305.

[53] *Ibid., 1912*, pp. 85, 121–122; *1913*, pp. 178–179; *1915*, pp. 734, 751; *Harvester World*, 3: 32 (January, 1911).

pany's Milwaukee Works explained in 1910, it was impractical to have interpreters on hand to explain these matters each time that ditch diggers and other casual laborers were hired for a day or two. On the other hand, he said, it "don't seem . . . quite right to employ him and thrust an insurance contract under his nose and say 'sign this' without his knowing anything about it."[54]

Thomas Darlington, the welfare secretary of the American Iron and Steel Institute, found that even if translations were provided, care had to be taken to prevent misunderstanding. One of the institute's first circulars dealt with personal hygiene—the fact that the common fly found a ready breeding place in the "dirty and nasty conditions" in many neighborhoods, where garbage was not collected and where "wash water, slop, everything goes out of the back door." Though Darlington thought that he had made a clear case against the fly in each of nineteen different languages, he failed to reckon with so simple a question as, "Why were flies so bad if God made them?"[55] The welfare secretary responded that flies "were wisely ordained, but we ought not to need their services; where filth and waste are allowed to accumulate flies are needed to aid in their decomposition and disposal, but if filth and waste are removed, the necessity for the fly is removed." This explanation also was translated, sometimes with ludicrous results. The Bulgarian version read: "Flies are ministers of God, but we don't need them."[56]

Teaching immigrants safe working habits faced an additional obstacle—stereotyped assumptions about the nature of foreign-born employees. A Denver mining engineer expressed one version of it: When Mexican pit workers said, "No sabe," they really meant that "they don't want to 'sabe.' "[57] Likewise, a representative of the Youngstown Sheet

[54] "Proceedings of the Committee on Industrial Insurance," April 14, 1910, p. 958.

[55] *Proceedings of the National Safety Council, 1912*, pp. 310–311.

[56] *Ibid.*, 311.

[57] *Ibid.*, 100.

and Tube Company in Pennsylvania believed that foreign-born workers had the highest accident rate and a high incidence of ignorance and feeble-mindedness. In such circumstances, he thought, a comprehensive educational program was not feasible. Their primitive European agricultural backgrounds and their low intelligence, he argued, made many immigrants unable to cope with American technology. It was pitiful indeed, he reported, to see "men 20 to 50 years old attempting to put a square block into a round hole." As further substantiation of his appraisal, he recounted that the four-year-old daughter of the United States surgeon at Ellis Island had successfully completed "without the least hesitation" every one of the tests given to immigrants.[58]

Other observers cited practical barriers to an effective safety program embracing immigrant workers. Some argued that companies employing more than 3,000 men had such a rapid turnover of green hands that using interpreters was futile. Suppose, said one company spokesman, "you had fifteen interpreters in your employment. If you have three or four employment offices . . . you simply cannot have fifteen interpreters at every such office at the plant . . . nor can you secure a man who speaks every language when you have . . . a heterogeneous mass of workers coming in."[59] Smaller firms, employing fewer than 300 men, argued that they could not afford interpreters, and companies which relied heavily on workmen's committees and bulletin boards felt that immigrants were not "high class" enough to use on committees, and that it took too much time to translate information for bulletin boards.[60]

On the other hand, those persons most convinced of the value of safety programs found none of these obstacles insurmountable. The Wisconsin Industrial Commission, for example, used both propaganda and decisions in workmen's

[58] *Ibid., 1914,* p. 132.
[59] *Ibid., 1913,* pp. 162–163, 177. See also the "Proceedings of the Committee on Industrial Insurance," April 14, 1910, p. 258.
[60] *Proceedings of the National Safety Council, 1913,* pp. 173–174; *1915,* p. 751.

compensation cases to urge employers to tackle the difficult problem of educating immigrants. The commission distributed hundreds of leaflets to manufacturers, superintendents, and foremen urging the education of all workers, native- as well as foreign-born. The task "should be done in a frank and kindly manner," the commission advised, in order to make each employee "appreciate the part which the company is doing and the larger part which he alone can do in protecting himself and his fellows."[61] Behind this advice lay the commission's power to hold negligent companies responsible for industrial accidents.

In 1913, the Plankinton Packing Company of Milwaukee was charged with ignoring the commission's instructions. Plankinton had hired Mike Magda, a newly arrived Hungarian immigrant who neither spoke nor understood English. Magda joined a crew which caught, shackled, and butchered hogs. Since neither the foreman nor any of the other workers spoke Hungarian, the foreman instructed Magda through signs. Magda understood the sign language to mean that he was to keep busy, to work harder, and to help the butchers. On one occasion, mistakenly assuming that he was to kill hogs when the regular butcher was absent, Magda cut his hand. The commission held the company responsible on the ground that Magda had been inadequately instructed.[62]

The commission and the Milwaukee Merchants and Manufacturers Association recommended special techniques for teaching immigrants. Employers were advised to use interpreters, either men specially hired for this purpose or other employees, and to translate all signs and rules into as many languages as necessary. The commission itself also educated foreigners. In 1914, it supplied employers with safety movies. The motion picture, the commission thought, "at once entertains and instructs. It speaks a universal tongue. If the

---

[61] Wisconsin Industrial Commission, *Report on Allied Functions, 1914,* pp. 6–7.

[62] Mike Magda *v.* Plankinton Packing Company, in Wisconsin Industrial Commission, *Workmen's Compensation, Annual Report, 1912–1913,* pp. 63–64.

worker of foreign birth is not well enough schooled in the English language to 'catch the drift' of the safety pamphlet given to him, the safety movie does for him what cold type could never do." With the co-operation of a number of industrial firms, the commission also sought the assistance of churches in promoting safety among immigrants.[63]

The Wisconsin Industrial Commission found a particularly useful ally in the National Safety Council, an organization whose membership, recruited from industrial organizations, government agencies, and other groups, climbed from 40 in 1912 to 3,300 in 1917. The commission encouraged Wisconsin firms to take advantage of the council's services, and its own staff worked closely with the council. It was probably not coincidence that the council's first national convention met in Milwaukee, or that George P. Hambrecht, one of the commission's early chairmen, presided over a number of council meetings, or that Price regularly chaired the council's discussion on safety education. Indeed, Price left the commission in 1916 to become the council's executive secretary, and when he began a two-year stint as general manager in 1919, he was succeeded as secretary by a field worker from the Wisconsin commission.[64]

The efforts of Wisconsin to provide for the industrial safety of immigrants were strongly supported by other government employees and independent social workers. The United States Department of Labor and the Bureau of Mines, for

[63] *Civics and Commerce,* April, 1913, p. 11; October, 1913, p. 10; December, 1913, p. 12; February, 1914, p. 15; January, 1915, p. 16; Wisconsin Industrial Commission, *Report on Allied Functions, 1915,* pp. 7–8; *Proceedings of the National Safety Council, 1913,* p. 164.

[64] Commons, *History of Labor,* 3: 369; Witte, in Haferbecker, *Industrial Safety,* v; *Proceedings of the National Safety Council, 1912,* pp. 60, 63–64; *1913,* pp. 153, 179; *1915,* p. 734; *1919,* p. 23; Hambrecht, "Industrial Accidents," 5–6; Altmeyer, *Industrial Commission,* 151, 178. In 1921, Price resigned from the council and dropped out of safety work entirely. Cameron maintains that Price brought the council to the verge of bankruptcy. When the council's executive committee asked him to return to his earlier position, Price refused. Interview with Cameron. I have tried to trace Price's whereabouts after 1921, but with little success.

example, sent representatives to the meetings of the National Safety Council, where they denied that immigrants were too feeble-minded to comprehend safety education. In 1913, L. W. Channey vigorously protested the notion that "the foreign element is not approachable." On the contrary, he argued, immigrant workers were neither childish nor inept but rather intelligent. "If you get to it," he insisted, "results will be forthcoming; but if you do not do so, the fault does not lie at [the immigrants'] door."[65] Dr. Hamilton, the Hull House industrial hygienist, turned the stereotyped view of immigrants into a weapon in the safety crusade by contending that employers in the lead industry who thought that their foreign-born workers were feeble-minded had an even greater than usual responsibility for their safety. "You are after all," she told employers in 1914, "getting the benefits of a force that accepts low wages, . . . that is willing to work for longer hours, [and] that is docile. . . . Then, having the advantage of these child-like and docile employees you ought to be willing to treat them as children." She insisted that employers should not "look upon [their children] as entirely responsible for their own stupidity and their own obstinacy that comes from slow wittedness—defects which are in the very virtues for which you have employed them."[66]

Several companies demonstrated before 1917 that immigrants could be trained to work safely. The Commonwealth Steel Company used an ingenious system of providing immigrant newspapers with translations of articles on safety methods. The company then purchased a hundred copies of each paper, had them marked by its interpreter, and distributed them to its Hungarian and Bulgarian employees. This arrangement helped the company to educate both the worker and his family and was judged to be exceptionally beneficial by the company's safety engineer.[67]

---

[65] *Proceedings of the National Safety Council, 1913,* p. 162. For the comments of Joseph A. Holmes, see *ibid., 1912,* pp. 8, 13, 15.

[66] *Ibid., 1914,* pp. 170–171.

[67] *Ibid., 1915,* p. 753.

The New Jersey Zinc Company, a firm which employed immigrants almost exclusively, succeeded in adapting the safety-committee system to its particular needs. It rotated membership in order to allow each class of worker to partici-pate. The rotation began with the general foreman and end-ed with the "humble man," the Hungarian, Polish, Lithua-nian, and other foreign-born workers. Committee members were designated by red-bordered badges, former members by blue-bordered ones. "This permanent badge designates the prestige they enjoyed in having fulfilled such a position," observed a company spokesman, "and as the men appreciate prestige, we profit accordingly."[68]

Another firm which successfully adapted its safety program, particularly the committee system, to its immigrant employees was the Illinois Steel Company. Indeed, some of its com-mittees were composed entirely of "foreign-speaking men." They were thoroughly indoctrinated in safety procedures, and were especially encouraged to suggest even safer methods. These seeds of caution were sowed so well that immigrant committeemen became the company's "best safety propagan-dists," and they campaigned for accident prevention "more ef-ficiently than the average English-speaking men." Illinois Steel saw another benefit in the committee system—the useful exchange of ideas and points of view between English and non-English-speaking workers and between workers of varying skills and education.[69]

The same firm published a multi-language edition of its safety rule book, required all workers to be thoroughly con-versant with the rules, and in 1912 began marking all danger spots in its mill with such symbols as red circles, a system of identification readily understood by immigrants. The company also called on the immigrant press and immigrant churches for assistance. Priests agreed to encourage the work-ers to follow safety rules, and immigrant newspapers then

[68] *Ibid.*, 736–738. See also *ibid.*, *1912*, pp. 86–88; *1913*, pp. 178–179; *1915*, pp. 747–749.
[69] *Ibid.*, *1912*, pp. 302–303; *1913*, p. 179; *1915*, p. 734.

printed their remarks "along with other little schemes to foment interest." Throughout its efforts, Illinois Steel made extensive use of professional interpreters. By 1913, within a single year, a safety worker at the Joliet plant came to regard his interpreter as indispensable. "We lost him once for a month," he reported, "and the foremen in the plant were asking in a quandary: 'Where is the interpreter, where is the interpreter?' "[70]

Though firms like Illinois Steel, New Jersey Zinc, and Commonwealth Steel clearly recognized that effective safety programs were in their self-interest, their efforts to educate immigrant workers also involved, no matter how dimly perceived, a growing sense of humanity. Frances Perkins, a member of the New York Committee on Safety, both contributed to and reflected this growing American awareness of the social value of each human life. Addressing the second convention of the National Safety Council in 1913, she argued that people gradually were coming to realize that the Russian, Italian, Irish, and American girls burned in factory fires "represented a value in the community which did not mean only dollars and cents and profits and loss." Indeed, she implored the delegates, "if we want our community, our nation, our democracy to succeed . . . we must . . . preserve the life and health, the arms and legs, the happiness of the people who work in our factories."[71]

Frances Perkins was not alone in concerning herself with the place of the immigrant in America's factories and cities, but few shared her high-minded patriotism and compassion. By 1913, more Americans looked upon the immigrant worker with misgivings, and when war came to Europe these misgivings turned to fear about the nation's vitality and unity of purpose. As a consequence, employers, their welfare and safety practitioners, and social workers such as Miss Perkins

---

[70] *Ibid., 1913,* pp. 161–164, 174–175; *1915,* pp. 303, 750, 751–753.
[71] *Ibid., 1913,* p. 67.

had increasingly to cope with the more militant nationalists, who attempted to use the nation's factories and mills as instruments in their crusade to Americanize the immigrant labor force.

6

Americanization at the Factory Gate

THOUGH THEY WERE INTERTWINED with the education of immigrants, welfare and safety programs did not aim to convert foreign-born workers into loyal, patriotic, English-speaking Americans. Pioneering companies such as Illinois Steel, Allis-Chalmers, and International Harvester did not, in their efforts to promote welfare and safety, seek to solve the problem of the hyphenated American. Nor did the later comers to safety education. Between 1910 and 1914, employers increasingly emphasized the "human side" of manufacturing, but few sought to clothe welfare and safety in patriotic garb. Indeed, their programs were rooted in self-interest and were designed to foster loyalty to the company and harmony between labor and capital rather than loyalty to the nation and harmony among its citizens.

In the decade of World War I, the militant wing of the Americanization movement tried to impose its solutions for national vigor and harmony upon welfare and safety programs which were designed to make industrial relations less exploitive and wasteful. Convinced that the teaching of English and civics was essential for the nation's welfare, militant Americanizers used the war in Europe to launch a campaign for disciplining the loyalties and languages of America's immigrants. This crusade brought Americanizers to factories employing large numbers of newcomers. They tried to make existing welfare and safety programs instruments of their crusade, and they sought to institute practices to make immigrant workers learn English and civics. Though they failed to make welfare and safety programs an integral part of the Americanization movement, militant Americanizers helped shape the educational programs that large employers were developing for their workers.

The Americanization movement developed in the context of the nativism of the late nineteenth century. In the 1880's and 1890's, concern about the changing composition of the nation's population gripped many native Americans and former immigrants.[1] By the turn of the century, many influential people had joined in a clamor for legislation to restrict immigration from southern and eastern Europe. Among them were New Englanders, who spun out racist arguments, and eugenicists, who perverted the science of genetics to fit their preconceptions about immigrants not of Anglo-Saxon or Teutonic stock.[2] Numerous attempts were made to require immigrants to pass a literacy test. In 1907, Congress established the Immigration Commission which, under the chairmanship of Vermont's Senator William P. Dillingham, labored for three years to secure adoption of effective restrictive legislation to "protect" the country against southern and eastern Europeans.[3]

The growing agitation against foreign-born persons reflected widespread misgivings about the workings of the long-cherished concept of the melting pot, a concept which Americans had inherited from their simpler, agricultural days.[4] Something was wrong with the entire absorption process, for obviously the nation could no longer create the American

---

[1] Merle E. Curti, *The Roots of American Loyalty* (New York, 1946), 75, 184–187; Higham, *Strangers in the Land*, 1–182.

[2] *Ibid.*, 131–157; See also Oscar Handlin, *Race and Nationality in American Life* (New York, 1957), 57–73.

[3] *Ibid.*, 79.

[4] "In the crucible of the frontier," wrote Frederick Jackson Turner in 1893, "the immigrants were Americanized, liberated and fused into a mixed race, English in neither nationality or characteristics. The process has gone on from the early days to our own." See his "The Significance of the Frontier in American History," in the *Proceedings of the State Historical Society of Wisconsin*, 41: 98–99 (December 14, 1893).

idealized by Hector St. John de Crèvecoeur. The nation no longer fused into his New World man the tired, the poor, "the huddled masses yearning to breathe free." Their faith in an unregulated system of immigration shaken, Americanizers proposed to replace the melting pot with a pressure cooker.

The impetus to accelerate and intensify the process of absorbing the foreign-born into American society came from social settlement workers, from militant nationalists in the patriotic societies, and from public-spirited businessmen. Each group had its own particular goals, and each sought to lead the Americanization movement.

The settlement workers came into contact with immigrants through their neighborhood approach to urban problems. They sought to treat and, if possible, to heal the social sores on the nation's industrial body, but they did not believe that the remedy lay in isolating the immigrant from the rest of America or in ending the threat of contagion by halting admission of the newcomer. They had not lost faith in the beneficent operation of the melting pot. Instead of abandoning it, they sought to modify it to allow for the development of cultural pluralism. They felt that love and understanding would catalyze the absorption process and make it operate more smoothly. They stressed the value of immigrant traditions and customs to America, and they attempted to make immigrants feel proud of their heritage. They preached "the doctrine of immigrant gifts . . . and . . . concentrated less on changing the newcomers than on offering them a home." During the Americanization crusade, the social settlement workers fought a rearguard action against the militant nationalists.[5]

Militant nationalists attempted to change the immigrant. Around 1900, they launched enthusiastic crusades through such patriotic societies as the Daughters of the American

[5] Higham, *Strangers in the Land*, 121–122, 236, 240, 250–254; Curti, *Roots of American Loyalty*, 238; Edward George Hartmann, *The Movement to Americanize the Immigrant* (New York, 1948), 31–36, 38–63. During the war the Committee on Public Information "most consistently applied" the view of the social settlement workers. Higham, *Strangers in the Land*, 252.

Revolution, the Society of Colonial Dames, and the Sons of the American Revolution. In 1907, the S.A.R. spent half its annual income trying to make aliens "good citizens." In their propaganda campaigns, these groups urged a common effort to make immigrants embrace their versions of Americanism: use of the English language and reverence toward the Constitution and founding fathers, and above all reverence toward their version of law and order.[6] With the outbreak of war in Europe, the militant nationalists, together with powerful aggregates of businessmen, came to dominate the Americanization movement.

Public-spirited businessmen in New England turned to Americanization largely because they feared for their economic order. Since the 1890's this region had experienced a rapid change in the national origin of its population, and more recently it had witnessed a marked increase in the recruiting activities of socialists and other radical groups.[7] Reluctant to advocate restricted immigration because of their dependence on foreign-born labor, the businessmen turned instead to a campaign to minimize the impact of radicalism.[8] The instrument of their efforts was the North American Civic League for Immigrants, founded in 1908, three years after the establishment of the Industrial Workers of the World.

Initially, the league sought to protect, to disperse, and especially to educate the immigrants. It worked particularly hard to enlist the support of employers in a drive to enlarge facilities for teaching adult immigrants both English and civics. This goal was crucial to the league, since it assumed that ignorance accounted for the supposed success enjoyed by foreign-language labor organizers.[9]

Few people in the nineteenth century would have denied

[6] Hartmann, *Movement to Americanize the Immigrant*, 31–36.
[7] *United States Census, 1910*, 2: 853; *Proceedings of the Socialist Party, 1908*, pp. 313–314; *1910*, pp. 20, 307; *1912*, pp. 237–242; Kipnis, *The American Socialist Movement*, 272–274.
[8] Hartmann, *Movement to Americanize the Immigrant*, 88–90.
[9] *Ibid.*, 38–63; Higham, *Strangers in the Land*, 240.

that courses in English and citizenship affected the absorption process. Indeed, immigrants, employers, and interested observers everywhere looked on the public school as the prime flux in the melting pot. School officials, however, paid little attention to the needs of the first- or second-generation student; they seemed to assume that the education of native Americans was somehow sufficient for all. Toward the end of the century, a number of cities in the East and Midwest instituted evening classes in English and citizenship. Milwaukee, for example, offered courses for three months each year, but in 1897 the school board abandoned the program in a fit of economy.[10] Nevertheless, a beginning had been made, and all those interested in Americanization looked increasingly to the schools to facilitate the absorption of immigrants into the nation's life.

These groups agitated for expansion of public school facilities. Partly because the federal Bureau of Naturalization made the schools the focal point of its Americanization program, various communities expanded their efforts to educate immigrants. Beginning in 1911, Milwaukee's school board supplemented its evening classes with offerings at various social centers in the city, and within four years it was conducting language classes in thirteen different locations as part of its effort to assist immigrants to become naturalized Americans. Both New York and Chicago had similar programs.[11]

The more enthusiastic proponents of Americanization, however, soon concluded that the nation's schools could not by themselves cope with the problem. They claimed that state and local efforts fell far short of the objectives of Americanization. Legislators and school officials, they charged, lit-

[10] *Ibid.*, 236; Hartmann, *Movement to Americanize the Immigrant*, 25–36.

[11] Richard M. Campbell to Peter Roberts, January 11, 20, 1916, in Record Group 85, case file 27671/614, in the National Archives; H. H. Wheaton, "Survey of Adult Immigrant Education," in *Immigrants in America Review*, 1: 51–53 (June, 1915); *Milwaukee Leader*, February 3, 1914; broadside issued by the Social Center Publicity Department of the Milwaukee Board of Education, in a scrapbook in the board's archives; Wisconsin State Council of Defense, Minutes of Meetings, May 25, 1917, Series 76/1/10, in the Wisconsin State Archives; Higham, *Strangers in the Land*, 235–236.

tle understood the problems and functions of adult education. Textbooks were selected carelessly, and there was a desperate shortage of materials specially prepared for teaching English to adult foreigners. Moreover, the evening school calendar too often was determined by factors other than the needs of immigrant workers. Only Rochester and Cleveland, it was claimed, had recognized that programs of evening education required specialized supervision. In New York, Boston, Philadelphia, Providence, Buffalo, Chicago, and Detroit, by contrast, the night classes were supervised and taught by administrators and teachers as a means of supplementing their regular incomes. These men, it was charged, had too many daytime responsibilities to give proper attention to the evening program.[12]

Beset with these difficulties, and knowing that attendance in public schools was voluntary, some Americanization groups began to agitate for English classes in factories. The first phase of this movement was started by Peter Roberts, a Welshman who had spent some years among immigrants in Pennsylvania's coal fields. In 1907, when the industrial safety movement began, he became head of the industrial department of the national council of the Y.M.C.A. He launched that organization's language and citizenship program for immigrants. The geographic focus of his drive was an area which he called the "immigrant zone," the industrial region bounded on the west by the Mississippi River and on the south by the Potomac and Ohio rivers. By 1915 the "Y" had about 500 branches operating in this region; more than half were engaged in educating immigrants. The program had recruited about 1,900 language instructors from various walks of life: men who lived in "Y" homes, Bible class members, factory workers, business and professional men, civil servants, and students in colleges, universities, and seminaries. These instructors were supplied with material Roberts had prepared

---

[12] Peter Roberts to Raymond F. Crist, January 6, 1916; Roberts to Campbell, January 17, 1916, both in Record Group 85, case file 27671/614, in the National Archives; Wheaton, "Survey of Adult Immigrant Education," 51–53.

for teaching English to immigrant workers and with literature selected by the "Y" from such organizations as the Sons of the American Revolution, the National Temperance League, and the National Safety Council.[13]

The Y.M.C.A. operated under a number of handicaps. Many workers considered it a tool of employers, and Catholic workers eyed it suspiciously as a Protestant organization. Though Roberts tried to halt proselytizing, many Catholics hesitated to participate in "Y" activities.[14] Temperance propaganda did not set well with immigrants who traditionally drank wine and beer, and patriotic speeches and songs extolling the blessings of American life seemed not to describe the lives that immigrants led. One Italian workman, puzzled by the phrase "sweet land of liberty," concluded that the song was in error.[15]

But in spite of such handicaps, the "Y" was more successful than other private groups in establishing English classes in industry. Roberts had the advantage of working for an organization which was endorsed by powerful interests, and his enthusiasm convinced many employers of the value of his proposals. Too, he knew how to adjust his program to the needs of corporations, and especially to existing welfare and safety programs.

Roberts frowned on irrelevant content and abstract teaching methods. He divided his curriculum into three interrelated parts—introductory, intermediate, and advanced. Most significant was the introductory course of thirty lessons, since

[13] Edith T. Bremer, "Development of Private Social Work with the Foreign-born," in the *Annals of the American Academy of Political and Social Science,* 257: 140 (March, 1949); Peter Roberts, "The Y.M.C.A. Teaching Foreign-Speaking Men," in *Immigrants in America Review,* 1: 18–19, 21 (June, 1915); Leiserson, *Adjusting Immigrant and Industry,* 121–122.

[14] *Proceedings of the National Conference on Americanization, 1919,* pp. 20–23; Peter Roberts, *The New Immigration: A Study of the Industrial and Social Life of Southeastern Europeans in America* (New York, 1912), 320. See also Howard K. Beale, "Teaching English to Foreigners," and "A Y.M.C.A. English Class," undergraduate themes written in 1918 and 1920. Originals in the author's possession.

[15] Society for Italian Immigrants, *Annual Report, 1913,* pp. 11–12.

few immigrants went beyond this stage. It stressed the practical and the necessary, ten lessons being devoted to common phrases used at home, ten to words related to factory employment, and ten to words for buying, selling, traveling, and trading. The lessons were taught by acting out words and sentences: one "Y" worker all but undressed himself in order to teach English equivalents for various pieces of clothing. The intermediate and advanced courses focused on reading lessons in history, geography, and civics; the advanced course of thirty-five lessons was devoted almost entirely to preparing immigrants for naturalization and good citizenship.[16]

Roberts designed the introductory lessons so that they would fulfill a social purpose. Though he preferred to speak of "coming Americans" rather than "Americanization," and though he rejected the approach of the militant nationalists, he shared the view common to many settlement workers that "new immigrants" could become a dangerous problem if left to themselves. Men like himself, he believed, had to go into the immigrant's homes and places of work if the newcomer was to be exposed to the influences which Roberts considered to be healthily American. "Shun the foreigner, leave him to himself, let him alone in dirt and disease and unseen by an appreciative eye," he declared in 1915, "and he will simply drift. We would do the same."[17]

International Harvester adopted the Roberts' method in 1910, following a presentation to the company's advisory board of welfare by the Chicago Y.M.C.A. Some superintendents liked the idea of a practical program designed to teach "the first necessary English required in getting a job and taking hold," and they thought that it would reduce the accident rate and improve the relations of the workers to the community. The company's chief social secretary also en-

---

[16] Roberts, "Y.M.C.A. Teaching Foreign-Speaking Men," 18–21; Peter Roberts, *The Problem of Americanization* (New York, 1920), 97, 107; Beale, "Teaching English to Foreigners."

[17] Roberts, "Y.M.C.A. Teaching Foreign-Speaking Men," 18–21; Roberts, *New Immigration,* viii, 306–307; *Harvester World,* 1: 29 (December, 1910). By 1920 Roberts had come to oppose militancy and coercion.

dorsed the proposal. She argued that English classes would increase both productivity and the potential value of immigrant workers to the company.[18]

The "Y" began teaching English to Greek and Lithuanian men and women at International Harvester's Weber plant in 1911. Though the company was well pleased with the results and especially with the willingness of the workers to pay a nominal fee after the first ten free lessons, the plant superintendent took over the program in January, 1912. Within three months two other Harvester plants in Chicago had joined the program, which was now oriented to shop discipline, welfare work, and safety. To be sure, the company wanted the immigrants to become good American citizens, but it also wanted them to become good employees who would "think and talk intelligently about all the important operations in the works."[19]

Two of the company's English lessons stressed discipline, welfare, and safety work. The first was devoted exclusively to matters of discipline:

> I hear the whistle. I must hurry.
>
> I hear the five minute whistle.
>
> It is time to go into the shop.
>
> I take my check for the gate board and hang it on the department board.
>
> I change my clothes and get ready to work.
>
> The starting whistle blows.
>
> I eat my lunch.

[18] *Harvester World,* 1: 29 (December, 1910); 2: 28 (September, 1911); 3: 32 (January, 1912); 5: 30 (March, 1914).
[19] *Ibid.,* 3: 30–32 (January, 1912).

It is forbidden to eat until then.

The whistle blows at five minutes of starting time.

I get ready to go to work.

I work until the whistle blows to quit.

I leave my place nice and clean.

I put all my clothes in my locker.

I go home.[20]

This lesson was followed by a series on the various parts of the works and on the names, use, and care of various tools. These lessons, too, dealt with the familiar, in keeping with Roberts' method.[21] One of them combined elements of the welfare and safety program under way at the company:

The Employee Benefit Association is composed of the employees of the International Harvester Company.

When you are sick or hurt report to your time-keeper and the doctor at once.

If you get sick at home send word at once to your timekeeper or foreman.

You are paid one half of your regular daily earnings for every day you are sick after one week.

[20] *Ibid.*, 3: 31 (March, 1912).

[21] For examples of other uses of the familar in teaching English to foreigners, see Lillian P. Clark, *Federal Textbook on Citizenship Training* (Washington, 1924); Isaac Price, *The Direct Method of Teaching English to Foreigners* (New York, 1909); Sarah R. O'Brien, *English for Foreigners* (New York, 1909); William E. Chancellor, *Reading and Language Lessons for Every School* (New York, 1904).

While you are sick do not leave the city without first seeing the doctor and telling him about it.

The doctor takes care of all accidents that happen in the works.

You should call on the doctor when you are able; do not wait for him to call you.

When the door of the doctor's office is closed, knock and wait for him to say, "come in," before you open the door.

Do not try to take slivers out of the hand or cinders out of the eye for yourself or another but go directly to the doctor's office.

When you are hurt in the Works, you will be paid on half wages for all the time you are disabled, provided you report the accident at once to your timekeeper and the doctor.

No benefits will be paid if you are hurt while scuffing or fooling.

No benefits will be paid if you are hurt or get sick as a result of having been drinking.[22]

Safety education for immigrants employed by the United States Steel Corporation also was influenced by Roberts. Indeed, it was he who drafted the original language lessons with their heavy emphasis on safety matters. Though the bulletins on safety, welfare, and sanitation which the corporation began circulating among its subsidiaries in 1910 did not openly espouse an Americanization program, they did reflect the Roberts approach to the teaching of English to immigrant workers.[23]

[22] *Harvester World,* 3: 31 (March, 1912).
[23] United States Steel Corporation, Committee of Safety, *Bulletin,* October, 1910, n.p.; November, 1913, p. 8; Roberts, *Problem of Americanization,* 99.

The Ford Motor Company attempted to build its safety program on a multi-language base and even went so far as to issue a safety bulletin in forty-two languages, but it soon abandoned this approach as too cumbersome and costly. Instead, it made English the sole working language, then instituted English classes in May, 1914, the substance of which was safety, shop discipline, welfare, and the company's benevolence. Though the welfare program was tied directly to hiring and firing practices and to wage increases—practices in which International Harvester never indulged—in all other respects it was much the same, including the use of lesson plans designed by Peter Roberts and the employment of volunteer teachers trained by him. When the militant Americanizers launched their language campaign in Detroit in 1915, they were therefore able to turn Ford's existing safety classes to their use.[24]

Thus the first phase of language education for immigrants in factories emerged from an industrial context, from the same demands that had resulted in welfare and safety activities. The classes dealt primarily with only one sphere of the immigrant's surroundings: factory life. Most Y.M.C.A. teachers began their English classes with the noblest of ambitions—the desire to teach the immigrant basic language skills and how to cope with America. The "Y" worker dedicated to these goals required considerable stubbornness and resourcefulness to prevent the program's being turned exclusively to the benefit of the employer. It took all the ingenuity of an in-

---

[24] *Immigrants in America Review*, 1: 6 (September, 1915); Hartmann, *Movement to Americanize the Immigrant*, 129. The Committee for Immigrants in America had been instrumental in beginning Detroit's drive. Esther E. Lape, "The English First Movement in Detroit," in *Immigrants in America Review*, 1: 46–50 (September, 1915); Nevins and Hill, *Ford*, 1: 513–515, 520–522, 532–545, 551–554, 556–557; 2: 332–341; John R. Lee, "So-called Profit Sharing System in the Ford Plant," in the *Annals of the American Academy of Political and Social Science*, 65: 297–310 (May, 1916); Higham, *Strangers in the Land*, 248; Robert H. Shaw, in the *Proceedings of the National Safety Council, 1916*, p. 225. For the comments of W. Ernest William, safety engineer at Packard, see *ibid.*, 236, 795. Henry Ford to Detroit Y.M.C.A., December 2, 1914, in *The Association among 59 Nationalities*, in Record Group 85, case file 27671/614, in the National Archives.

structor at a "Y" class of Illinois Steel to convince the foreman that the company's shop lessons were of little value or
interest to men and women seeking to learn English for general use.[25]

The outbreak of war in Europe and America's eventual
involvement gave the Americanization movement a sense of
urgency. Suddenly its goals seemed synonymous with national
interest and national defense. Militant patriots eagerly seized
this opportunity to mount a campaign for disciplining loyalties and languages, for shaping and directing American nationalism. At a time when the spread of welfare work and
other practices for systematizing human relations in factories
also was gaining momentum, American industry was unusually susceptible to the pressures of militancy.[26]

One of the most influential persons in the Americanization
crusade was Frances Kellor, a lawyer turned social worker and
a woman who made the position of executive secretary a sort
of personal career by assuming that post for a number of social
action groups. She injected into Americanization a zeal for
making the nation's economy and body politic function more
rationally. Miss Kellor began her career in public service. In
1904 she published an analysis of employment offices in New
York City, paying particular attention to immigrants and to
the chaotic distribution of labor. In association with Theodore Roosevelt and other Progressives, she investigated social
problems for municipal and state agencies and became an
authority on urban immigrants and immigrant legislation.[27]

In the midst of her activities for the New York Commission
on Immigration, Miss Kellor obtained the support of two
wealthy New Yorkers, Frank Trumbull and Felix Warburg,
for Americanization work. In 1909, they established a branch
of the North American Civic League, but from the beginning

---

[25] Beale, "A Y.M.C.A. English Class" and "Teaching English to Foreigners."
[26] Wittke, *The German-Language Press in America*, 252–254.
[27] Higham, *Strangers in the Land*, 239–241; Frances Kellor, *Out of Work: A Study of Employment Agencies, Their Treatment of the Unemployed, and Their Influence upon Homes and Business* (New York, 1904), *passim*.

they approached Americanization in their own way, for they wanted to change the general environment of America. Between 1912 and 1914, the differences between the parent body and the New Yorkers increased, in part because the activities of the Industrial Workers of the World at Lawrence, Massachusetts, Paterson, New Jersey, and elsewhere in the Northeast so heightened the league's fear of foreign-born radicals that it eventually resorted to spying and similar tactics in its effort to block strikes and the unionization of immigrants. Early in 1914, the New Yorkers broke with the parent body and established the Committee for Immigrants in America. Miss Kellor became its vice-chairman and guiding light. In 1915, she began editing the *Immigrants in America Review*, a journal published by the committee and entirely devoted to Americanization. Miss Kellor now had the means—an organization and a journal—to shape public opinion. She also had the support of a number of well-known intellectuals, including Herbert Croly, Walter Lippmann, and Felix Frankfurter, all of whom served on the journal's advisory board.[28]

The absence of a clearinghouse for Americanization activities gave the Kellor group an opportunity. With the help of the United States Bureau of Education, the committee created, staffed, and financed the Division of Immigrant Education within the bureau, thereby obtaining official endorsement of much of its propaganda.[29] In May, 1915, the United States Bureau of Naturalization held a mass naturalization celebration in Philadelphia at which President Woodrow Wilson delivered his "too proud to fight" speech.[30] For the next two months the committee worked furiously to create the National Americanization Committee and to make Independence Day the occasion for mass celebration of naturalization in a hundred American cities. The subsequent success of the Independence Day campaign helped the Committee for

[28] Hartmann, *Movement to Americanize the Immigrant,* 56–63, 91–97; *Immigrants in America Review,* 1: 1–2 (March, 1915).

[29] *Ibid.,* 1: 3–4, 15, 30–32 (September, 1915); Hartmann, *Movement to Americanize the Immigrant,* 97–100, 112–114.

[30] *Ibid.,* 107–111; *Immigrants in America Review,* 1: 30–32 (September, 1915).

Immigrants in America establish itself as the leading Americanization organization.[81]

Miss Kellor was a nationalist of the Croly-Roosevelt persuasion, a believer in "social welfare and national discipline," and an energetic advocate of systematizing industrial production, distribution, and personnel. She looked toward the day when the population would be more or less homogeneous and when the economy would be so regulated as to minimize conflict between labor and capital.[82]

The committee's official statement of purpose reflected these views. It considered Americanization as a domestic immigration policy designed to reduce unemployment, eliminate discriminatory state and municipal legislation, raise the immigrants' standard of living, distribute alien workers according to their abilities and the needs of the economy, protect immigrants, particularly their savings, and improve educational facilities for newcomers, including opportunities for industrial training.[83] The *Review* regularly devoted two sections to these goals. "The Record of Progress" discussed unemployment, legislation, and education, while the book review section listed and discussed pertinent books, including ones on industrial service work.[34]

With the first issue of *Immigrants in America Review* in March, 1915, however, the militant nationalist in Miss Kellor began to emerge. She urged a "conscious effort to forge the people of this country into an American race that will stand together for America in time of peace and war." By September, she sounded frightened about the potentialities of un-Americanized immigrants. "Because of our lack of patriotism, efficiency, and consideration we have failed to inspire our better conditioned immigrants and their sons with a love for this country which supplants that of other countries." This failure was a serious weakness, she argued, for

[81] *Ibid.;* Hartmann, *Movement to Americanize the Immigrant,* 112–124.
[82] Higham, *Strangers in the Land,* 239.
[83] *Immigrants in America Review,* 1: 3–15, 17–86 (March, 1915).
[34] *Ibid.,* 90–94; 1: 76, 87, 94 (June, 1915); 1: 98, 108 (September, 1915); 2: 110–111 (June, 1916).

many immigrants and often their children retained deep attachments to their homelands. The attachments were "more widespread than we know," she claimed, warning that "in case of war we would have in this country if not actual traitors, a division of forces such as would make a victory precarious in any prolonged warfare." In January, 1916, she declared that America faced a crisis. The big problem was not "whether we need a larger army and navy, but whether we shall have a United America back of that army and navy, and whether America, with her many races and divided allegiances, will survive as a great nation."[85]

Miss Kellor's militant Americanism evoked sharp criticism in some quarters. Among the most telling was an article in the *Review* by Horace M. Kallen, a social psychologist who had long been developing concepts of cultural pluralism.[86] Kallen's piece was a careful statement on the evolution and meaning of such American ideals as liberty, union, and democracy. He attacked militants like Miss Kellor for their "vicious abstractionism," a term he borrowed from William James. The whole issue of immigrants' double loyalties, Kallen maintained, had gotten out of hand because of the failure to distinguish between treason and differences in values and beliefs. He charged that those obsessed with the issue were distorting the meaning of American democracy. "In essence democracy involves not the elimination of differences but the perfection and conservation of differences. It aims through union, not at uniformity but at variety."[87]

However, Miss Kellor had moved too far toward militant nationalism to heed Kallen's criticism. In 1916 she espoused her "America First" position in a book, *Straight America,*

[85] *Ibid.,* 1: 15 (March, 1915); 1: 3, 4–5 (September, 1915); 1: 3 (January, 1916).

[86] Horace M. Kallen told the author in 1962 that he began to develop his ideas about cultural pluralism just after the turn of the century. Kallen was then studying philosophy under William James at Harvard. See also his *Culture and Democracy in the United States: Studies in the Group Psychology of the American Peoples* (New York, 1924), *passim.*

[87] Horace M. Kallen, "The Meaning of Americanism," in *Immigrants in America Review,* 1: 12–19 (January, 1916).

and these views rather than those of the social settlement workers gave Americanization its main direction, especially in industry.[88]

During the winter of 1915–1916, Miss Kellor and three other leading members of the Committee for Immigrants in America took their campaign to the United States Chamber of Commerce, which then established an Immigration Committee with Frank Trumbull as chairman, William F. Morgan as treasurer, and Miss Kellor as assistant to the chairman. This group became an effective organ for Miss Kellor's views, though the link between the two groups was not at first known even by such knowledgeable people as the deputy commissioner of the Bureau of Naturalization.[89] The new committee quickly attached itself to the growing industrial service movement. "The nation-wide Americanization movement," it explained to members of the Chamber of Commerce, "is part of the present-day trend toward humanizing industry. It aims to take what is commonly called welfare work out of paternalism and make it a part of legitimate business organizations everywhere. . . . There is no agreement among American employers now as to the extent and manner of its organizations or where it really belongs. There are no recognized standards. What we need is to extend scientific methods to the human phase of industrial organizations. . . ."[40]

By linking Americanization to the "trend toward humanizing industry," the committee showed a keen appreciation of the strategic role that autocratic industrial organizations could play in the crusade. Miss Kellor applauded the actions of leading Detroit employers, who were among the first to require

[88] Higham, *Strangers in the Land*, 242–244.

[89] *Immigrants in America Review*, 1: 9, 2 (June, 1915); 1: 2 (September, 1915); 1: 86 (January, 1916); Hartmann, *Movement to Americanize the Immigrant*, 113–132; Richard M. Campbell to Eliot H. Goodwin, August 18, September 8, 1917; Frances A. Kellor to Campbell, September 5, 1917, all in Record Group 85, case file 27671/1832, in the National Archives.

[40] *Report of the Committee on Immigration of the Chamber of Commerce of the United States of America, Fifth Annual Meeting, 1917*, p. 2, in *ibid*.

immigrants to attend English and civics classes in the public schools or in the factories. Indeed, by 1916, she even argued that coercion was one of the few ways to force immigrants into educational programs.[41] As she supported this use of power, so too she accepted one of the basic assumptions behind the "humanizing trend." In her words: "It will mean . . . industrial peace. So long as our industrial communities are made up of large groups of un-Americanized immigrants, without the English language, without understanding American conditions, too helpless to bring their grievances to the attention of their employers, too ignorant to force them in legitimate ways . . . able to understand only the radical agitators addressing them in their own language—just so long will the industrial history of America be blotted out by Calumets, Ludlows, Lawrences, and Wheatlands. The road to American citizenship, to the English language, and [to] an understanding of American social and political ideals is the road to industrial peace. Even now in peace, our country is honeycombed with industrial strife, disorder and disputes involving the destruction of life and property."[42]

From 1916 to 1918, Frances Kellor and her supporters intensified their campaign to convince employers that Americanization was a natural part of the humanizing efforts being carried on by industrial organizations. In March, 1917, the Committee for Immigrants in America created still another group, the Committee on Industrial Engineering, staffed by experts from universities and industry. The group published a bulletin on industrial service work, a subject which the now defunct *Immigrants in America Review* had stressed. At the same time, the Immigration Committee of the Chamber of Commerce continued its drive to establish factory classes for immigrants. In the spring of 1918, as America entered its second year of war, the Kellor group centralized much of its work in agencies of the federal government. It

[41] *Immigrants in America Review,* 1: 16 (September, 1915); 1: 6 (January, 1916).

[42] *Ibid.,* 1: 4.

expanded the facilities of the Bureau of Education, enlisted the support of the Department of the Interior, and convinced the National Council of Defense to accept its Americanization program.[43]

Miss Kellor's views made slow headway among safety inspectors, employment managers, visiting nurses, and others active in safety and welfare work. At first, the National Safety Council paid little attention to Americanization, but militant nationalists were soon urging the council to issue its safety and health bulletins in only one language—English. As Dr. J. W. Schereschewsky of the United States Public Health Service put it in 1917, "we ought not to give [immigrants] the opportunity for perpetuating their native speech, but make them understand that now is the time for them to become true American citizens and learn to speak the language of this country."[44] Stephen W. Tener of the American Steel and Wire Company in Cleveland supported Schereschewsky's position, in part because his company's failure on one occasion to publish its safety literature in a particular foreign language had provoked a strike. The omission had kindled national animosities because the excluded group, and particularly its national aspirations, had been ridiculed by members of other ethnic groups. For these and other reasons, said Tener, "it is best to confine work to English and we have pretty well abandoned the idea of using any other language."[45]

J. B. Douglas of the United Gas Improvement Company in Philadelphia, chairman of a sectional meeting of the Na-

[43] *Ibid.*, 1–2, *passim;* Frank P. Walsh saw clearly the relationship between Kellor's Americanization drive and the efforts to humanize industry. He also sharply attacked Kellor's group for not including unions in their campaign. *United Mine Workers Journal*, 25: 7 (February 3, 1916); United States Chamber of Commerce, Immigration Committee, *Bulletin*, February 15, March 1, 15, April 15, June 15, 1917; January 2, 1918; Hartmann, *Movement to Americanize the Immigrant*, 165–166, 187–205.

[44] *Proceedings of the National Safety Council, 1917*, p. 235. For an example of establishing a linkage between safety and Americanization before 1915, see *ibid., 1912*, pp. 13–15.

[45] *Ibid., 1917*, pp. 235–236.

tional Safety Council, cautiously supported Americanization, partly because the Pennsylvania Department of Labor and Industry had required foremen overseeing hazardous work to speak the language of their workers. "While this ruling may be termed progressive," said Douglas, "I am in doubt as to how it will work out in practice." He thought that the ruling showed the importance of all employees being able to speak English, and hoped that "all progressive employers" would give the Americanization of their employees the attention it deserved.[46]

Others also pleaded for the use of safety and health literature as teaching devices for Americanization. Charles B. Milner of the Hammersmill Paper Company of Erie, Pennsylvania, urged that multi-language cards be tacked to bulletin boards instructing immigrants to have English bulletins translated for them.[47] Charles A. Prosser, director of the United States Board of Vocational Education, agreed that safety bulletins could "be made a very practical drill in English."[48] The most outspoken advocate of militancy was undoubtedly J. R. de la Torre Bueno, a naturalized citizen and editor of the house organ of the General Chemical Company, a firm that had twenty plants in the United States and Canada.[49] Assuming that foreign languages perpetuated national allegiances, he maintained that all foreigners should be taught English, that the nation "must do away with foreign languages," and that the foreign-language press must be suppressed. To him such measures were prerequisites for a successful Americanization program.[50]

The council's staff and most of its members greeted these proposals with marked coolness, mainly because they were still committed to the multi-language approach which had been so common in the factory. They preferred that signs marking danger spots in factories carry foreign-language cap-

[46] *Ibid.*, 484–485.
[47] *Ibid., 1918*, pp. 563–564.
[48] *Ibid.*, 296.
[49] *Ibid.*, 409.
[50] *Ibid.*, 417–418.

tions, and many of them urged the council to translate safety literature for its members. The council's general manager, William H. Cameron, resisted the request for a translating service on the grounds of its expense and complexity. Anyway, he argued, the council's officers were "more or less in sympathy with the Americanizers." Bowing to pressure from the membership, in 1917 the council began translating "into any one of a dozen languages."[51]

To be sure, in 1915 the council's special education committee had asked Peter Roberts to work out special lessons devoted to safety, and within a year it had English lesson plans available on technical subjects as well as on such topics as "Health and Safety," and "Safety First and Sober Always."[52] But these lessons were similar to the ones Roberts had worked out for individual firms—that is, language education rooted in the job of the immigrant.

Welfare and safety practitioners at Illinois Steel and at other firms in the council who supported the Americanizers usually did so in the spirit of their factory programs, not in the spirit of militant nationalism. In response to the Americanizers, Illinois Steel required each job applicant to give his race, place of birth, the race and place of birth of his parents, the number of years he had lived in the United States, his naturalization status, and his ability to read both English and a foreign language.

These social characteristics of his firm's workers, however, held little interest for Arthur H. Young, the employment manager. He frankly admitted that the "answers to some of [these questions were] of far more interest to Uncle Sam than to plant executives." Young's approach to Americanization was in the spirit of the settlement house worker: "America is the melting pot she is," he said in 1916, "because each individual plant, each social settlement, and each civil center in her

<hr />

[51] *Ibid., 1916*, pp. 125–126, 131, 365–366; *1917*, pp. 25–37, 234. B. B. Folger, chairman of the Safety Committee of the Manufacturers Association of Ludlow, Massachusetts, was among this group. *Ibid., 1916*, pp. 365–366.

[52] *Ibid.*, 53–54.

broad expanse, is in itself a melting pot, and the employment chief is like unto a chef, in charge of the mixture at the particular plant [where] he refines a product of American manhood. . . . The melting pot is there and the executive who neglects a proper supervision of its activities neglects a profitable and patriotic service." Young spoke in this spirit even after America had entered the war. Emphasizing the safety movement at the expense of militant nationalism, he explained that immigrants "are transplanted suddenly into the center of a very busy plant" from farms, from streetcar work, from occupational hazards far different from those in the factory. He thus urged that immigrants be interviewed in their own language, and when unable to speak or read English be instructed in their own language. These aspects of an immigrant's occupational education were too important to be used for teaching the newcomer English and the values espoused by militant Americanizers.[53]

Florence S. Wright, a visiting nurse employed by the Clark Thread Company in Newark, New Jersey, also continued to work with immigrants as if oblivious to militancy: "I find the Italian family taking boarders. . . . The father has his chest examined, is found to be an incipient tuberculosis case, and after a period of rest and education is given outdoor work suited to his strength. The mother is taught to buy and cook. The children are sent to an open air school. It takes time but in the end the boarders are no longer there, and the father is well and doing suitable work, the children are going to school, and the mother is making a home of which the family and the nurse are proud. . . . I have increased my Italian vocabulary and have six firm friends. Needless to say, the unseen employer who sent me also has six loyal friends although he may never know of their existence."[54]

On the other hand, Miss Nesta C. Edwards of Wisconsin's Kimberly-Clark Company, who helped place nurses in various companies in the state and elsewhere, became a mili-

---

[53] *Ibid.,* 522, 526.
[54] *Ibid.,* 545–553. The quotation may be found in *ibid.,* 548–549.

tant Americanizer. Arguing that English-language classes had
no place in the factory, Miss Edwards urged employers to
adopt the coercive measures of Ford and other automobile
manufacturers in Detroit: Give an increase in pay to every
man who acquired a speaking knowledge of English; do not
promote a man until he has learned the required amount of
English; make attendance at night school a requisite for employment. These methods, she felt, lay within the province
of the employer and were also a "Safety First Measure."[55]
Few industrial organizations joined the militant Americanizers as enthusiastically as Ford. At the Ford School,
initially established as a result of the safety movement, the
first thing the immigrant learned to say was "I am an American." Pageants dramatizing this conversion had newcomers
enter the stage dressed in Old World clothing and leave the
stage dressed in American clothing.[56] By the end of 1916,
Ford had about 2,700 immigrants receiving language instruction from some 160 volunteer teachers who used Roberts'
methods. The immigrant student was expected to attend
classes for six to eight months before or after his work shift.
At the end of his course of seventy-two lessons, a printed di-
ploma qualified him for his first naturalization papers without further examination by federal authorities.[57]
But even at Ford, the expansion and functions of the school
were determined by the needs of the entire work force and
by the firm's economic requirements. At the end of 1916, the
school added mathematics, psychology, and public speaking to
the curriculum. These courses were attended by about 300 native-born workers. In the same year the company established
the Henry Ford Trade School, and this institution increasingly outweighed the language school in importance in the
company's educational scheme. When industrial considera-

---

[55] *Ibid., 1917,* 424–425. The use of economic power to affect the styles of life
outside the workshop was not, of course, limited to immigrants. A frank
statement about its use in "holding . . . colored labor" can be found in *ibid.,*
1294–1295.

[56] Higham, *Strangers in the Land,* 248.

[57] Nevins and Hill, *Ford,* 1: 557.

tions came into conflict with those of the Americanizers, the industrial ones triumphed. In 1917 the allotment of rooms for English classes was cut from twenty-two to three, and after that English-language education was continued on a limited scale at the Ford plants, with some five hundred students and thirty instructors.[58]

When the United States Steel Corporation and a number of its subsidiaries joined the Americanization crusade, it was clear that Americanization was but an adjunct of programs already in operation. In 1916 the company's Bureau of Safety, Sanitation, and Welfare commented on its work and noted that the corporation's English-language classes—Roberts' instruction program—taught foreign labor "the principles of clean, wholesome living" and good citizenship.[59] In 1917, immigrant education was entirely ignored. In its 1918 employee publication issue, which included a special section devoted exclusively to Americanization, the bureau discussed movies used in safety work. One of these, a film made in 1912, was oriented entirely toward the immigrant, but it was not discussed in the Americanization section. The bureau described the film as being about an "ignorant Hungarian peasant . . . stupid and uneducated" who became a forward-looking, industrious workman at a plant in Gary, Indiana, because of U. S. Steel's program of safety and welfare education.[60]

Only in the special section of the bureau's publication of 1918 was militancy reflected. The education and Americanization of foreign-born workers had become a "national problem of vital importance." It was necessary to have a "hundred per cent America." The Bureau of Safety, Sanitation, and Welfare insisted that "we must help the foreign-born laborer improve the opportunities afforded to him for

[58] *Ibid.*, 2: 340–341.
[59] United States Steel Corporation, Committee of Safety, *Bulletin*, December, 1916, pp. 52–53. Americanization in the steel industry is discussed in a different context by Brody in his *Steelworkers in America*, 189–192.
[60] United States Steel Corporation, Committee of Safety, *Bulletin*, December, 1918, pp. 5–6.

education and training, so that, through knowledge of the language and familiarity with the standards of living in this country, his condition will be improved."[61] Now, in the midst of war, the bureau had for the moment accepted concerns outside the industrial framework. The help to be given a foreign-born worker would, according to the bureau, "awaken in him a respect for and love for American ideals which . . . would develop strong loyalty towards his adopted country."[62]

Subsidiary companies of U. S. Steel implemented Americanization work in different ways.[63] Shop language and safety language classes were supplemented by others in English and citizenship at the Y.M.C.A. and the public schools. Some subsidiaries helped to pay for these evening classes. The American Bridge Company added English lessons to its curriculum in mathematics, mechanics, and drawing, and used pictorial charts with descriptive texts giving sketches of the names and uses of the various tools and other equipment in and around the plant. Taught by employees, the English classes were designed to improve the skill and "mental alertness" of the firm's immigrant workers. Americanization posters took their place beside safety posters; naturalization was stressed.

The Illinois Steel Company also added English to its general education curriculum, which in 1918 included courses in machine shop, mechanical drawing, electricity, English for foreigners, shop mathematics, mathematics, woodshop, high school English, forge, bookkeeping, stenography, and eighth grade chemistry. The English classes were given by the Y.M.C.A., and though attendance was voluntary, the instructor was required to report absentees to the company. Fore-

---

[61] *Ibid.*, 95.

[62] *Ibid.*

[63] The discussion of Americanization activities at United States Steel subsidiaries is based on *ibid.*, 95–103. See also *Proceedings of the National Safety Council, 1916,* pp. 1009–1010; *1917,* pp. 237–238, 1206.

men checked attendance and attempted to orient the lessons to actual operations in the shops.[64]

Some of the plants of the American Steel and Wire Company engaged in elaborate Americanization activities. The Americanization committee at its Waukegan works consisted of the superintendent, the personnel manager, the safety inspector, four Finns, three Austrians, three Swedes, three Lithuanians, two Armenians, two Poles, one Dane, and one German. This group organized three Americanization parades, four mass meetings, and a thirty-eight-piece band. Another committee, comprised of the foreman and representatives from each nationality in a given department, kept in close touch with all men needing instruction in English, helped immigrants to file for citizenship, and encouraged foreign-born workers to attend evening school. The committee also arranged English classes at a public school.

The International Harvester Company took little interest in the early development of the Americanization movement. Partly because of its many international connections, in November, 1914, the firm endorsed President Wilson's policy of neutrality, and reminded its foreign-born employees that, despite their natural sympathies for one side or the other, "this country and this company has only one interest in the present struggle: an early termination of hostilities."[65] Nevertheless, a spirit of militant Americanization gradually came to influence company policy. In May of 1916, the foremen's club at the company's Weber works began assisting foreign-born employees to become citizens. A special committee compiled a list of those who had not taken the initial legal steps towards citizenship, and checked on the progress of those who had.[66] To facilitate filing procedures for naturalization, the committee arranged with the clerk of the superior

[64] Interview with Howard K. Beale, 1956. He was a "Y" instructor at the Illinois Steel Company in Chicago in 1918.

[65] *Harvester World*, 5: inside of the front cover (November, 1914).

[66] *Ibid.*, 7: 30 (May, 1916).

court of Cook County to meet the applicant group in a body at a time and place arranged to prevent loss of wages. All this was done in the name of the community and country. As the *Harvester World* said, this work was "demanded by the best interest of the city and the nation."[67]

By February, 1917, the company was becoming increasingly involved in Americanization. The Weber and other plants encouraged naturalization and English classes, and the Keystone works proudly announced that all but two of its immigrant employees had become, or were in the process of becoming naturalized employees.[68] Keystone also sponsored an English class which met twice weekly in evening sessions of one and a half hours each, and provided a mock naturalization court to prepare candidates for the citizenship examination. A typical exchange between "judge" and "applicant" went as follows:

> *Teacher*: Who was the first president of the United States?
> *Alien*: George da Wash.
> *Teacher*: Who is president now?
> *Alien*: Mr. da Wils.
> *Teacher*: Could you be president?
> *Alien*: Excuse me please, I got pretty good job on the Keystone.[69]

By the summer of 1918, classes in English and citizenship had become common at International Harvester's branches, especially in the Chicago area. Some of the factories conducted classes during two noon hours each week; other units, such as the works in St. Paul, Minnesota, preferred to have Y.M.C.A. teachers come to the factory for twenty minutes during the noon hour.[70] Y.M.C.A. classes were thought to be

[67] *Ibid.*
[68] F. F. Trigg, "Keystone Works—100 Per Cent American," in *ibid.*, 9: 8 (June, 1918).
[69] *Ibid.*, 8–9.
[70] *Ibid.*, 9: 13 (July, 1918); A. E. Conrath, in the *Proceedings of the National Safety Council, 1918,* pp. 582–583.

more effective than classes taught as part of regular shop schools.[71] Special naturalization campaigns were also conducted at various branch installations. The Deering works, for example, used questionnaires to determine the number of citizens among its workers, and used its clubhouse facilities for issuing first papers.[72]

The *Harvester World's* safety and welfare section became filled with Americanization propaganda, often in the form of pictures of employees surrounded by flags. The *World* devoted one double-page spread to special patriotic ceremonies, published pictures of workrooms which foreign-born workers had bedecked with flags, publicized Liberty Bond drives by reporting how this or that plant had exceeded its goal, and supported Herbert Hoover's campaign to conserve food. The *World* also reproduced pictures of honor boards dedicated to company men in military service, and it printed stories about employees sending Christmas packages to the front.[73]

The editor of the *Harvester World,* like the editors of other house organs, found that the workers liked these patriotic articles and that personalizing the war effort helped to identify the individual workers with the company and the nation. By 1918, the Americanization movement and other war activities had become linked under the slogan "100 per cent Americanism." Espousal of this cause, so it was believed, would stimulate production still further by developing harmonious relations within the shop.[74]

The *Harvester World* also printed editorials and superpatriotic speeches in its campaign for "100 per cent Americanism." An editorial in August, 1918, for example, urged the election of loyal and patriotic congressmen. "If a weak or bad man sits in the next Congress—a stupid man, a mere self-seeker, or a shifty sneaking pacifist—the blame will be on

[71] *Harvester World,* 9: 13 (July, 1918).
[72] *Ibid.*
[73] *Ibid.,* 8: 5–7, 17 (September, 1917); 8: 12–13, 16 (October, 1917); 9: 9, 11 (February, 1918); 9: 10 (March, 1918); 9: 16–17 (July, 1918).
[74] For a frank discussion by house-organ editors of the methods they used, see "The Employee's Publication," a round-table discussion in the *Proceedings of the National Safety Council, 1918,* pp. 409–430. See also *ibid.,* 345–346.

his district," warned the journal, perhaps in an effort to defeat Socialist Victor Berger, who was seeking re-election from Milwaukee, a city in which International Harvester had important interests.[75]

A month later, the Milwaukee superintendent, Paul Schryer, urged the plant's employees to support the fourth Liberty Bond drive. Preceded by flag-raising ceremonies, Schryer's speech was built around the flag and the war effort. Though many Harvester workers initially had sided with the Central Powers, Schryer declared that it was no longer material who started the war. What mattered was that America was going to finish the war. Emphasizing the theme of full participation in the bond drive, he announced that he would be most disappointed if he could not report to the Chicago office that "Milwaukee Works' employees are not simply loyal but are absolutely 100 per cent loyal." So great was the impact of this speech that an employee years later recalled that German and Hungarian workmen huddled in corners as the superintendent tried to shame them into patriotism. "If there is one man in this organization who would hesitate to alleviate or lessen the suffering of [the men at the front]," Schryer concluded, "I would advise him to go somewhere out on the prairie away from the gaze of civilization and drain the yellow blood out of his heart."[76]

This militant declaration marked the zenith of International Harvester's Americanization campaign. Language and naturalization classes continued after the war, but the company's enthusiasm for superpatriotism soon waned, to be replaced by support for an industrial council, a system which was intended to provide the "machinery for solving differences between management and labor and also give workers a share in the planning and execution of matters in their immediate interest." International Harvester also established

---

[75] *Harvester World,* 9: 3 (August, 1918).

[76] The writer had asked the employee, over 65 years old, what he remembered about the days of World War I. The first thing that came to his mind was Schryer's talk. Interview with A. F. Leidel, 1956.

an industrial relations department and broadened its industrial service work.[77]

The different outlook at International Harvester reflected changes in the viewpoint and activities of Frances Kellor. With the end of the war, all federal agencies except the Bureau of Naturalization withdrew from Americanization work, and the bureau chose to work exclusively through the public schools.[78] This obliged Miss Kellor to become executive secretary of still another private organization or to abandon her Americanization work entirely. She chose the former course, replacing her old employer, the now defunct Committee for Immigrants in America, with a new one, the Inter-Racial Council.

Founded late in November, 1918, on the eve of the great steel strike, the new group soon represented hundreds of industrial corporations. For the next three years the council worked "to save America from Bolshevism" and to strengthen the industrial loyalties of immigrant workers. Miss Kellor sought industrial harmony and stability through managerial efforts to systematize human relations, counseled employers to use techniques of veiled coercion in the place of shrill nationalism, and, through her control of the American Association of Foreign Language Newspapers, flooded the immigrant press with "patriotic articles, admonitions against emigration to Europe, and anti-radical propaganda."[79]

In 1920, she told the convention of the National Association of Manufacturers that it was essential to encourage the foreign-language press to take a friendly, pro-American interest in national affairs. She believed such a policy to be "one of the best antidotes to Bolshevism," and thought that

[77] *Harvester World*, 10: 10 (March, 1919); Cyrus McCormick, Jr., "Cooperation and Industrial Progress," an address to the National Safety Council, published in its *Proceedings, 1919*, pp. 40–50. See also *Harvester World*, 10: 1–2 (August, 1919); Cyrus McCormick, Jr., "The Advantages of a Superintendent of Labor," in *ibid.*, 9: 4 (April, 1918); *ibid.*, inside of the front cover; *ibid.*, 11: 24 (December, 1920); Hartmann, *Movement to Americanize the Immigrant*, 220, n7.

[78] *Ibid.*, 228–234, 236–237.

[79] *Ibid.*, 220–225; Higham, *Strangers in the Land*, 257–258.

articles about industrial good works should be substituted for attacks on capital. This approach, she argued, would get immigrant workers "interested in Americanism."[80]

Thus, Frances Kellor mirrored the changing attitude toward the treatment of the foreign-born worker. She began her career as a progressive, then turned militant Americanizer, and finally, in the postwar era, became a spokesman for a brand of welfare capitalism—the corporate brand, to be achieved through educational programs imposed on industrial workers.

[80] Quoted in Hartmann, *Movement to Americanize the Immigrant*, 222–223.

7

The Milwaukee Synthesis

MILWAUKEE did not promote Americanization until 1917. In the prewar years the education of immigrants in English, civics, and citizenship was limited to night classes and community center activities in the public schools, the state's continuation school, social settlements, and a few patriotic groups.[1] These recruited but a small proportion of foreigners. In 1914, for example, few Italians and Poles even knew of the existence of the educational facilities that had been created in their behalf, and in 1915, when Milwaukee began to conduct elaborate naturalization ceremonies, these did not cause civic groups and manufacturers to enlist in the Americanization crusade, as they had in Detroit.[2]

Milwaukee did not offer fertile soil for militant Americanizers, in part because its two largest and most influential immigrant groups opposed their aims. Germans and Poles, led by journalists and churchmen, insisted on the right to perpetuate their languages and cultures; each group forced the city to include its language in the school curriculum; each fought for national self-determination within the Catholic

[1] Isabella Laura Hill, "Americanization Work in Milwaukee" (unpublished bachelor's thesis, University of Wisconsin, 1920), 1–3; Woman's Advisory Committee and Executive Committee, State Council of Defense, Minutes of Meetings, May 25, 1917, Series 76/1/10, in the Wisconsin State Archives.

[2] La Piana, *The Italians in Milwaukee*, 5; Harold O. Berg to Milton C. Potter, September 3, 1918, in the *Proceedings of the Milwaukee Board of School Directors, 1918–1919*, p. 68; *Survey Magazine*, 34: 390 (July 31, 1915).

Church; and each sought to advance its interests through political activity. The outcry against hyphenated Americans and demands for substituting English for foreign languages met with firm opposition.[3]

The attempts to shroud Americanization in the garb of preparedness also encountered hostility. Germans in Milwaukee, like those elsewhere, supported strict neutrality. In the past the German-language press had reflected German foreign policy, had criticized Great Britain, and had given scant attention to the growing friction between the United States and the Fatherland. Now these newspapers emphasized the German side of the conflict because, so they said, England had cut off Americans from German telegraph reports from the front.[4]

The national preparedness crusade favorable to the Allies secured little support in Wisconsin from two influential groups: United States Senator Robert M. La Follette and his followers, and the Social Democratic party, then in control of both the Milwaukee government and the local Federated Trades Council. These groups did not oppose Americanization, but they refused to align themselves with militant elements.[5] La Follette viewed the European conflict as an imperialist war and opposed American involvement. He particularly feared that intervention would distract attention from serious problems at home.[6] He fought for a policy of genuine neutrality, was one of twelve senators who opposed arming American merchant vessels, and was one of six senators who voted against the declaration of war. The Social Democratic party in Milwaukee also opposed preparedness

---

[3] On legislation requiring parochial schools to teach English, see Milwaukee County Council of Defense, *Official Bulletin* (1918), March 7, p. 7; March 21, p. 1; April 11, p. 4; September 12, p. 2; October 3, pp. 2–3; November 2, p. 2; unidentified newspaper clipping, in the Algie Simons Papers, in the State Historical Society of Wisconsin; interview with Lescohier.

[4] Wittke, *The German-Language Press in America*, 236–261.

[5] *La Follette's Magazine*, 9: 8 (July, 1917).

[6] *Ibid.*, 8: 5 (January, 1916); 8: 5 (October, 1916).

and intervention, a position which was endorsed by most members of the Federated Trades Council.[7]

Nevertheless, the gradual deterioration of relations with Germany gave the forces of militant Americanism an opening wedge. The *Milwaukee Journal,* supporting the Wilson Administration, gradually marshaled public opinion against a pro-German policy and worked vigorously to imbue the community with "America first sentiments." The effectiveness of its efforts can be judged from the fact that in 1916, when the wives of some of the city's industrialists helped organize a German war-relief bazaar, they received rings bearing iron cross insignia for their services. Another bazaar proposed for February of the following year had to be abandoned because of public hostility, and in March 7,000 citizens protested charges that Milwaukee was disloyal.[8]

Under this mounting pressure even the Catholic Church in Milwaukee found it necessary to urge "true Americanism" on its Polish-American communicants. Early in 1917, the Nowiny Publishing Company, a firm which printed official Catholic publications in the Polish language, prepared a special Easter Sunday edition of *Nowiny Polski* containing patriotic articles by Archbishop Sebastian Messmer, the superintendent of schools, Milton C. Potter, United States Senator Paul O. Husting, John Cudahy of Cudahy Brothers, Otto Falk of Allis-Chalmers, and others. The editor explained to Husting that there was "so much agitation going on between the different factions all over the country [that] his Grace, the Archbishop, as well as the Catholic clergy feel this is the opportune time to come out and show the Pole that his best interests lie in being loyal to his employer and keeping away from all agitation; to have in his heart a love for America and American institutions. In other

[7] Gavett, *Development of the Labor Movement in Milwaukee,* 126–127. Still, *Milwaukee,* 459–460.

[8] Statement of Martha Huettlin, February 19, 1918, in State Council of Defense, Milwaukee, Series 76/1/1, in the Wisconsin State Archives; *Milwaukee Journal,* February 9, March 17, 18, 1917.

words to divorce him from his associations across the seas, and to bring home to him the benefits to be derived from being loyal to his country and to his employer, and doing his share to help make this the greatest country in the world."[9]

Once war was declared, most Milwaukeeans tried to convince the nation that disloyalty had not triumphed in the city of Pabst, Schlitz, and *Gemütlichkeit*.[10] German-Americans, socialists, and La Follette became special targets. The largest German-language paper in the city felt obliged to renounce its earlier support of Germany, and superpatriots set up a machine gun in front of the Pabst Theater to prevent a performance of *Wilhelm Tell*.[11] German family names, names of clubs, business establishments, and foods were changed to English-sounding ones.[12] The *Milwaukee Journal* became famous for discrediting sympathizers of the Central Powers and "detecting" German spies and disloyal sentiments.[13] The Wisconsin Loyalty Legion, a self-appointed vigilante organization, urged the suppression of the German and socialist presses and the jailing of socialist leaders, and used strong-arm methods to promote the sale of Liberty Bonds.[14] Superpatriots hounded La Follette for his prewar

[9] M. Paruch to Paul O. Husting, March 19, 1917, in the Husting Papers. During the war the Catholic and Lutheran churches insisted that it was unnecessary to use force to secure the substitution of English for Polish and German in the parochial schools. Father Boloeslaus E. Goral of St. Hyacinth, a leading Polish priest, insisted in June, 1919, that Poles opposed the use of the "*Faustrecht* of Prussia" in Americanization work. *Milwaukee Journal*, June 2, 5, 1919.

[10] Demonstrating to the nation that Milwaukee was loyal affected all of the city's war work. Compare Charles D. Stewart, "Prussianizing Wisconsin," in *La Follette's Magazine*, 11: 6–8 (January, 1919); Milwaukee County Council of Defense, *Official Bulletin*, April 25, p. 1; August 8, 1918, p. 1.

[11] *Ibid.*, May 23, 1918, p. 2; *Milwaukee Germania Herold*, January 1, 1921, where the paper also said that its editor and publisher in 1917 had no other choice but to renounce its position. "*Deutsch sein heisst treu sein*, no matter how heart-breaking it might be to live up to the dictum."

[12] Still, *Milwaukee*, 459–460. See also *Milwaukee Journal*, September 29, 1917, for a letter to the editor demanding that the Pabst Theater not open for German-language plays.

[13] For a good summary of the *Journal*'s activities see the statement awarding the paper the Pulitzer Prize for journalism. *Milwaukee Journal*, June 3, 1919.

[14] Stewart, "Prussianizing Wisconsin," 8.

views and for his continuing criticism of the administration. Grand juries charged Congressman Victor Berger with disloyalty, and the *Milwaukee Leader,* his socialist paper, lost its mailing privileges.[15] Truly, a local patriot did not exaggerate when he declared that he was confident that "public opinion would speedily take care of any malcontents who show their racial bias."[16]

In the fall of 1917, the Milwaukee County Council of Defense (M.C.C.D.) launched its Americanization campaign. A small steering committee soon spawned a sprawling but influential organization with first six, then twenty subcommittees and a steadily growing advisory board.[17]

The council's crusade was organized by May Wood Simons, a woman whose background scarcely foreshadowed a commitment to militant nationalism. She and her husband, Algie M. Simons, were prominent socialists and had sought to advance their beliefs by their writings, by translating German and French socialist literature, and by attending international socialist meetings. The Simonses had been social settlement workers in Chicago, and in 1913, after a brief and unsuccessful venture with a socialist publication in Kansas, they came to Milwaukee—Simons to join the editorial staff of Victor Berger's *Leader,* his wife to become a teacher at the Riverside High School.[18]

With the outbreak of war in 1914, they became ardent opponents of Germany and sharp critics of sympathizers with the Central Powers. Mrs. Simons reacted bitterly to her pupils' pro-German sentiment at the time of the sinking of the *Lusitania.*[19] Her husband turned against Victor Berger

[15] *Milwaukee Journal,* September 25, October 4, October 8, November 24, 1918; *La Follette's Magazine,* 9: 1 (June, 1917).

[16] Willits Pollock to A. H. Melville, June 9, 1917, State Council of Defense, Milwaukee, Series 76/1/2, in the Wisconsin State Archives.

[17] Pollock, "Weekly Report," December 1, p. 2; December 6, 1917, p. 2; April 11, 1918, pp. 2–3. The council was established on April 30, 1917. *Official Bulletin,* January 3, 1918, p. 4.

[18] D. D. Egbert and Stow Person, *Socialism and American Life* (2 volumes, Princeton, 1952), 1: 312, 469, n9, 499, n13; 2: 81, 84, 200, 242, 381, 398; Algie Simons to Mrs. Emmons Blaine, June 19, 1900, in the Emmons Blaine Papers, in the McCormick Collection.

[19] May Wood Simons, Diary, August 12, September 18, 1914; May 30, 1915,

and the other so-called German socialists in the city, charging that they were strict neutralists and sympathetic to the Central Powers because of their ideological and filial connections with Germans and Austrians.[20] By 1916, Simons had become an enthusiastic war socialist and had thrown his entire support behind the Allies. He complained to J. Ramsay MacDonald, a prominent English socialist, for example, that Milwaukee reflected the sentiments of Berlin. He also claimed that he had heard Milwaukee socialists rejoice when the *Lusitania* was sunk.[21]

When the United States entered the conflict, the Simonses supported the war effort with organizational work and journalism, and readily joined forces with interests that they had formerly opposed. Long committed to the idea of a planned democratic society, they now preached the doctrine of national discipline. Algie Simons promoted the war effort within the international socialist movement, and in Milwaukee he took an active part in the Wisconsin Loyalty Legion recruitment drive.[22] May Wood Simons turned her abilities to Americanization work for the Milwaukee County Council of Defense. In October, 1917, she became chairman of its newly created Americanization Committee and its most active crusader.[23]

---

in the Simons Papers, in the State Historical Society of Wisconsin.

[20] Simons to *Labour Leader,* July 17, 1918, in *ibid.;* Simons in the *Milwaukee Journal,* December 2, 9, 1917.

[21] J. Ramsay MacDonald to Simons, October 4, 1916; Simons to *Labour Leader,* July 17, 1918, both in the Simons Papers.

[22] Simons to wife and daughter, June 29, 1918; M. Van Antwerpen to Simons, January 19, 1918, both in *ibid.; Milwaukee Journal,* October 1, 8, 1917; Simons to Richard M. Campbell in Record Group 85, case file no. 27671/6305, in the National Archives. Some of Algie Simons' wartime activities may be followed in the papers of the Wisconsin Loyalty Legion, in Series 83/0/8, in the Wisconsin State Archives. War socialists had their troubles in the legion with colleagues from management. See the charges leveled against W. R. Gaylord by the Cutler-Hammer Company. A. W. Berresford to Herman A. Wagner; to George S. Kridl, both April 6, 1918, in *ibid.*

[23] Walter Distelhort to George Creel, March 19, 1918, in Correspondence of the Committee on Public Information, CPI-I-A3 (I), in the National Archives; Chicago Chief Examiner to Raymond F. Crist, August 30, September 19, 1918, in Record Group 85, case file no. 27671/4773, in the National Archives; Milwaukee County Council of Defense, *Official Bulletin,* April 11, 1918, p. 3.

When Mrs. Simons began her work for the M.C.C.D., a number of organizations, including the Loyalty Legion, had for some time been engaged in Americanization activities. Harold O. Berg, superintendent of the extension department of the city's public school system, had opened the new school year with war enthusiasm; patriotic organizations affiliated with the State Council of Defense had been actively promoting Americanization among immigrants; and patriots, manufacturers, and others had been drawn into the work of the M.C.C.D.[24]

In this context of rising patriotism the Loyalty Legion became especially influential. Together with the *Milwaukee Journal,* it gave socialists, pacifists, and followers of La Follette little choice but to acquiesce in the actions of superpatriots; it forced the public schools to supply "loyal" teachers for English and civics classes for immigrants; and it overcame socialist opposition to militancy in the classroom. The public schools were made instruments of national policy and purpose: alien and new teachers were carefully screened, all teachers were required to sign loyalty oaths, and foreign languages were dropped from the elementary school curriculum.[25] At the same time Loyalty Legionnaires became members of the advisory board of the Americanization Committee which Mrs. Simons had organized to promote militant nationalism and "a common language and a united and intelligent citizenship." Under her chairmanship, the M.C.C.D. unfurled banners reading "America 100 per cent American" and "Milwaukee 100 per cent American" over the entire community.[26]

From the outset, Mrs. Simons attempted to make factories

[24] *Milwaukee Journal,* September 25, October 14, 1917; Distelhort to George Creel, March 19, 1918, in the National Archives; *Final Report of the Wisconsin State Council of Defense, 1917–1919,* p. 62; Mrs. Henry M. Youmans to Mrs. H. H. Morgan, September 4, 1918; report of the Women's Advisory Committee of the State Council of Defense, August 20, 1917, Correspondence Folder, both in Series 76/1/10, in the Wisconsin State Archives.

[25] *Milwaukee Journal,* September 26, October 6, October 17, December 4, 1917.

[26] *Announcement of Americanization Conference,* November 18–22, 1918, in the Lighty Papers; Milwaukee County Council of Defense, *Official Bulletin,*

instruments of Americanization. Familiar with the work of the Ford Motor Company, U. S. Steel, and International Harvester, she appreciated that factories were autocratic organizations capable of encouraging or coercing their workers to attend classes in English, civics, and history, and to become naturalized citizens.

But Ford in Detroit and U. S. Steel in Chicago were not Milwaukee manufacturers, and in Milwaukee things were different. The success of industrial Americanization programs of the sort advocated by Miss Frances Kellor and Mrs. Simons depended on the co-operation of employers and the existence of systematized welfare programs. In Milwaukee, neither condition was wholly present.

This is not to say that Milwaukee manufacturers lacked patriotism. Manufacturers acted with great dispatch in raising the national banner over their factories once the war broke out, in part because they feared that a reputation for disloyalty would result in a boycott against the city.[27] In March, 1917, the A. O. Smith Corporation went as far as appealing to Senator Husting for a rousing statement on "True Americanism" addressed to its 2,000 employees, in order to encourage those who "think right," and to stiffen the spines of those out of step with the nation.[28] Manufacturers were well represented in war agencies and organizations from the time America joined the conflict. They were particularly strong in the Milwaukee County Council of Defense, where August H. Vogel (leather), Charles Allis (metal

December 2, 27, 1917, p. 4; January 3, p. 4; January 17, p. 1; January 31, pp. 2–3; August 15, 1918, p. 1. The council's general campaign may be followed in *ibid.*

[27] For concern about Milwaukee's reputation and a possible boycott, see George H. Russell to Harold H. Seaman, April 20; Seaman to Russell, April 23; Guy F. Gregg to Morris F. Fox, April 25; George F. Kull to Gregg, May 4, 1918, all in Series 83/0/15, in the Wisconsin State Archives; *Civics and Commerce*, April, 1918, 20–21; Stewart, "Prussianizing Wisconsin," 5.

[28] Advertising and Sales Manager, A. O. Smith Corporation, to Husting, March 1, 12, 1917, in the Husting Papers. The typescript of the article, dated March 10, 1917, is also in *ibid.*

trades), and Robert Uihlein (brewing), served on the executive committee. One of the industrialists' early patriotic endeavors was to join thirteen other executive committee members to oust Mayor Daniel D. Hoan as chairman of the council, over the votes of the five Socialist members.[29] Afterwards,
Allis and Vogel each served as chairman.[30] Employers established a department of manufacture within the council that
nominally included a representative from organized labor,[31]
but unions actually had little voice in its operation and
throughout the war they looked with distrust upon the activities of the M.C.C.D.[32]

Manufacturers played similar roles in other war organizations and activities. They helped open the city bond drives
and organized their factories for bond subscriptions, participated in Red Cross drives, and often helped organize their employees for other activities characteristic of the home front
in 1917 and 1918.[33] At least fourteen companies—including
International Harvester, Cutler-Hammer, Briggs and Stratton
Engineering, Pfister and Vogel, Cudahy Brothers, and the
Weinbrenner Shoe Company—established factory chapters of
the Wisconsin Loyalty Legion.[34]

[29] Milwaukee County Council of Defense, *Official Bulletin,* August 2, 1917,
p. 3; June 6, 1918, p. 3.

[30] Pollock, "Weekly Report," March 16, 1918. Hoan's sharp protest may be
found in his letter to the Milwaukee County Council of Defense, March 13,
1918, in the Hoan Papers; for examples of Hoan's co-operation with Vogel
and Allis on behalf of the war effort in Milwaukee, see Minutes, 1: 152–
153 (1917–1919), State Council of Defense, Series 76/1/1, in the Wisconsin
State Archives.

[31] Milwaukee County Council of Defense, *Official Bulletin,* June 6, p. 4;
July 25, 1918, p. 3; Report of the *Wisconsin State Council of Defense, 1917–
1919,* p. 58.

[32] Pollock, "Weekly Report," June 2, June 16, July 5, December 17, 1917;
Milwaukee County Council of Defense, *Official Bulletin,* November 29, 1917,
p. 2; Gavett, *Development of the Labor Movement in Milwaukee,* 128–130.

[33] *Harvester World,* 9: 9 (February, 1918); 9: 10 (March, 1918); 9: 2 (July,
1918); 9: 10 (October, 1918); *Milwaukee Journal,* October 8, 14, 1917; Pollock,
"Weekly Report," September 22, 1917.

[34] See *Record of the Wisconsin Loyalty Legion,* April 10, 1919, pp. 22–23,
a pamphlet preserved in the Simons Papers.

Nor had efforts to establish systematized welfare programs been lacking. To the extent that they had developed, however, they had evolved in the context of a partnership between manufacturers who were changing industrial relations in the interest of private enterprise and a state government which was changing industrial relations in the interest of all its citizens. And a basic part of that partnership, from the manufacturers' point of view, was that decisions about what was good for the workers should be left to the employers, not to the workers—and particularly, not to the labor unions.

Milwaukee employers since the troubles of 1886 had fiercely maintained their opposition to organized labor. The stronghold of this hostility was in the metal trades, which employed the largest share of the work force and where, at the turn of the century, owners had pooled their resources in a local branch of the National Metal Trades Association. In 1901, 1906, and 1916 they defeated machinists and foundry workers in their drive for an eight-hour day and for the principle of a union shop. To William W. Coleman, president of Bucyrus and head of the Milwaukee Metal Trades Association, it eventually appeared that employers in Milwaukee had freed themselves from the "menace of unionism."[85]

During the war, despite new difficulties, employers in the metal trades continued their traditional resistance to organized labor. The Briggs and Stratton Engineering Company, for example, spied on labor organizers, partly because it considered the government derelict in not preventing "labor agitators" from hindering production. According to Briggs-Stratton, union organizers were stirring up the men to demand higher wages and were claiming that President Wilson supported their aspirations.[86]

[85] Rau Appraisal Company, compiler, "Wisconsin, Region 17, Resources and Conversion Section, War Industries Board, Classification and Index of Manufacturing Industry," bound typescript volume (Milwaukee, 1918), Labor Data Section, 1–15, in the Milwaukee Public Library; Williamson and Myers, *Designed for Digging*, 62–63, 72–73, 127.

[86] Briggs and Stratton to Commonwealth Steel, May 15, 1918, Committee on Public Information, in the National Archives.

In the summer of 1918, tension in the city became serious. August brought a breakdown in negotiations between labor and management at a firm manufacturing war materials. Though told that they would be joining the Kaiser's side if they went out on strike, workers struck for higher wages and the eight-hour day.[37] Metal trade manufacturers in Milwaukee rallied to support the strikebound plant. They sought to convince federal mediators not to change working conditions in the Milwaukee area, even though wage scales were lower in the city than in its environs and even though the Wilson Administration had urged government contractors to adopt the eight-hour day. William W. Coleman, Otto Falk (president of Allis-Chalmers), and R. P. Tell (president of the National Brake and Electric Company) insisted that any strike settlement should preserve the right of the employer to pay each workman according to his ability, and refused to abandon the open shop principle.[38]

Yet, while Milwaukee employers sternly and effectively opposed organized labor, they continued earlier paternalistic practices. "Old Julius," the owner of the Heil Company, would have nothing to do with unions, but his wife, "Mama Heil," bustled about at company picnics and brought flowers and goodies to the homes or hospital beds of injured workmen.[39] Theodore Vilter, a member of the Milwaukee Metal Trades Association and later vice president of the Merchants and Manufacturers Association, urged a similar approach on his fellow employers. Recognizing that the wartime boom eventually would come to an end and predicting that there might then be a danger of labor disturbances, he advised manufacturers to prepare their workers for the eventual substitution of the traditional sauerkraut and sausage for the

[37] "Brief of Workers," typescript, in Hearing of the National War Labor Board, Record Group 2, case file no. 163, in the National Archives.

[38] "Brief of Employers and Testimony," typescript, 128, 152, 222, 226, 238, 240, in *ibid*. This brief includes wage data from the metal trades. See also Pollock, "Weekly Report," July 28, 1917.

[39] Interview with Elmer Kreutzer, Employment Manager, International Harvester Company, Milwaukee Works, 1959.

turkey and duck that he claimed they were then eating. "Talk to Jack or Jim or Dick about your mutual relations and do not be afraid to talk to their wives. Tell them that you desire their husbands to be in fit condition to be on the job in the morning. Tell them when a man comes home tired from his job . . . he wants to be greeted with a good meal and friendly face—and with a kiss on the side."[40]

Even in the face of such attitudes, some systemized welfare work and up-to-date methods in industrial service had developed in Milwaukee as the outcome of the interaction between private and state interests. During the war decade many large enterprises, especially in the metal trades, expanded their welfare activities because of their hostility to organized labor and the growing number of female employees. The National Civic Federation, now hostile to trade unions, encouraged Milwaukee employers to organize welfare programs for women employees. In 1914 a field representative established a local branch with 150 members.[41]

The Wisconsin Industrial Commission, following practices established between 1911 and 1914, continued to press for implementation and expansion of industrial service work. It still insisted that welfare activities could not replace organized labor or be a substitute for higher wages and reduced hours. But because it was committed to improving the conditions of employment and strengthening industrial welfare programs for all workers, the commission had no choice but to co-operate in this fashion with management. Organized labor was simply too weak to be of any significant assistance.[42]

The commission tried to make employers and the state partners in executing protective labor legislation. It pointed to welfare and industrial service practices already successfully in operation in some companies as proof that they could be utilized in all factories, and its advisory council, the group

---

[40] *Milwaukee Free Press,* February 27, 1916.

[41] *Milwaukee Leader,* January 24, 1914.

[42] This evaluation was confirmed in an interview with Professor Selig Perlman, for many years a close associate of Commons. For a statement of Commons' own approach to this subject, see his *Industrial Goodwill, passim.*

organized by Commons, Price, and others, then developed a standard code of practice. Working closely with the Pfister and Vogel Leather Company and International Harvester, for example, both of which firms had open shop policies, the commission experimented with lighting standards in its efforts to reduce accidents, protect eyesight, and improve production. Out of this and another experiment came the commission's 1916 lighting code for Wisconsin factories.[43] Similarly the commission continued Price's policy of providing deputies of the Department of Safety and Sanitation to those employers who intended to inaugurate or expand industrial services.[44]

Beginning in 1917, the commission supplemented its assistance to employers with special conferences. Organized for manufacturers, superintendents, employment managers, welfare and service workers, safety engineers, physicians, and nurses,[45] the conferences were intended to provide up-to-date information on safety, sanitation, employment, hours of labor, health conservation in industrial productivity, and labor-management relations.[46]

Except for Sumner Slichter, then at the University of Chicago, and Kate Kohlstadt, who represented Milwaukee's Visiting Nurses Association, the second conference, held in April, 1918, attracted experts exclusively from the ranks of management. Arthur H. Young, employment manager of Illinois Steel and director of the American Museum of Safety, read a paper on employment problems and labor turnover

[43] Altmeyer, *Industrial Commission,* 116–121, 151, 153; Commons, *Myself,* 161; Charles W. Price, "Co-operation for Safety between the Wisconsin Industrial Commission and the Manufacturers and Workmen," an address to the National Association of Manufacturers, May 19, 1914, reprinted by the Industrial Commission; Price in the *Proceedings of the National Safety Council, 1916,* pp. 322–323; interviews with Perlman, Elizabeth Brandeis, 1959, Lescohier, 1958. See also Wisconsin Industrial Commission, *First Aid, A Handbook for Use in Shops* (Madison, 1915), *passim.*

[44] George P. Hambrecht, "Industrial Accidents," 8–9; John R. Commons in the *Milwaukee Journal,* September 7, 1919.

[45] Wisconsin Industrial Commission, *Industrial Service Conference, Milwaukee, April 25–27, 1918,* program of the conference, in a folder marked "State Officers," Series 76/1/10, in the Wisconsin State Archives.

[46] Hambrecht, "Industrial Accidents," 8–9.

and John W. Schmidt, employment manager of the Northwestern Malleable Iron Company of Milwaukee, led the discussion of it. Richard Feiss of Clothcraft Shops in Cleveland, a company long a leader in welfare work, spoke on employment and service work; Arthur S. Ross, employment and personnel director at the Milwaukee Coke and Gas Company, led a discussion on physical examinations; B. Rosing of the A. O. Smith Corporation spoke about organizing a factory service department; and Howard D. Plimpton, representing the Aetna Insurance Company of Milwaukee, talked on safety and output.[47]

Ross and Rosing were products of the prewar industrial service trend in Milwaukee. Ross's work at the Milwaukee Coke and Gas Company went back to the heyday of the safety campaign. The firm's house organ, *Conveyor*, which Ross edited, was an outgrowth of the company's campaign for "boosting safety."[48] In the metal trades, where most of the large firms were engaged in some aspects of welfare, A. O. Smith's program resembled those at International Harvester, Bucyrus, and Allis-Chalmers.[49] Since 1910, the work at these three firms had become increasingly elaborate and centralized. International Harvester and Bucyrus had established departments of industrial relations; Allis-Chalmers had compartmentalized its work into employment management, safety, sanitation, and welfare, and mutual benefit departments.[50] Other firms in the metal trades had similar but less elaborate programs. The programs included ones at the Chain Belt Company, Pawling and Harnischfeger, the Falk Corporation, and the Harley-Davidson Company.[51] Outside the metal

[47] Wisconsin Industrial Commission, *Industrial Service Conference*.

[48] A. S. Ross in the *Proceedings of the National Safety Council, 1918*, p. 414.

[49] R. C. Mullinex in the *Milwaukee Journal*, September 4, 5, 1919. Mullinex, an instructor at Lawrence College, did a series of twenty articles on welfare work in Milwaukee for this paper. See also Wisconsin Industrial Commission, *First Aid*, 2–3.

[50] Mullinex in the *Milwaukee Journal*, September 11, 19, 20, 1919; *Harvester World*, 9: 4, inside of the front cover, (April, 1918); 10: 24 (December, 1920); Williamson and Myers, *Designed for Digging*, 128–132.

[51] Mullinex in the *Milwaukee Journal*, September 6, 21, 1919; *Proceedings of the National Safety Council, 1916*, pp. 1314–1316; *Proceedings of the Milwaukee Board of School Directors*, March 6, 1919.

trades, a number of firms also engaged in welfare work. By the end of the decade, the Pfister and Vogel Leather Company had an industrial relations department and employment managers for each of its three plants in the city. The Nunn and Bush and the Weinbrenner shoe companies and three large knitting mills, Phoenix Hosiery, Holeproof Hosiery, and Monarch Manufacturing Company, directed their welfare programs particularly at their female employees.[52]

Yet as late as 1917, industrial service work had not become common in Milwaukee, and it still lacked professional status. Few companies had specialists in employment, personnel, or industrial management. Employment managers usually functioned also as welfare workers, and their hiring offices were often little more than shacks.[53] Service secretaries were usually self-styled social workers or visiting nurses who often flitted from position to position. For example, between December, 1917, and March, 1918, Avis Ring of the Holeproof Hosiery Company served as employment manager, social worker, and service worker, and in March she left the company for a position in the state's vocational educational program.[54] Others had no preparation at all. At the Robert A. Johnston Candy Company in 1918, Maynard Downes, a young lady with a graduate degree in American history from the University of Wisconsin, was the head of the welfare depart-

[52] Mullinex in the *Milwaukee Journal,* September 11, 19, 26, 29, 1919; statement by Mrs. William B. Kittle, Chairman, Women in Industry Committee, State Council of Defense, August 29, 1918, in Correspondence Folder, Series 76/1/10, in the Wisconsin State Archives; *Harvester World,* 9: 4 (April, 1918); interview with Kreutzer; Williamson and Myers, *Designed for Digging,* 128.

[53] Interview with Kreutzer. At the Pawling and Harnischfeger Corporation, Thomas J. Kelly had the title of employment and welfare manager. Mullinex in the *Milwaukee Journal,* September 21, 1919.

[54] Typescript report of meeting of the Women in Industry Committee, State Council of Defense, December 10, 1917; June 7, 1918; Frank L. Glynn to Mrs. William Kittle, February 26, 1918; Mrs. William Kittle to Miss Tracy Copp, March 27, 1918, in Correspondence Folder, Series 76/1/10, in the Wisconsin State Archives; Mullinex in the *Milwaukee Journal,* September 16, 26, 1919; *Proceedings of the National Safety Council, 1917,* pp. 272, 428. The company replaced her with Alice B. Smith, a self-styled service secretary. Alice B. Smith to Mrs. William Kittle, August 26, 1918, in Correspondence Folder, Series 76/1/10, in the Wisconsin State Archives.

ment, and she seemed to view military drill for girls as essential for the workers' well-being.[55]

It was to this largely unprofessional and limited base of industrial welfare work that the Americanization program in Milwaukee was grafted. Thus, whereas Mrs. Simons and the public school board supported militant patriotism on behalf of what they thought to be the national interest, employers, to the extent that they participated at all, did so out of self-interest. Industrial spokesmen explained clearly how and why Americanization fitted into their scheme of things. John W. Maple, assistant to the vice-president at Pfister and Vogel, who in October, 1917, attributed the acute labor shortage in the city to the virtual halt in immigration from Europe and enlistment of many workers in military service. "Soon women will be forced into the ranks of industries," he said. "The only solution . . . is to increase the efficiency of the workers we now have by Americanization." Americanization was necessary, he explained, because as much as a quarter of the labor force in some large factories spoke no English. The laborers "could not be expected to have the American spirit," he declared, "because they were too slow to learn the trade. A foreman," said Maple, "cannot explain to them how to work to the best advantage nor how to protect themselves from possible dangers as he can to English-speaking employees. They therefore do not get advancement, they become discouraged and go somewhere else to work." This in turn led to serious labor problems, for the "foreigner was at the heart of manufacturing." Maple explained that training new men was expensive, especially in a period during which the labor turnover was so high that if a firm needed 1,000 men for its operations, it had in many instances to hire about 1,500 during the course of a year to keep all positions filled. "Speaking English will have a tendency to stabilize labor and therefore reduce the turnover percentage,"

[55] Louise F. Brand to William H. Lighty, August 19, 1918, in the Lighty Papers. Miss Downes received her master's degree under Professor Frederick L. Paxson in 1913.

Maple predicted. "Under present conditions every manufacturer should be interested in this Americanization proposition as we hire the men today and they hire ours tomorrow."[56]

Shortly after the M.C.C.D. established its Americanization committee, the council's department of manufacture began to assist Mrs. Simons' group.[57] In December of 1917, Chester F. Rohn, general manager of the Weinbrenner Shoe Company and secretary of the department of manufacture, began to send letters to Milwaukee employers, soliciting their support for propaganda activities within their plants. He mentioned safety and efficiency as industrial problems related to the teaching of English, but his emphasis was on labor unrest: "There should be but one common language in this country, and the accomplishments of this purpose will lessen accidents and increase efficiency. By encouraging foreigners to become American citizens and to learn the English language you are taking them outside of the influence of irresponsible agitators. The phenomenal results obtained in Detroit, Kansas City and other large cities may also be accomplished in Milwaukee providing the manufacturers will lend their assistance." Rohn closed by extending his "best wishes for improved labor conditions, safety and efficiency."[58]

The Wisconsin Industrial Commission and the influential John R. Commons expressed similar sentiments about the relationship between Americanization and industrial conditions. In 1918, Chairman George P. Hambrecht ranked the teaching of English with an adequate and up-to-date first-aid room and employment department, improved sanitation, lunchrooms, and factory training classes as the more important "phases of industrial betterment work which are now generally recognized as having an important relation to the accident rate." The deputies of the commission's safety and

---

[56] *Milwaukee Journal,* October 14, 1917; Milwaukee County Council of Defense, *Official Bulletin,* February 7, 1918, p. 2.

[57] *Ibid.,* January 17, 1918, p. 2; Pollock, "Weekly Report," December 1, 1917.

[58] Chester F. Rohn, typescript circular letter to Milwaukee employers, December 17, 1917, Series 76/1/2, in the Wisconsin State Archives.

sanitation department encouraged manufacturers to engage in all these activities.[59] Commons supported such policies, for he not only had advocated industrial service work, but was also convinced that employers owed it to the republic to use their coercive force to teach English to the foreign-born workman, in part because they could reduce the threat of radicalism.[60]

Since the fall of 1917, Mrs. Simons, Berg, manufacturers on the M.C.C.D., and the Milwaukee Merchants and Manufacturers Association had been pursuing similar goals. They used the familiar techniques of the safety campaign—noonday meetings, posters, bulletin boards, slips in pay envelopes, and personal solicitations by superintendents and foremen— to increase enrollment in night school classes in English and civics.[61] By the spring of 1918, however, it became clear to Mrs. Simons that this campaign had not succeeded, for one firm reported that only 4 of its 500 immigrant workers spoke English and other firms reported similar though much lower deficiencies.[62] Workers, Mrs. Simons then concluded, were too tired to attend night school. Classes inside the factories were the only alternative.

To achieve this, Mrs. Simons' group organized a special committee representing ten of Milwaukee's largest industries. Through Berg's efforts, the Milwaukee School Board assigned some of its extension department teachers to factory classes, but, despite the urging of the local Association of Commerce, perhaps no more than five companies participated in the

[59] Hambrecht, "Industrial Accidents," 8–9.

[60] Milwaukee County Council of Defense, *Official Bulletin,* May 2, p. 1; May 9, 1918, p. 2; John R. Commons, scrapbooks, 5: 445, in the University of Wisconsin Archives; and his *Industrial Goodwill,* 129–131.

[61] Pollock, "Weekly Report," December 1, 1917; April 11, 1918; Rohn, circular letter; *Milwaukee Journal,* September 25, 1917; Milwaukee County Council of Defense, *Official Bulletin,* December 5, 1917, p. 2.

[62] *Ibid.,* January 17, 1918, p. 2; unidentified newspaper clipping, November 10, 1918, in the Algie Simons Papers; *Proceedings of the Milwaukee Board of School Directors, 1917–1918,* p. 335; *Milwaukee Journal,* September 25, 1918.

well-publicized but poorly received educational program.[63]

Equally important, Mrs. Simons found that even when companies wanted to co-operate, they simply did not have the necessary personnel to implement her Americanization program, a condition which had been recognized by the United States War Industries Board when it established two courses to train social service workers. In July, 1918, she sought to overcome the shortage by getting William H. Lighty, acting dean of the University of Wisconsin Extension Division, to arrange courses in the Milwaukee area. Though the University could not co-operate at that time because it had no competent teacher available, it hired her husband eighteen months later to lecture on personnel relations in industry.[64]

While trying to obtain the help of the University, Mrs. Simons sought to dramatize her objectives by proposing a national Americanization conference in Milwaukee. To this end she tried to obtain the support of the United States Bureau of Naturalization; but when disputes developed over both the location of the convention and whom to invite, she arranged for a less spectacular conference consisting of local community leaders and, at the expense of the M.C.C.D., six experts from outside Milwaukee.[65] Following a postpone-

[63] Pollock, "Weekly Report," February 2, 1918; Milwaukee County Council of Defense, *Official Bulletin,* February 14, p. 3; April 11, p. 2; May 9, p. 2; May 16, p. 3; September 19, 1918, p. 3; Hill, "Americanization Work," 3–4; *Proceedings of the Milwaukee Board of School Directors, 1917–1918,* pp. 68, 335; Final Report, 1917–1919, Women's Committee, State Council of Defense, Series 76/1/10, in the Wisconsin Archives.

[64] Mrs. A. M. Simons to William H. Lighty, July 6, 1918; Lighty to Simons, July 16, 1918, both in the Lighty Papers; Milwaukee County Council of Defense, *Official Bulletin,* June 27, 1918, p. 1; M. E. McCuffey to A. M. Simons, December 4, 1919; January 22, 1920; May Wood Simons, Diary, January 20, 1920, all in the Algie Simons Papers.

[65] W. H. Wagner to Richard M. Campbell, September 19, 1918; Campbell to All Examiners, September 19, 1918; Weber to Chief Examiner, Chicago District, September 25, 1918; W. H. Wagner to Campbell, November 23, 1918, all in case file no. 27671/4773, in the National Archives; May Wood Simons to Algie Simons, August 3, 1918, in the Algie Simons Papers. In

ment because of 1918 influenza epidemic, the convention assembled during the third week in November, just after the Armistice.[66]

The conference stressed the place of Americanization in industry, two of the outside participants being experts on this subject. One of them was Winthrop Talbot, who had both taught and evaluated English classes in factories, and had also edited a study of Americanization methods.[67] Shortly after the conference, he gave an Americanization course for the Extension Division of the University of Wisconsin, and he persuaded Mrs. Simons, Berg, and the Pfister and Vogel Leather Company that he had a novel and successful method for teaching English to foreigners. Pfister and Vogel, in turn, persuaded the University of Wisconsin to pay Talbot's salary, and he began the course in the spring of 1919.[68]

Each sponsor hoped to benefit from Talbot's work. Pfister and Vogel had for some time been engaged in industrial service activity, and the officers of the company viewed the firm's large numbers of immigrant employees as an obstacle blocking the success of these efforts, on the ground that the absence of a common language prevented effective communication between the company and its workers. It wanted its immigrant workers to have classes, but not the type that the

---

August she hoped to have President Wilson at the conference, but if not Wilson, then William Howard Taft or Secretary of the Interior Franklin K. Lane.

[66] *Announcement of Americanization Conference*; Milwaukee County Council of Defense, *Official Bulletin*, August 8, 1910, p. 1; October 24, 1918, pp. 2–3.

[67] *Ibid.*, August 8, p. 1; November 4, 7, p. 2; November 28, 1918, p. 3; Winthrop Talbot in the *Proceedings of the National Safety Council, 1917*, p. 236; *Milwaukee Journal*, November 18, 1918; Talbot in transcript of Winthrop Talbot Hearing, 22–23, in the Lighty Papers; unidentified newspaper clipping, November, 1918, in the Algie Simons Papers.

[68] Report of Professor Don D. Lescohier on the investigation of classes for teaching English to foreigners at the Pfister and Vogel plants, Milwaukee, 5; Talbot Hearing, 7, 15, 18–19, 23, 25, 27; interview with Lescohier; *Milwaukee Journal*, November 19, 1918; *Proceedings of the Milwaukee Board of School Directors, 1918–1919*, p. 344.

extension department of the local public school provided. Instead, the company wanted them to study industrial English applicable to the conditions of the firm.[69]

The Extension Division of the University had for a number of years provided specialized courses in various aspects of manufacturing and social work. During the war it began offering short courses in Americanization and soon became so involved that it had to hire a specialist on Americanization and civic education. The man chosen was Don D. Lescohier, a former student of John R. Commons, an expert on employment agencies, and in 1918 the industrial safety specialist for the State of Minnesota.[70] Lescohier quickly became associated with Americanization and other war agencies in Wisconsin, and in the fall of 1918 he was drawn into the language project at Pfister and Vogel. He acquiesced in the Extension Division's judgment that it had found the Talbot approach a sound method for teaching English to immigrants. In the co-operative arrangement which developed, the company agreed to pay the wages of its workers attending the classes, printing costs for Talbot's materials, and all incidentals. The University paid Talbot's salary, and the Milwaukee School Board paid the salaries of all other teachers in the program, including those of two teachers transferred to the Pfister and Vogel project.[71]

[69] *Milwaukee Journal,* October 14, 1917; Mullinex, in *ibid.,* September 29, 1919.

[70] Lighty to John L. Elliot, June 26, 1918; Charles R. Van Hise to Commons, Ely, and Lighty, July 2, 1918; Robert H. Woods to Van Hise, June 29, 1918, all in the Lighty Papers; interview with Lescohier; Woods wrote that he was too committed in his work in Boston but suggested Allen T. Burns for the position. Woods to Van Hise, June 29, 1918, in the Lighty Papers.

[71] Lighty to Louis E. Reber, August 29, 1918; Lescohier to Percy E. Pope, June 5, 1919; C. H. Powell to Lighty, November 26, 1918; Lescohier to Pope, June 5, 1919; report on the English classes at Pfister and Vogel, 5; Talbot Hearing, 9, 19, 30, 36, 42, all in the Lighty Papers; *Milwaukee Journal,* November 22, 23, 1918. On November 23, 1918, Wagner wrote Campbell that Lescohier's "aims" included the development of a "visualization" course for immigrants. Case file 27671/4773, in the National Archives. By September, Lescohier, whose formal title was Associate Professor in charge of Americanization, had been appointed executive secretary of the State Council of

The Milwaukee School Board's extension division had a similar stake in the project. If successful, Talbot would train a number of instructors in his methods of teaching industrial English, and the school system would have a model program for other industrialists to copy.[72]

Talbot began his ten-week course on April 28, 1919, but after a few weeks those concerned with the project became alarmed. In the first week in June and in the name of the company, Mrs. Simons asked Lescohier to investigate; for she, Berg of the city's extension department, and Percy E. Pope, Pfister and Vogel's industrial service manager, considered Talbot's course to be unsatisfactory. Lescohier held a formal hearing as the representative of the University and obtained the company's promise that it would abide by any decision reached by him and the local school authorities.[73]

The evidence against Talbot was overwhelming. Though hired to teach a well-prepared short course of industrial English, his supply of leaflets illustrating English words on one side and foreign-language equivalents on the other was completely inadequate and made it difficult to implement his visual approach to language teaching. To make matters worse, instead of employing "industrially minded" teachers, Talbot hired any teacher who came along, including, Berg charged, unemployed soldiers and sailors, whom he then grossly overpaid. Nor had Talbot lived up to his promise of giving these instructors technical training, and he had refused to show his teaching materials to a language instructor from the University.[74]

Defense's Committee on Americanization. See minutes of the council, 1: 6, 1917–1919, Series 76/1/1, in the Wisconsin State Archives. Lescohier claimed in an interview in 1959 that he knew from the start that under Talbot's direction the project would fail. He says he so advised Dean Reber, but the "University" thought support of the project would be "good for public relations."

[72] *Milwaukee Journal*, April 16, 1919; Talbot Hearing, 43; *Proceedings of the Milwaukee Board of School Directors, 1918–1919*, p. 344.

[73] Report on the English classes at Pfister and Vogel, 1; Talbot Hearing, 9.

[74] *Ibid., passim*, but especially pp. 18–19, 43; *Milwaukee Journal*, April 16, 1919.

On the basis of his investigation, Lescohier recommended that Talbot be dismissed and that the classes be turned over to the city schools' extension department. The University of Wisconsin, which had invested $1,000 in the project, stopped paying Talbot's salary on June 11, but despite the company's promise to abide by Lescohier's recommendations, Pfister and Vogel retained Talbot to complete the ten-week course. Pope admitted that the results were unsatisfactory, but explained that his firm wished to give Talbot an opportunity to prove himself, and that it thought that there was little to be gained by changing management for the five weeks remaining. Anyway, Pfister and Vogel had invested some $2,000 in the program, not including the wages paid to workers while they attended classes. Berg then joined Lescohier in washing his hands of the entire affair.[75]

As an educational undertaking, Talbot's work was a fiasco, but the company gave the impression of being well pleased with the results. Those interested in industrial management and Americanization in industry were informed that 600 employees had received a ten-week course in speaking, reading, writing, and calculating in English, and that they had attended four one-hour classes for five days each week. The directors declared themselves to be extremely gratified with the results. "It was undoubtedly one of the biggest experiments of its kind ever carried on in an American industry and will probably be followed elsewhere," their spokesman proclaimed. Among Milwaukee employers, Pfister and Vogel thereby acquired a reputation as the leader and authority on Americanization in factories. However, the company did not again embark on such a project. It held no more language classes for almost a year, and its new program consisted of a small class taught by the city's extension department for sixty-odd Mexicans who were living on Pfister and Vogel

[75] Lescohier to Pope, June 5, 1919; Pope to Lescohier, June 7, 1919; Harold O. Berg to Lescohier, June 10, 1919, all in the Lighty Papers. In 1918 Lescohier estimated that the classes cost about $400 a day. Talbot Hearing, 21. In 1959 he estimated that the entire project cost the company around $35,000.

property adjacent to one of its Milwaukee factory buildings.[76]

That the gap between industry and public education had not been closed was further demonstrated in June, 1919, when the Y.M.C.A.'s Peter Roberts arrived in Milwaukee hoping to get employers to adopt his language program. He found himself unwelcome; the industrial secretary of the local Y.M.C.A. believed that Roberts' method was not entirely successful and that it might jeopardize the Americanization program in the city.[77]

Roberts addressed a number of groups, including the influential City Club, but his brand of Americanization made little headway. In September, Pfister and Vogel considered but did not adopt Roberts' method of teaching language. The Chain Belt Manufacturing Company permitted Roberts to start a program of industrial English later in the year (an arrangement the company had with Talbot having failed to materialize), but this was one of his few successes. Clearly, most Milwaukee employers were little interested in language programs, whether the Roberts or Talbot variety, and neither of the two extension programs—the University's or the city's—had much success in promoting Americanization.[78]

In the fall of 1919, the Association of Commerce became the chief sponsor of Americanization work. Its president, A. T. Van Scoy, created a subcommittee comprised of Berg, J. B. Modesitt of the Y.M.C.A., and Mrs. Simons, but it soon became clear that there was no consensus in the committee, or indeed in Milwaukee, about its objectives. Though the crucible of war had enabled essentially incompatible interests to forge an alliance in the drive for victory, peace and particularly the Red Scare fractured the harmony within the ranks of the Americanizers. Mrs. Simons had broken with the So-

[76] *Milwaukee Journal*, September 26, November 30, 1919; May 15, 1920; Caroline A. Whipple, *Americanization in Industry* (New York, 1919), 22; Mullinex, in *Milwaukee Journal*, September 29, 1919.

[77] W. H. Bennett to Lescohier, June 11, 1919, in the Lighty Papers.

[78] *Milwaukee Journal*, April 16, September 20, 22, 23, 1919; Milwaukee Y.M.C.A., *Annual Report, 1920*, p. 7; unidentified newspaper clipping, October 7, 1919, in the Simons Papers.

cialist party but she had renounced neither socialism nor the labor movement, and she was quick to perceive that the Americanization Council which the Association of Commerce established was dominated by what she called "a group of extreme reactionaries." By February, 1920, they had succeeded in keeping her off all the council's committees, and the rupture was complete. "Think of that," she told her daughter, "after all I did. I don't care. I tell them to go whistle."[79]

The war and its aftermath in fact demonstrated much else. Clearly many citizens wished to change industrial relations in various ways, especially where immigrants were involved, but no less clearly most employers had not drifted from their industrial moorings. In Milwaukee, by 1921, a new Employers' Council had enlisted the employers of more than half of the city's industrial workers beneath the banner of the metal trades association to battle resurgent local unionism.[80] Though the criteria for handling the work force were changing, the foreign born were still treated simply as workingmen of varying capacities and potentials rather than as Europeans whose divergence from the American norm required that they be handled in special ways. Milwaukee industrialists, like those in the rest of the nation, were now relating the aims of militant Americanization to their opposition of trade unions. In short, Americanism, industrial service, and the open shop had coalesced into welfare capitalism.

What had happened? In Milwaukee as elsewhere in the nation, the men and women who formulated industrial policies affecting immigrants usually had little training, and they were often quite unaware of the social complexity of indus-

---

[79] *Milwaukee Journal,* September 30, November 30, 1919; *Civics and Commerce,* December, 1919, p. 3; unidentified clipping, October 7, 1919; May Wood Simons, Diary, November 28, 1919; May Wood Simons to daughter, February 21, 1920, in the Simons Papers. Miss Hill claims that the Milwaukee County Council of Defense committee came to an end with the Americanization Pageant of May 17 and 18, 1919. Hill, "Americanization Work," 3. On the pageant, see *Milwaukee Journal,* May 15, 16, 17, 18, 1919; and May Wood Simons, Diary, May 12, 1919, in the Simons Papers.

[80] Gavett, *Development of the Labor Movement in Milwaukee,* 139.

trial life. During the Progressive era, men like Frederick W. Taylor, John R. Commons, Sumner Slichter, and Herbert Croly suggested solutions intended to rationalize social relations in the nation and especially in industry. Many manufacturers shared this desire to change industrial relations, but America had few trained persons capable of carrying such a program into effect. Industrialists who wished to make changes were therefore forced to make do with amateurs—presidents of stenographic associations, bookkeepers, secretaries, visiting nurses, schoolteachers, safety enthusiasts, and self-styled social workers. Such people gave shape and direction to the changing pattern of industrial relations, and often did so through their day-to-day decisions as company employees.

In their efforts to confer stability and rationality on the industrial world, they struggled with the complexities of factory life, setting up ad hoc committees and organizations and gradually educating themselves for the emerging profession of industrial relations. Thus native- and foreign-born workers alike found factory life shaped by decisions other than those made by the production manager and his foreman. They were also subjected to the decisions of social workers and indirectly to those of public servants and academicians who shared a concern for creating order out of what seemed to be the chaos of American industrial life.

By 1921 these rationalizers of social relations—often in concert, often in their own spheres, but almost always through union-free workshops dominated by a paternal management—had taken giant strides toward refashioning factory life in the United States.

True, this was not immediately apparent. In the next few years, under the aegis of a permissive government, the conditions of employment improved, but so did the techniques of paternalistic employers. Then, on the eve of the Great Depression, the New Deal, and industrial unionism, the consequences of the earlier efforts became clear, at least to Sumner Slichter, who had helped launch the modernization process. The personnel methods of the 1920's—Slichter called them "one of the most ambitious social experiments of the age"—went after the mind of the "average and subaverage worker" to prevent him from "becoming class conscious, and . . . organizing trade unions." Corporate programs offered him security—steady work, protection against arbitrary discharge, an old-age pension, and sometimes insurance against illness—and encouraged him to rely so much on the employer that he would become dependent on him for resolving his legal problems and handling his real estate transactions, and for curing the aches of his head, teeth, and feet.[81]

Slichter understood that some kind of paternalism had become necessary in the industrial economy. How else could the wage earner secure protection against the hazards of modern life and obtain the benefits of scientific discoveries and the services of professional experts? But in 1929, when the scope of corporate management's campaign for the mind of the worker was obvious, Slichter questioned assumptions he and other reformers had held about the source of that paternalism. They had accepted the employer as the primary source of paternalism and had encouraged him to administer their programs and policies inside his factory as part of his own welfare activity. Thus, in the twentieth century, native American and immigrant workers had continued to share a factory life in which employers sought to capture their minds. If paternalism was inevitable, Slichter asked, "would it not be more satisfactory from the point of view of the community, that it be paternalism of the government rather than the paternalism of employers?"

But instead of choosing between the employer and the government as the primary sources of paternalism, in succeeding decades Americans used both and added yet a third. They retained employer paternalism, accepted the New Deal's

---

[81] For Slichter's ideas, see his article, "The Current Labor Policies of American Industries," in the *Quarterly Journal of Economics*, 43: 432–435 (May, 1929).

social welfare legislation, and in time established the paternal features of mass-production unions. As Americans groped their way towards our contemporary system of industrial and labor relations they provided forms of paternalism which both complemented and competed with those of the employer. In short, they followed the ways of the Progressives.

8

Conclusion

IN THE LAST thirty-four years of the nineteenth century
the distinctive ethnic composition of Milwaukee's leadership
and patterns of industry crystallized. Each had emerged between 1866 and 1871. The Americans, Scots, and Germans
who had earlier built the commercial economy and small
processing and manufacturing establishments were now the
leaders of the industrial sector, the holders of skilled occupations in brewing, tanning, and metalwork, and the dominat-
ing elements in the trade unions, in the churches, and—with
the Irish—in politics and municipal government. The emerging industrial sector had also set patterns for the future. By
erecting its rolling mills and blast furnaces on the lake shore
just beyond the city's limits, the Milwaukee Iron Company
had made Bay View the city's first center of steam-powered
heavy industry. Within the decade of the 1860's medium
heavy industry had established itself along the banks of two
of the city's rivers—the Menominee and the Milwaukee—
and at their juncture developed another distinct center of
Milwaukee's industrial sector. These and related developments in cigar making and other small shop endeavors remained essentially unchanged until the end of the century
when electricity made it possible to establish industrial suburbs.

The initial years of industrialization in Milwaukee had
apparently slammed ethnic locks on many occupations associated with factory production. The flood of immigrants

after the depression of 1873 had increased the diversity of the city's work force without altering the ethnic composition of the leadership of the newly established industrial sector. The Poles, who had by far outnumbered each of the other groups coming from eastern and southern Europe, had joined the ranks of the unskilled and semi-skilled. Like others of that immigration—Italians, Greeks, Russians, Hungarians, Austrians, and Bulgarians—they had usually found inaccessible a factory's skilled occupations and supervisory positions above the rank of assistant foreman, a condition extending well beyond the years of first settlement.

From the beginning, then, English- and German-speaking factory masters and their minions, coming from one set of backgrounds, had to learn how to recruit, organize, and discipline a worker who often spoke a different language and identified himself with a different culture and different customs. Recruitment tasks had been relatively simple, since the foremen had only to search out the strikebreaker or the man whose skill they especially required. Besides, the recruitment efforts of foremen and other individual employees, contractors, employment agents, and private non-profit organizations had usually sufficed to supplement those labor needs not adequately provided by work-hungry men applying at the gates. But if much of the labor procurement had remained outside the direct control of the factory, still the tasks of organizing and disciplining a heterogeneous work force had remained in the hands of its masters. And by the 1880's these tasks had become complex. In addition to facing the uncertainties of the competitive product market, factory masters had to cope with ever-larger numbers of employees: now thousands found work in factories employing between 360 and 1,800 men.

Enabled by government and by weak trade unions to manage their men arbitrarily, factory masters had coped with their labor problems by assigning most of them to their foremen, who were responsible for meeting the production schedules of the work shops. Taking full advantage of the breadwinner's compulsion to obey him, the foreman had been an artful juggler of bits of information derived from his factory's labor market and from his conceptions of behavior among Milwaukee workers. The consequences of his key role had been manifold. Holding the keys to the kingdom of employment, he had manipulated workers spontaneously, and often shrewdly, within a shop's economic and social groups, usually sustaining and reinforcing the ethnic patterns formed during the early 1870's. He had improvised the ways and means, the symbols and rituals for instructing and controlling workers whose language he did not know and whose cultures he often despised. Still, these casual, unsystematic responses to markets and workers had produced both products and profits, partly because Poles and other immigrants from eastern and southern Europe did not challenge the system which entrapped them.

But the system had also worked because of abundance—the fortunate intersection of plentiful supplies of capital, material, inventions, entrepreneurial skills, workers, and customers. The immigrants had accepted their occupational fate, often exploiting it by trying to monopolize even the most menial of tasks for their ethnic kinsmen, because abundance had made it possible to use money rather than occupational status for improving their general lot. Abundance had cushioned the impact of unsafe and exhausting working conditions and had prevented the mustering of a systematic program for improving them. So in the years of rapid industrial growth the voices of social protest had been unable to produce a legislative attack on existing industrial relations, and the phenomenal expansion of productive capacity had precluded questioning the methods used in handling labor. Thus, when factory masters had showed concern for the well-being of their workers, it had usually been in the form of random responses to the stimuli of conscience, townsite development, or the attack of a trade union. In the nineteenth century this response had meant financial help to families of injured workers, anniversary celebrations, company outings and free beer, donations of church sites, the services of building-and-loan associations, and the support and formation of benevolent aid societies.

Even as they had so ruled their workers, Milwaukee's factory masters had become enmeshed in economic and political forces which created the demand for handling labor in a deliberate and rationalized fashion. Their very triumphs in applying technological innovations and expanding factory production had involved factory masters in the process of integration and centralization which had changed the competitive character of the nation's industrial economy, fostered industrial specialization, and diffused administrative authority. For example, by 1905, when 27 per cent of Milwaukee's manufacturing establishments employed 78 per cent of its industrial work force, New York's House of Morgan, Pittsburgh's United States Steel, and Chicago's International Harvester were pivotal in the city's economy, especially in her metal trades sector, which E. P. Allis, Illinois Steel, Bucyrus Erie, Milwaukee Harvester, and others had made the primary industrial producer and employer.

As economic developments created these changes for the city's factory masters, political circumstances in Wisconsin had fostered demands for changing the ways of handling industrial labor. After Robert La Follette's followers gained control of the state Republican party they began to pass legislation for effective participation of the state in Wisconsin's economic affairs, a legislative development which had culminated in 1911 with the establishment of the Wisconsin Industrial Commission and a constitutional workmen's compensation law. Consequently Milwaukee's factories became subject to two complementary pressures which fostered new techniques for educating and controlling the work force. One set of pressures came from the internal affairs of International Harvester and firms such as Allis-Chalmers, Bycyrus Erie, and A. O. Smith. The other set came from the agencies of state government charged with enforcing the letter and spirit of the 1911 legislation.

Events at International Harvester demonstrated how the management of that company had responded to internal factory pressures for changing the methods used to govern a large, heterogeneous work force. The McCormicks had looked for an inexpensive welfare program that would least disturb the authority of the managers of production. In their search they had sought guidance from such diverse individuals as Gertrude Beeks, Henry Bruère, S. M. Darling, and Charles W. Price. Under the aegis of benevolent despotism the McCormicks, in time, had developed a comprehensive welfare program designed to develop company loyalty, employment stability, and harmonious relations with workers.

Events at International Harvester had also demonstrated that three unanticipated by-products had resulted from its welfare work. The self-trained practitioners of welfare work had converted International Harvester into one of a number of nurseries for the new governors of labor: industrial safety experts, employment managers, and directors of personnel departments. In the case of Charles W. Price, International Harvester had prepared him for his role as industrial safety crusader on behalf of Wisconsin's Industrial Commission. The novices had also begun to educate the superintendent and foreman, for the novices' subordination to the production manager had forced superintendent and foreman to participate in welfare work. Finally, companies like International Harvester had pointed the way for developing welfare programs which could absorb innovations demanded by the reformers once these had become incorporated into protective labor legislation.

In Wisconsin that incorporation had become effective when the state adopted workmen's compensation and established the industrial commission as its administrative agency for modernizing industrial relations. Using the coercive features of workmen's compensation and the persuasive abilities of Charles W. Price, International Harvester's welfare and safety expert, the commission turned to the industrial safety movement for propagandizing on behalf of modernization.

These choices facilitated obtaining from management the co-operation which the industrial commission sought. Both groups had begun to appreciate the high cost of labor turn-over, and both had come to recognize the place of such inter-related activities as welfare and industrial safety programs in reducing labor turnover and increasing the efficiency of in-dustrial production. Consequently public servants, working on behalf of the state's well-being, and management's welfare and safety experts, working on behalf of their companies, had experimented with techniques that could transmit to all workers—natives as well as immigrants—rudiments of health, safety, and other aspects of industrial service work. To-gether they had begun to change the relationship between themselves and industrial workers and between superinten-dents, foremen, and industrial workers. Together they had also started to spin the web of rules and practices which made government agencies the partners of management in develop-ing more sophisticated techniques for controlling the work force.

While Milwaukee factory masters responded to pressures from the workshop and state capitol, World War I had un-leashed militant nationalists who had tried to use the factory for teaching their gospel of Americanism. The heteroge-neous character of the industrial work force had attracted Americanizers to the pedagogical experiments of factories and state agencies, and by the time war broke out in Europe welfare and safety practitioners had begun to develop tech-niques for instructing immigrants. To Americanizers, con-cerned with the general question of linguistic diversity or convinced that diversity complicated industrial discipline and fostered radicalism, factories had appeared as logical classrooms for teaching English to migrants and for starting them on the road to citizenship.

As long as Americanizers had remained free of the urgent desire to mobilize nationalism, Americanization ventures in industry had been dominated by Peter Roberts of the Y.M.C.A. By working through United States Steel and such other large industrial organizations as International Harvester and Ford, Roberts had tried to facilitate company efforts to promote industrial discipline, welfare, and safety. However, by 1916 the shrill tones of Francis Kellor's militant nationalism had come to dominate the Americanization crusade, and subsequently Americanizers had sought to organize factories on behalf of an English-language and citizenship campaign in the interest of nationalism and defense. They had failed, but all Americanizers looking to factories to implement their programs had increased the pressure on corporations to educate workers systematically. The militant nationalists had, in addition, infused such efforts with the nationalism of the war effort, namely Americanism.

Local circumstances had prevented militant nationalists from seriously affecting Milwaukee's industrial economy before 1917, but once the United States entered the war they had sought to enmesh their teachings with developing welfare and safety programs. With Milwaukee eager to demonstrate that it was the citadel of American loyalty, the Milwaukee County Council of Defense launched its Americanization drive under the direction of May Wood Simons, a socialist whose husband had by this time become an ardent worker for the Wisconsin Loyalty Legion. The militant Mrs. Simons, trying to enlist factories to her campaign, quickly discovered that only employers who had introduced the techniques and organization essential for welfare and safety programs could co-operate with her in establishing Americanization programs. In effect this meant the larger companies in the metal trades, the big knitting mills, some of the shoe manufacturers, and the Pfister and Vogel Leather Company.

Since by 1917 industrial service work still lacked professional status, efforts to identify Americanization with it simultaneously became ventures for introducing and expanding welfare and safety programs. With the help of the Wisconsin Industrial Commission and the manufacturers associated with the Milwaukee County Council of Defense, Mrs. Simons linked English-language education to the problems of labor turnover and efficiency of production. By 1919 Milwaukee's Americanizers had succeeded in gaining support for special programs to foster both Americanization and industrial service work; in direct response to Mrs. Simons' request the Extension Division of the University of Wisconsin hired Algie Simons to teach short courses on the subject of industrial service, and Pfister and Vogel, in conjunction with the Milwaukee public schools' extension department, the M.C.C.D., and the University's Extension Division, launched a language program for the firm's immigrant workers.

These ventures into industrial Americanization failed, but in the process militant Americanism became fused to industrial service work. More important still was the fact that the companies co-operating with reformers and Americanizers were usually committed to the open shop. The industrial commission, the extension departments of the public schools and of the University, not to mention the M.C.C.D., had assisted anti-union managements in developing their programs to improve the conditions of employment, and to educate and control workers.

All this had transpired before most of the nation turned to welfare and safety programs, protective labor legislation, and the more sophisticated techniques of industrial relations. Years would elapse before the programs at International Harvester, Allis-Chalmers, and Bucyrus Erie would become commonplace in American industry, and the protective labor legislation of Wisconsin a characteristic of all industrialized states. In time, however, factory masters in all major cities would encounter the forces which their Milwaukee counterparts felt so early. Then they, too, would reveal their ability to adapt to government-sponsored reform programs. But by then management and government, together, would have demonstrated their remarkable capacity for evolving ever-new techniques and governors for educating and controlling a heterogeneous work force.

Bibliography

Unpublished Primary Sources

A. *Business Archives*
    Allis-Chalmers Company, West Allis
    International Harvester Company, McCormick Collection, State Historical Society of Wisconsin
    International Harvester Company, Milwaukee
    Milwaukee Harvester Company, McCormick Collection, State Historical Society of Wisconsin
    Phoenix Hosiery Company, Milwaukee
    Wisconsin Power and Electric Company, Milwaukee

B. *Institutional Archives*
    Young Men's Christian Association, Milwaukee

C. *Public Archives*
Milwaukee Public Library, Milwaukee
    Rau Appraisal Company, compiler, "Wisconsin, Region 17, Resources and Conversion Section, War Industries Board, Classification and Index of Manufacturing Industry," 1918.
National Archives, Washington
    Committee on Public Information: CPI–I–A7 (I).
    Department of Justice: Record Group 60, Central Files 4929–5053, Immigration and Naturalization Service, Files 53246/206, 53498/9, 51388/4, 51405; Record Group 85, Records of the Immigration and Naturalization Service, Division of Citizenship Training, Americanization Section, Case Files 27671/614, 1832, 4758, 4773, 4848, 6268, 6305, 7576.
    Department of Labor: Record Group 174, unpublished studies and investigations of the United States Commission on Industrial Relations (1912–1915).
    Department of State: Diplomatic Register, Letters to the Department, Vols. 1–10 (1870–1905); Index to Exequaturs, 1863–1910; Record File, Cases 6132–6156; Numerical Files 6917–6947, 9488–9510.
    National War Labor Board: Record Group 2, Case File 163.

State Historical Society of Wisconsin, Madison
Manuscript United States Census, 1870, 1880, Milwaukee, Village of Bay View (microfilm).

Wisconsin Legislative Reference Library, Madison
Testimony, Proceedings, and Reports (1909–1911), Wisconsin Legislature, Special Joint Committee on Industrial Insurance, 6 vols.

Wisconsin Secretary of State, Madison
Manuscript Wisconsin Census, 1905, Milwaukee, Bay View, West Allis, Cudahy, South Milwaukee.

Wisconsin State Archives, Madison
Executive Department, Administration: Strikes and Riots, 1858–1909, Series 1/1/8–9; Immigration, 1852–1905, Series 1/1/1–4; Industrial and Insurance Commissions, 1895–1915, Series 1/1/7–11.
Secretary of State: General Records, Wisconsin Legislative Papers, Petitions and Remonstrances, Series 2/2/2.
State Council of Defense: Series 76/1/1–10.
War History Commission: Wisconsin Loyalty Legion, Series 83/0/8, 15, 17.

C. *Personal Papers*
Milwaukee County Historical Society, Milwaukee
Daniel D. Hoan Papers

Newberry Library, Chicago
Graham Taylor Papers

State Historical Society of Wisconsin, Madison
John G. Gregory Papers
Paul O. Husting Papers
Elisha W. Keyes Papers
Robert M. La Follette Papers
William H. Lighty Papers
Alexander Mitchell Papers
John L. Mitchell Papers
Jeremiah Rusk Papers
Robert Schilling Papers
Algie M. and May W. Simons Papers
Ellis P. Usher Papers
William F. Vilas Papers

Published Primary Sources

A. *Bulletins, Proceedings, Reports*
Amalgamated Association of Iron and Steel Workers of the United States. *Proceedings,* 1885, 1895, 1901.

Amalgamated Meat Cutters and Butcher Workmen of North America. *Proceedings,* 1899–1904.

Chicago, Milwaukee and St. Paul Railway Company. *Annual Reports,* 1881–1891.

Deutsche Gesellschaft von Milwaukee. *Annual Reports,* 1881–1905.

Industrial Removal Office, New York City. *Annual Reports,* 1904– 1917, 1921.

————— *Distribution,* July, 1914–June, 1916.

Iron Molders' Union of North America. *Proceedings,* 1863–1865, 1867–1868, 1882, 1888.

Knights of Labor. *Proceedings,* 1885–1887.

Milwaukee Board of Trade. *Annual Reports,* 1854–1856.

Milwaukee Chamber of Commerce. *Annual Reports,* 1856–1910.

Milwaukee Club. *Annual Reports,* 1883–1884, 1898.

Milwaukee Industrial Exposition. *Reports,* 1881–1882, 1901–1902.

Milwaukee Young Men's Christian Association. *Annual Reports,* 1880–1885, 1887–1892, 1894, 1896, 1904, 1910, 1920.

Milwaukee Young Women's Christian Association. *Annual Report,* 1897.

National Civic Federation. *Conference on Welfare Work,* 1904.

National Conference on Americanization in Industries. *Proceedings,* 1919.

National Safety Council. *Proceedings,* 1912–1921.

Socialist Party of America. *Proceedings,* 1908, 1910, 1912.

Society for Italian Immigrants. *Annual Report,* 1913.

Staatverbandes der Deutsch Roemisch Katholischen Unterstuetzungs und Juenglings Verein von Wisconsin und Ober Michigan. *Reports,* 1908– 1914.

United Brewery Workmen. *Proceedings,* 1900–1917.

United States Chamber of Commerce, Immigration Committee. *Bulletin,* 1912, 1918.

United States Steel Corporation, Committee of Safety. *Bulletin,* 1910–1925.

B. *Government Documents*

New York

New York Emigration Commissioner. *Annual Reports,* 1880–1886.

United States

Commission on Industrial Relations. *Final Report and Testimony,* 11 vols., 1916.

Department of Commerce and Labor, Bureau of the Census: *Census Bulletins* nos. 145 (1902), 3 (1903), 56 (1905), and 105 (1907); *Special Reports,* Employees and Wages (1900), Street and Electric Railways (1902), and Manufacture (1905).

Department of the Interior, Bureau of the Census: *Census Bulletins* nos. 205 (1882), 11 (1890), 19 (1890), and 230 (1892); *Report on Manufacturing Industries in the United States,* 1890.

Department of Labor, Bureau of Labor Statistics: *Bulletins* nos. 31 (1900), 196 (1916), 234 (1918), 250 (1919), and 518 (1930).

Federal Reserve Board. *Production Index, 1830–1886.*

Immigration Commission. *Immigrants in Cities: A Study of the Population of Selected Districts in New York, Chicago, Philadelphia, Boston, Cleveland, and Milwaukee,* 2 vols., 1911.

Industrial Commission. *Reports,* 19 vols., 1901–1902.

Wisconsin

Blue Book of the State of Wisconsin, 1911.

Hambrecht, George P. "What Wisconsin Is Doing to Prevent Industrial Accidents," mimeographed address to meeting of Industrial Accident Board, Madison, January 1, 1918.

Houser, Walter H. *Tabular Statement of the 1905 Census,* 1906.

Milwaukee Board of School Directors. *Proceedings,* 1916–1921.

Milwaukee Citizens Committee on Unemployment and the Milwaukee Free Employment Office. *Annual Reports,* 1912–1921.

Milwaukee Common Council. *Proceedings,* 1882–1883, 1885, 1886.

Milwaukee County Council of Defense. *Official Bulletins,* 1917–1918.

Milwaukee School Board. *Proceedings,* 1882–1886.

Wisconsin Bank Examiner. *Annual Reports of the Condition of the Loan and Building Association of Wisconsin,* 1898–1901.

Wisconsin Board of Immigration. *Annual Reports,* 1880–1882, 1884–1886, 1898, 1900.

————. *Wisconsin, What It Offers to the Immigrants,* 1879.

Wisconsin Bureau of Labor and Industrial Statistics. *Biennial Reports,* 15 vols., 1883–1910.

Wisconsin Commissioner of Immigration. *Annual Reports,* 1871–1876.

————. *Een Verlage der Bevolking, des Bodens, en Klimaats en van Handel en Nyyerheid, van dezen Staat in het Nordwesten der Nordamerikaanische Unie,* 1870.

————. *Ein Bericht ueber Bevoelkerung Boden, Klima, Handel und die industriellen Verhaeltnisse dieses reichen Staates im Nordwestern der nordamerikanischen Union,* 1868.

————. *Ein Bericht ueber Bevoelkerung, Boden, Klima, Handel und industriellen Verhaeltnisse dieses Staates in Nordwestern der nordamerikanischen Union,* 1870.

————. *Exhibiting the History, Climate, and Production of the State of Wisconsin,* 1870.

Wisconsin Industrial Commission. *Bulletins,* vols. 1–2 (1912–1913).

————. *First Aid: A Handbook for Use in Shops,* 1915.

————. *Report on Allied Functions,* 1914, 1915, 1917, 1918.

————. *Workmen's Compensation, Annual Reports,* 1912, 1913, 1915, 1920.

Wisconsin Legislature. *Statistics Exhibiting History, Climate and Production of the State of Wisconsin,* 1867.

Wisconsin State Board of Arbitration and Conciliation. *Biennial Reports,* 1895–1904, 1908–1910.

Wisconsin State Council of Defense. *Final Report, April 2, 1917–June 30, 1919.*

C. *Newspapers*

    Chicago Tribune, 1902.
    Freie Presse, Milwaukee, 1880.
    Germania, Milwaukee, 1880–1883.
    Herold, Milwaukee, 1886.
    Kuryer Polski, Milwaukee, 1893.
    Milwaukee Abendpost, 1897.
    Milwaukee Free Press, 1916.
    Milwaukee Germania Abendpost, 1897.
    Milwaukee Journal, 1879, 1900, 1907, 1914, 1917–1920.
    Milwaukee Journal of Commerce, 1879–1880.
    Milwaukee Labor Review, 1887–1888.
    Milwaukee Leader, 1914.
    Milwaukee Sentinel, 1876, 1880–1883, 1888, 1893.
    Record Herald, Chicago, 1906.
    Social Democratic Herald, Chicago, 1907.
    Staats Zeitung, New York, 1880–1886.

D. *Periodicals*

    Annals of the American Academy of Political and Social Science, 1915–1916.
    Civics and Commerce, 1910–1920.
    Fortschritt der Zeit, 1879–1891.
    Harvester World, 1909–1921, 1936.
    Immigrants in America Review, 1915–1916.
    Industrial World, 1885–1886.
    Iron Age, 1880–1883, 1886.
    La Follette's Magazine, 1914–1920.
    Merchants and Manufacturers Bulletin, 1906–1910.
    Northwestern Mechanic, 1889–1890.
    Pep [International Harvester, Milwaukee], 1920–1921.
    Survey Magazine, 1915.

E. *Articles and Books*

    Amalgamated Meat Cutters and Butcher Workmen of North America. *50 Progressive Years.* Milwaukee, 1948.

    Anderson, William J., and Julius Bleyer, eds. *Milwaukee's Great Industries.* Milwaukee, 1892.

    Barton, E. E. *Industrial History of Milwaukee.* Milwaukee, 1886.

    Bloomfield, Daniel. *Labor Maintenance: A Practical Handbook of Employee's Service Work.* New York, 1920.

    Brandenburg, Broughton. *Imported Americans.* New York, 1904.

    Bremer, Edith T. "Development of Private Social Work with the Foreign-born." *Annals of the American Academy of Political and Social Science,* 257 (March, 1949).

    Bruce, William G. *I Was Born in America.* Milwaukee, 1937.

    Chancellor, William E. *Reading and Language Lessons for Every School.* New York, 1904.

Clark, Lillian P. *Federal Textbook on Citizenship Training.* Washington, 1924.

Commons, John R. *Industrial Goodwill,* New York, 1919.

————. "Labor Conditions in Slaughtering and Meat Packing." *Quarterly Journal of Economics,* 19 (January, 1904).

————. *Myself.* New York, 1934.

————. *Races and Immigrants in America.* New York, 1907.

————. " 'Welfare Work' in a Great Industrial Plant." *American Monthly Review of Reviews* (July, 1903).

Cudahy, Patrick. *Patrick Cudahy: His Life.* Milwaukee, 1912.

Cudahy Bros. Co. *Thirty Years of Progress, 1892–1922.* Milwaukee, 1922.

De Witt, Benjamin Parker. *The Progressive Movement: A Non-Partisan Comprehensive Discussion of Current Tendencies in American Politics.* New York, 1915.

Emerson, Harrington. *The Twelve Principles of Efficiency.* New York, 1912.

Feiss, Richard A. "Personal Relationships as a Basis of Scientific Management." *Bulletins of the Taylor Society,* 1 (November, 1915).

[Flower, Frank A.]. *History of Milwaukee, from Prehistoric Times to the Present Day.* Chicago, 1881.

Gilbreth, Frank B. *Primers of Scientific Management.* New York, 1912.

Glazier, Willard. *Peculiarities of American Cities.* Philadelphia, 1881.

Harrison, Shelby M. *Public Employment Offices: Their Purpose, Structure and Methods.* New York, 1924.

Ingersoll, Ernest. "Milwaukee." *Harper's Magazine,* 62 (April, 1881).

Kallen, Horace M. *Culture and Democracy in the United States: Studies in the Group Psychology of the American Peoples.* New York, 1924.

King, Charles. "The Cream City." *Cosmopolitan,* 10 (March, 1891).

Kruse, Horace, W. *Americanizing an Industrial Center.* Colfax County, New Mexico, 1920.

Kellogg, Paul Underwood, ed. *The Pittsburgh Survey.* 5 vols, New York, 1910–1911.

Kellor, Frances. *Out of Work: A Study of Employment Agencies, Their Treatment of the Unemployed, and their Influences upon Homes and Business.* New York, 1904.

La Follette, Robert M. *La Follette's Autobiography: A Personal Narrative of Political Experiences.* Madison, 1912.

La Piana, G. *The Italians in Milwaukee, Wisconsin.* Milwaukee, 1915.

Larson, Laurence M. *The Log Book of a Young Immigrant.* Northfield, Minnesota, 1939.

Lee, John R. "So-called Profit Sharing System in the Ford Plant." *Annals of the American Academy of Political and Social Science,* 65 (May, 1916).

Leiserson, William M. *Adjusting Immigrant and Industry.* New York, 1924.

Milwaukee City Directory, 1880.

Milwaukee Blue Book, 1894, 1905–1906.

Milwaukee Elite Directory, 1892.

Milwaukee Society Blue Book and Family Directory, 1884–1885.

Mumford, Kimberly John. "This Land of Opportunity: The Heart of a 'Soulless Corporation'." *Harper's Magazine,* 52 (July 18, 1908).

O'Brien, Sarah, R. *English for Foreigners.* New York, 1909.

Price, Isaac. *The Direct Method of Teaching English to Foreigners.* New York, 1909.

Ramsey, Oliver E., and William George Bruce. *A Half Century in Business Effort: History of the Merchants and Manufacturers Association.* Milwaukee, 1921.

Roberts, Peter. *The New Immigration: A Study of the Industrial and Social Life of Southern Europeans in America.* New York, 1912.

————. *The Problem of Americanization.* New York, 1920.

Roster of Members of Milwaukee Clubs. Milwaukee, 1898–1933.

Simons, Algie. *Personnel Relations in Industry.* New York, 1921.

————. *Production Management: Control of Men, Material and Machines.* Chicago, 1922.

Slichter, Sumner H. "The Current Labor Policies of American Industries." *Quarterly Journal of Economics,* 43 (May, 1929).

————. *The Turnover of Factory Labor.* New York, 1919.

Steffens, Lincoln. *The Autobiography of Lincoln Steffens.* New York, 1931.

Thomas, William I., and Florian Znaniecki. *The Polish Peasant in Europe and America.* 2 vols., New York, 1927.

Tolman, William. *Social Engineering: A Record of Things Done by American Industrialists Employing Upwards of One and One-half Million People.* New York, 1909.

Whipple, Caroline A. *Americanization in Industry.* Bulletin no. 693, University of the State of New York. New York, 1909.

Wright's Business Directory of Milwaukee, 1892. Milwaukee, 1892.

Wright's Directory of Milwaukee for 1905. Milwaukee, 1905.

Wright's Milwaukee County Directory, 1892. Milwaukee, 1892.

Turner, Frederick Jackson. "The Significance of the Frontier in American History." *Proceedings of the State Historical Society of Wisconsin,* 41 (December 14, 1893).

Secondary Sources

A. *Articles and Books*

Altmeyer, Arthur J. *The Industrial Commission of Wisconsin: A Case Study in Labor Law Administration.* Madison, 1932.

Andersen, Theodore A. *A Century of Banking in Wisconsin.* Madison, 1954.

Asch, Solomon E. *Social Psychology.* New York, 1952.

Baritz, Loren. *The Servants of Power: A History of the Use of Social Science in American Industry.* Middletown, Connecticut, 1960.

Barry, Colman J. *The Catholic Church and German Americans.* Milwaukee, 1953.

Berthoff, Rowland. *British Immigrants in Industrial America, 1790–1950.* Cambridge, Massachusetts, 1953.

Blied, Benjamin J. *Three Archbishops of Milwaukee:* Michael Heiss (1818–1890), Frederick Katzer (1844–1903), Sebastian Messmer (1847–1930). Milwaukee, 1955.

Borun, Thaddeus, comp. *We, the Milwaukee Poles: The History of Milwaukeeans of Polish Descent and a Record of Their Contributions to the Greatness of Milwaukee.* Milwaukee, 1946.

Bowen, Ian. *Population.* London, England, 1954.

Bowers, Claude G. *Beveridge and the Progressive Era.* Boston, 1932.

Brissenden, Paul F. *The I.W.W.: A Study of American Syndicalism.* New York, 1919.

Brody, David. *Steelworkers in America: The Nonunion Era.* Cambridge, Massachusetts, 1960.

Burnham, John Chynoweth. "Psychiatry, Psychology and the Progressive Movement." *American Quarterly,* 12 (Winter, 1960).

Callahan, Raymond E. *Education and the Cult of Efficiency: A Study of the Social Forces That Have Shaped the Administration of the Public Schools.* Chicago, 1962.

Carpenter, Niles. *Immigrants and Their Children.* Washington, 1927.

Caro, Leopold. "Auswanderung und Auswanderungspolitik in Oestereich." *Schriften des Vereins fuer Sozial politik,* 131 (Leipzig, Germany, 1909).

Child, Clifton J. *The German-Americans in Politics, 1914–1917.* Madison, 1939.

Clark, Victor S. *History of Manufactures in the United States.* 3 vols., New York, 1929.

Cochran, Thomas C. *The Pabst Brewing Company: The History of an American Business.* New York, 1948.

————, and William Miller. *The Age of Enterprise: A Social History of Industrial America.* New York, 1956.

Commager, Henry S. *The American Mind: An Interpretation of American Thought and Character Since the 1880's.* New Haven, 1950.

Commons, John R., *et al. History of Labor in the United States.* 4 vols., New York, 1918–1935.

Current, Richard N. *Pine Logs and Politics: A Life of Philetus Sawyer, 1816–1900.* Madison, 1950.

Curti, Merle E. *The Roots of American Loyalty.* New York, 1946.

————. *The Social Ideas of American Educators.* New York, 1935.

————, and Vernon Carstensen. *The University of Wisconsin: A History, 1848–1925.* 2 vols., Madison, 1949.

Derleth, August. *The Milwaukee Road: Its First Hundred Years.* New York, 1948.

Egbert, Donald Drew, and Stow Person, eds. *Socialism and American Life.* 2 vols., Princeton, 1952.

Eisenstadt, Samuel N. *The Absorption of Immigrants: A Comparative Study Based Mainly on the Jewish Community in Palestine and the State of Israel.* London, 1954.

Ellul, Jacques. *The Technological Society.* New York, 1964.

Erickson, Charlotte. *American Industry and the European Immigrant, 1860–1885.* Cambridge, Massachusetts, 1957.

Ernst, Robert. *Immigrant Life in New York City, 1825–1863.* New York, 1949.

Everest, Kate A. "How Wisconsin Came by its Large German Element." *Collections of the State Historical Society of Wisconsin,* 12 (1892).

Faulkner, Harold U. *The Quest for Social Justice, 1898–1914.* New York, 1931.

Feldman, Herman. *Racial Factors in American Industry.* New York, 1931.

Frank, Louis F. *The Medical History of Milwaukee, 1834–1914.* Milwaukee, 1915.

Gavett, Thomas W. *Development of the Labor Movement in Milwaukee.* Madison, 1965.

Gerth, Hans, and C. Wright Mills. *Character and Social Structure: The Psychology of Social Institutions.* New York, 1953.

Ginger, Ray. *Altgeld's America: The Lincoln Ideal Versus Changing Realities.* New York, 1958.

Gregory, John G. *History of Milwaukee, Wisconsin.* Chicago, 1931.

Grinstein, Hyman B. *The Rise of the Jewish Community of New York, 1654–1680.* Philadelphia, 1945.

Haber, Samuel. *Efficiency and Uplift: Scientific Management in the Progressive Era, 1880–1920.* Chicago, 1964.

Handlin, Oscar. *The American People in the Twentieth Century.* Cambridge, Massachusetts, 1954.

————. *Boston's Immigrants, 1790–1865: A Study in Acculturation.* Cambridge, Massachusetts, 1941.

————. *Race and Nationality in American Life.* Boston, 1957.

Hartmann, Edward George. *The Movement to Americanize the Immigrant.* New York, 1948.

Harkness, Georgia E. *The Church and the Immigrant.* New York, 1921.

Hawgood, John A. *The Tragedy of German-America.* New York, 1940.

Hays, Samuel P. *The Response to Industrialism, 1885–1914.* Chicago, 1957.

————. *Conservation and the Gospel of Efficiency: The Progressive Conservation Movement, 1890–1920.* Cambridge, Massachusetts, 1959.

Heming, Harry. *The Catholic Church in Wisconsin.* Milwaukee, 1895–1898.

Hense-Jensen, Wilhelm, and Ernest Bruncken. *Wisconsin's Deutsch-Amerikaner, bis zum Schluss des neunzehnten Jahrhunderts.* 2 vols., Milwaukee, 1900–1902.

Herberg, Will. *Protestant, Catholic, Jew: An Essay in American Religious Sociology.* Garden City, New York, 1956.

Higham, John. *Strangers in the Land: Patterns of American Nativism, 1860–1925.* New Brunswick, New Jersey, 1955.

Hoxie, Robert F. *Scientific Management and Labor.* New York, 1915.

Hughes, Everett Cherrington. *French Canada in Transition.* Chicago, 1943.

Hutchinson, E. P. *Immigrants and Their Children, 1850–1950.* New York, 1956.

Josephy, Fritz. *Die deutsche ueberseeische Auswanderung seit 1871.* Berlin, 1912.

Kallen, Bernard. *History and Importance of the German Control of Emigrants in Transit, 1884–1897.* Hamburg, 1922.

Kipnis, Ira. *The American Socialist Movement, 1897–1912.* New York, 1952.

Kirkland, Edward C. *Dream and Thought in the Business Community, 1860–1900.* Ithaca, New York, 1956.

————. *Industry Comes of Age: Business, Labor, and Public Policy, 1860–1897.* New York, 1961.

————. "You Can't Win." *Journal of Economic History,* 14 (December, 1954).

Korman, Gerd. "Political Loyalties, Immigrant Traditions, and Reform: The Wisconsin German-American Press and Progressivism, 1909–1912." *Wisconsin Magazine of History,* 40 (Spring, 1957).

Kruszka, Waclaw. *Historya Polska w Ameryce.* 13 vols., Milwaukee, 1908.

Lescohier, Don D. *The Labor Market.* New York, 1919.

Lindsey, Almont. *The Pullman Strike: The Story of a Unique Experiment and of a Great Labor Upheaval.* Chicago, 1942.

Lipset, Seymour, and Reinhard Bendix. *Social Mobility in Industrial Society.* Berkeley and Los Angeles, 1959.

Lubove, Roy. *Progressives and the Slums: Tenement House Reform in New York City, 1890–1917.* Pittsburgh, 1962.

Mack, Raymond W. "Ecological Patterns in an Industrial Shop." *Social Forces,* 32 (May, 1954).

Maxwell, Robert S. *La Follette and the Rise of the Progressives in Wisconsin.* Madison, 1956.

May, Henry F. *The End of American Innocence.* New York, 1959.

McDonald, Forrest. *Let There Be Light: The Electric Utility Industry in Wisconsin, 1881–1955.* Madison, 1957.

McKelvey, Jean T. *AFL Attitudes Toward Production, 1900–1932.* Ithaca, New York, 1952.

Merk, Frederick. *Economic History of Wisconsin During the Civil War Decade.* Madison, 1916.

Merrill, Horace S. *William Freeman Vilas: Doctrinaire Democrat.* Madison, 1954.

Millis, Walter. *Arms and Men: A Study in American Military History.* New York, 1956.

Moore, Wilbert E. *Industrial Relations and the Social Order.* New York, 1951.

Mowry, George. *The Era of Theodore Roosevelt, 1900–1912.* New York, 1958.

————. *Theodore Roosevelt and the Progressive Movement.* Madison, 1946.

Mueller, Theodore. "Milwaukee Workers." Milwaukee Writers' Project. *History of Milwaukee County.* Milwaukee, 1947.

Nevins, Allan. *Ford: The Times, the Man, the Company.* New York, 1954.

—————, and Frank Ernest Hill. *Ford: Expansion and Challenge, 1915–1933.* New York, 1957.

Regier, C. C. *The Era of the Muckrakers.* Chapel Hill, 1932.

Robinson, Jesse S. *The Amalgamated Association of Iron, Steel and Tin Workers.* Baltimore, 1920.

Roethlisberger, Fritz J., and William J. Dickson. *Management and the Worker: An Account of a Research Program Conducted by the Western Electric Company, Hawthorne Works, Chicago.* Cambridge, Massachusetts, 1959.

Schlesinger, Arthur M. *The Rise of the City, 1878–1898.* New York, 1933.

Schneider, Eugene V. *Industrial Sociology: The Social Relations of Industry and the Community.* New York, 1957.

Schrier, Arnold. *Ireland and the American Emigration, 1850–1900.* Minneapolis, 1958.

Slosson, Preston W. *The Great Crusade and After.* New York, 1930.

Smith, William C. *Americans in the Making: The Natural History of the Assimilation of Immigrants.* New York, 1939.

Still, Bayrd. *Milwaukee: The History of a City.* Madison, 1948.

Thernstrom, Stephan. *Poverty and Progress: Social Mobility in a Nineteenth Century City.* Cambridge, Massachusetts, 1964.

Thomas, Brinley. *Migration and Economic Growth: A Study of Great Britain and the Atlantic Economy.* Cambridge, England, 1954.

Ulman, Lloyd. *The Rise of the National Trade Union: The Development and Significance of its Structure, Governing Institutions, and Economic Policies.* Cambridge, Massachusetts, 1955.

Wachman, Marvin. *History of the Social-Democratic Party of Milwaukee, 1897–1910.* Urbana, 1945.

Warner, W. Lloyd, and Leo Srole. *The Social Systems of American Ethnic Groups.* New Haven, 1945.

Watrous, Jerome A., ed. *Memoirs of Milwaukee County.* 2 vols., Madison, 1909.

Weber, Adna Ferrin. *The Growth of Cities in the Nineteenth Century: A Study in Statistics.* New York, 1899.

Whitbeck, Ray Hughes. *The Geography and Economic Development of Southeastern Wisconsin.* Bulletin no. 58, Wisconsin Geological and Natural History Survey. Madison, 1921.

Whyte, William F. "The Bennett Law Campaign." *Wisconsin Magazine of History,* 10 (June, 1927).

—————, ed. *Industry and Society.* New York, 1946.

Wiebe, Robert H. *Businessmen and Reform: A Study of the Progressive Movement.* Cambridge, Massachusetts, 1962.

Wight, William W. *Henry Clay Payne: A Life.* Milwaukee, 1907.

Williamson, Harold F., and Kenneth H. Myers III. *Designed for Digging: The First 75 Years of Bucyrus Erie Company.* Evanston, 1955.

Wittke, Carl. *The German-Language Press in America.* Lexington, 1957.

————. *We Who Built America*. New York, 1940.

Woodward, C. Vann. *Origins of the New South, 1877–1913*. Baton Rouge, 1951.

Woolf, Harry, ed. *Quantification: A History of the Meaning of Measurement in the Natural and Social Sciences*. New York, 1961.

Wray, Donald E. "Marginal Men of Industry: The Foremen." *American Journal of Sociology*, 54 (January, 1949).

Young, Donald. *American Minority People*. New York, 1932.

B. *Theses and Dissertations*

Berthrong, Donald J. "Social Legislation in Wisconsin, 1836–1900." Ph.D., University of Wisconsin, 1951.

Hill, Isabella L. "Americanization Work in Milwaukee." B.A., University of Wisconsin, 1920.

Korn, Bernhard C. "The Story of Bay View." M.A., Marquette University, 1935.

————. "Eber Brock Ward: Pathfinder of Industry." Ph.D., Marquette University, 1942.

Olszyk, Edmund G. "The Polish Press in America." M.A., Marquette University, 1939.

Olson, Frederick I. "The Milwaukee Socialists, 1897–1941." Ph.D., Harvard University, 1952.

Perlman, Selig. "History of Socialism in Milwaukee." B.A., University of Wisconsin, 1910.

Rice, Herbert W. "The Early History of the Chicago, Milwaukee and St. Paul Railway." Ph.D., University of Iowa, 1911.

Scheft, Charles E. "The Tanning Industry in Wisconsin: A History of its Frontier Origin and its Development." M.A., University of Wisconsin, 1939.

Schmidt, Gertrude. "History of Labor Legislation in Wisconsin." Ph.D., University of Wisconsin, 1933.

Interviews

A. *General*

Howard K. Beale (Madison, 1955)
Elizabeth Brandeis (Madison, 1959)
W. C. Brice (Milwaukee, 1959)
George Bruce (Milwaukee, 1956)
William H. Cameron (Evanston, Illinois, 1959)
Michael Cudahy (Milwaukee, 1956)
John J. Dierbeck, Jr. (Milwaukee, 1956, 1958, 1959)
Rt. Rev. Monsignor Peter Leo Johnson (Milwaukee, 1956)
Elmer Kreutzer (Milwaukee, 1957, 1959)
A. F. Leidel (Milwaukee, 1957)
William M. Leiserson (Washington, 1956)
Don D. Lescohier (Madison, 1958)
Sam Leshin (Milwaukee, 1957)

Frank P. Olds (Milwaukee, 1956)
Frances Perkins (Ithaca, New York, 1964)
Selig Perlman (Madison, 1959)
T. C. Turner (Milwaukee, 1956)

B. *International Harvester Pensioners**
   Gaitano Balestriere
   John Balfanz
   James Bremmer
   George Bundschuh
   Arthur Carmichael
   Frank J. Felseeker
   Myron Halstead
   Charles Hanson
   Nicholas Hartman
   Emil Mantey
   William Marefke
   James Olson
   Michael Phair
   William J. Rodenbeck
   William Treichel
*All interviewed in Milwaukee during 1957.

Index

GERD KORMAN
is associate professor of history
New York State School of Industrial and Labor Relations
Cornell University